C2D1

An Examination of the Extreme Haunting and How the "Ghost Boy of Geneseo" Came To Be

An Urban Legend Explained

"Whoever fights monsters should see to it that in the process he does not become a monster. And if you gaze long enough into an abyss, the abyss will gaze back into you." — Friedrich Nietzsche

C2D1

An Examination of the Extreme Hauting and How the "Ghost Boy of Geneseo" Came To Be

An Urban Legend Explained

Christopher Di Cesare

With

Dale Kaczmarek
Mara Katria
Mark Allan Keyes
Alan D. Lewis
Charlie Manning
J. Jeff Ungar

CITA PRODUCTIONS
NEW YORK

www.citaproductions.com

Logo image designed by Kerry Lyon

This print edition to be catalogued as follows:

Di Cesare, Christopher.
C2D1: An Examination of the Extreme Haunting and How the "The Ghost Boy of Geneseo" Came To Be. A Western New York Urban Legend Explored / Christopher Di Cesare

ISBN-13: 978-0988554146 (trade paperback)

First Edition: February 2019
Second Edition: September 2019
Third Edition: March 2020

10 9 8 7 6 5 4 3 2 1

For Jeff, Paul, Beth, Linda,
Craig, Ed, Judy, and Fr. Charlie, with love

In Memory of Mary Rose Di Cesare,
who saw things others did not

8

Above - Geneseo images captured by J. Jeff Ungar using a 35mm Minolta SRT-201 camera in the spring of 1984. Ungar's photographic skills would be put to the test in early 1985 by fellow Erie Hall resident Christopher Di Cesare's whose claims of a ghost living inside his room next door, C2D1, would soon become the stuff of legend.

CONTENTS

10

Introduction

The Blair Witch Project, which became a cult movie classic shortly after its release in 1999, has likely done more to both encourage - and damage - the field of paranormal investigation than any other phenomenon in my lifetime. It's often jarring 'found footage' approach would set the tone for much of what paranormal television is today: A series of short, emotional, experiential, interactions that play on both the would-be-ghost hunters' - and the audience's - paranoia. It felt 'real'. Thus was set the powerful and effective tone for virtually every single episode, of every single 'ghost' television series, since. Never mind that almost nothing of substance is ever truly produced by the time most end credits roll.

The focus had moved, and in almost wholesale tectonic plate fashion, from what had typically been a private, introspective, and personal quest for meaning and understanding, to the very public and communal thrill of lucrative, organized entertainment.

With the multitude of television shows that began to spring up all over the 'Cableverse', came a noticeable societal by-product: acceptance. It was, by and large, a very positive one. Countless people who had been forever fearful of sharing their esoteric experiences and perspectives now found themselves – perhaps for the very first time – with a more tolerant and accepting general audience to share with, to work with, and to live with.

It was a New Awakening.

The once-thought-dangerous and taboo topic of the 'occult' began to transform and shift, in the conventional public mind. It soon became a celebration of creativity, diversity, gem stones, energy and magic. J. K. Rowling's Harry Potter film series and long running-television shows like *Charmed* assisted in re-casting society's viewpoint of 'the dark arts', especially among its younger viewers. The 'Old Ways' (paganism, witchcraft, divination) were once again rising up as a countervailing force to the often stodgy and canonical doctrines of organized religion. Publications once hidden away in the furthest, highest corners of book stores, were now gracing the Best-Seller lists. Hierarchical structures, that for centuries were viewed as the active Hand of God in the human world, were quietly and effectively being re-branded, in the minds of many, into places that were built by man and founded on claustrophobic restriction.

There was newfound freedom for many who had long felt consigned to the societal shadows: freedom of expression; freedom of practice and freedom of identity. This was a powerful about-face celebrating a new future, and some claimed it to be the culmination of an Age of Aquarius, bearing the fruit from seeds planted in the spirited sounds and smoke of events like the Woodstock festival held in the August of 1969.

Yet, there lingered a potential hazard that circled near its core, another freedom: The freedom from even the slightest hint of general practicality.

Whereas over the years Judaism, the Roman Catholic Church, and its Protestant offshoots had made slow and 'forced' steps towards reconciliation with the physical sciences and Natural Law, this unregulated and untested self-moralism often accompanied the loosening of traditional spiritual and religious bonds. A self-moralism that was, at times, devoid of the bothersome constraints of tested practice or societal expectations.

The world could be what you made of it, it was how you envisioned it. This exciting rush to spiritual self-determination, and its many intriguing alternate realities and projected possibilities soon began to rub abrasively against traditions and practices that had long served to help bind people together, which is an essential commonality during times of war, recession, and as part of the political process.

The communal chord began to fray.

The result of the inevitable impact – between the unstoppable force of inspirational progressivism and the immovable object of practical conservatism – would be an obvious one. People began to grow apart, moving into opposing tribes, polarizing families and communities.

A new politics (of identity) emerged. It was an almost unrecognizable by-product of the Civil Rights movement in the 1960's and the Feminist movement of the 1970's. Both of those movements declared, and in no uncertain moral tone, that neither race, nor gender, should be a disqualifying factor. Rather it should be a person's actions, and efforts, their moral compass, that should determine the strength of their mettle, their measure of their success, and their equality of opportunity. The new politics, which often fixates on one's skin color and/or gender preference, also tends to be in favor of eradicating unpleasant reminders of our shared human past (statues, monuments, words, phrases, customs) as one of its actionable tenets. In a frighteningly similar manner to those who, in years past, sought to eradicate opportunity, and in fact, the very humanity, of those people that they deemed to be too 'unpleasant' to recognize or consider. The United States once fought a civil war (1861-1865) over it.

One might argue that we find ourselves in danger of losing our hard-fought political balance, our societal equilibrium.

This New Way offers us the ability to view the world as we want to see it, as we feel it *should* be seen. We now have a shared, and almost expected, permission to fictionalize the factual in order to brand a greater number of outcomes as acceptable ones.

In the bombastic Age of Trump, this New Way helped to inspire a highly-acclaimed, award-winning, Broadway play: Hamilton. It has been almost universally lauded by critics for its vibrant sound track, compelling minority cast, and inspirational dance routines. Absolutely none of which embodies the focus of Hamilton's actual work, or the world and times in which he lived.

So what, then? Only our present views matters? The past is not to be considered – or valued – in full because it wasn't what we felt it should have been at the time that it occurred?

Today, if a person finds satisfaction and comfort in 'identifying' as an alligator-beaked Draconian living incognito amongst the human race in some swanky Los Angeles suburb after the crash-landing of their space flotilla following a hard-fought battle with the agents of Metatron, who are we to question that? Afterall, that is their own personal 'truth', and they are entitled to it.

Yet, living in a land of make believe (even when it creates an empowering sense of identity and purpose) only serves to 'cry wolf' in the long term. It increases the chance that, in doing so, we may inhibit our ability to recognize a true danger when it arises, because we have already agreed that it should not – and cannot – exist.

And that, my good reader, was perhaps the most disturbing aspect of The Blair Witch Project to me: The powerful cultural impact of the intentionally false and fabricated hype associated with it.

In what was certainly a stroke of organized genius, directors Daniel Myrick and Eduardo Sanchez helped push the film by coyly suggesting that the story was based on real people and real events. This interesting twist served to draw even more cash-paying bodies into the theater seats. By some accounts the film made close to 250 million dollars, and on a relatively small budget close to fifty thousand. To be sure, it was a financial success that has justifiably inspired countless others to begin creating their own masterpieces on 'shoestring' budgets. Sadly, what they sold us was a phony bill of goods, as none of it was real.

In fact, the general public has now largely come to accept, and without complaint, that movie studios are going to take – even *need* to take – certain 'liberties' in telling the story in order to (ironically) make it seem 'more real' for the viewer. We *expect* that factual events and occurrences will be fictionalized in order to provide us with a more 'realistic-feeling' overall experience.

It is Madness.

For you see, the winter months of 1985 taught me that things which defy our comfort or expectation certainly do happen. That they happen not for the sake of entertainment, and not because we 'willed' them to be, or not to be.

Sometimes things, very frightening things, things that work squarely against our systems of belief, are terrifyingly real.

They cannot be wished away, or hidden in the darkness.

Not even when we say they can. Not forever.

As far as I can tell, the reach of the haunting at Geneseo did not spread far beyond the confines of Western New York (the areas including and between Buffalo, Syracuse and Elmira). Although I have heard reference to an article that appeared in a Scranton, Pennsylvania area newspaper, it remained primarily a regional tale.

In his 2012 book *The C2D1 Haunting*, Tim Shaw writes:

> The C2D1 legend is about a student who became targeted by the mysterious and quite mischievous spirit of a young man. This ghost not only appeared to him, but also violently attacked him. For many years, paranormal enthusiasts have attempted to track down the key facts of this story, often visiting the Geneseo campus in order to interview anyone with knowledge of the actual incidents.

It also tended to be associated with another purported Western New York legend, that of the Haunted Hinsdale House, also known as the Dandy House. In later years I would visit that location.

However, unlike many who publicly claim to have endured some type of incredible paranormal experience, I initially chose to avoid the media, and did so for well over two decades. I was fearful of overt disclosures that might negatively impact my reputation, my career, and even my family.

There are still times when I think back to a particular overcast afternoon in the spring of 1985. The afternoon that a newspaper reporter from the *Democrat and Chronicle* (based out of nearby Rochester, NY) came calling. He was standing right in front of my dorm, Erie Hall, as I made my way back down the paved path from the College Union Hall.

"Excuse me. Have any of you heard of the Ghost Boy?"

"Does anyone know where I can find him?"

Startled, I stopping for a moment, then quickly maneuvered myself into relative obscurity by standing behind one of the large, free-standing, campus mailboxes. I studied his mannerisms, his appearance, his cadence.

He just wanted to 'have a talk', he repeatedly offered to any passersby willing to listen. On that particular day no one was willing, or perhaps knowledgeable enough, to give me away.

I believed him. I just didn't believe in myself yet. I didn't know how to make sense of things, how to define what had happened, how to share all of it in an effective, or even mildly comprehensible, manner. That would take time, and help from some very good people along the way.

In the summer of 2012, that same reporter's daughter posted a comment on a social media thread relating to my appearance on the recently aired SyFy "School Spirits" television series. The woman shared her father's disappointment that he had never found the student that he had so actively searched for. She was quite pleased when I responded that her father actually had found me, that I was just a few steps away from him. He just did not know it at the time. The physical description that I provided of her (now deceased) father was a match, and led her to reply that he always believed there was some actual truth behind the rumors.

In spite of my reluctance to publicly speak about the haunting, or to embrace the notion of what the 'Ghost Boy' was, the urban legend grew.

For ten years, then twenty, and without my assistance or approval, the story of the 'Ghost Boy of Geneseo' spread. The legend, I have been told, began much like any other, taking on various shapes and purposes along the way. My friend, and 1985 Erie Hall dormmate, Jeff Ungar always said that it was a story that wanted to be told; perhaps he was right.

The events were sometimes ascribed to differing dormitories (Genesee, Monroe, Livingston often before Erie was mentioned) and the general appearance and form of the ghost (a young boy; a skeleton; a deceased rugby player) could vary, but certain elements tended to remain constant in the tale when it was shared over drinks, or on dates, or at campsite sleepovers:

- There was a ghost who haunted a male student's dorm room
- It wore a blue and yellow-striped rugby shirt
- There was an actual photograph of the ghost, now lost
- Student and ghost were said to have conversed inside the room
- The ghost had attacked the student in a bathroom

On first inspection, it could be argued that these particular claims are fairly vague, and perhaps no different, and no more telling, than most standard ghost stories we hear growing up. Except, in each case, these 'constants' actually provide an accurate, if minimal, glimpse into the months-long terror that would reshape not only my world view, but eventually, my place in it.

Unlike most hauntings of renown, the location (SUNY Geneseo); the building (Erie Hall); and most of the people said to be involved (J. Jeff Ungar; Linda Fox; Fr. Charlie Manning; Craig Norris; Dr. Lawrence Casler; Beth Kinsman; and me, the so-called 'Ghost Boy', Christopher Di Cesare) can be verified. As can those who have sought, over time, to research the haunting at Geneseo and provide their own perspective on it, among them: Alan Lewis, Tim Shaw and Mark Allan Keyes (two of whom have graciously contributed to this book project).

And unlike many hauntings, the Geneseo 'Ghost Tape' was not the by-product of an exercise in recall made months (Amityville Horror), or possibly years, later. Nor was it born from hundreds of hours of listening for what might constitute a recognizable word or phrase, while scanning the airwaves, during the course of some public ghost hunt. Rather, it was a contemporary, on-site, recording – yielding arguable success – of communications with what was believed to have been an active spirit. Also unlike most paranormal literary offerings, which are weaved together, in large part, via hearsay, the C2D1 Journal Notes were chronicled daily during the very heart of the haunting, and by those involved in it. Whereas most cases offer very little in the way of compelling photographic material, the C2D1 event offers a collection of images, not limited to the so-called 'Skeletal Image Ghost Photograph', but others that help to capture the unusual environmental effects inside those college dorm rooms, and on the students themselves. This at a time before computer programs and cell phone apps allowed photos to pretend that they were something more than they actually were.

It should be noted, that by most objective standards, the C2D1 Haunting cannot hold a candle to better-known cases, like the Amityville Horror, in terms of its scope of influence and cultural impact. However, it might provide a student of the paranormal (or anyone for that matter) with a more meaningful glimpse of what might lie just beyond the edges of our understanding.

What you are about to read is not a work of fiction 'loosely based' on unverified material for the sole sake of entertainment or profit. Rather, it is meant to serve as a case study of reported experiences, from verifiable people, at known locations.

The goal isn't to change your mind, it is to challenge it.

1. "Ghost Boy"

Above – Photograph from the 1986 SUNY Geneseo college yearbook showing Christopher Di Cesare (background, right), the 'Ghost Boy of Geneseo', preparing for a 10K (6.2 mile) cross country meet on the Geneseo campus. Di Cesare, who would earn multiple varsity letters, was a Three-year Baccalaureate Student who attended the New York state college at Geneseo from September 1983 – May 1986. He would not 'go public' with his experience until twenty-five years later, in the summer of 2011.

"Ghost Boy."

I can no longer remember the first time I was called that, as more than thirty years have now passed. Recalling people staring and pointing towards me as they whispered it to their friends?

That's easier.

There was a pretty brown-haired girl, with a navy winter coat and white knit cap, whose eyes seemed to suggest that she understood the weight of being labeled, singled-out, judged. I only saw her on the path to class once. The rest? Well, they were young, impetuous, invincible.

We all were once.

Sometimes I wonder what it must have felt like to be on the other side.

For those who had heard the untenable rumors about some naïve student holed up in his dorm room, having conversations with something from beyond the grave. About claims of residents fleeing through the hallways, and talk of a priest quietly venturing into the darkness of night to face some type of unholy threat.

Or those who had listened to the cassette tape recordings, on which can be heard the sounds of my trembling voice, and the deep, guttural, groans of something else.

Sounds that I never wanted to hear again.

Or those who had seen the photographs. Photographs that looked to feature the effects of some unseen force, and a human-like shaped mist forming silently behind me. Photographs that featuring me, with arms outstretched, looking towards the photographer in awkward disbelief, completely overwhelmed.

Photographs I had asked to have destroyed.

There are many examples in history of those belonging to a minority population, an unpopular viewpoint or an uncommon practice banding together in solidarity, or brotherhood, or purpose. That there is strength in numbers cannot be understated. People can often join together with others of like mind, background or situation for safety, for comfort and for understanding.

In 1985, and in my world, there were no other 'ghost boys' to commiserate with. I was a minority of one. In the eyes of those who lived around me I was quickly and uncontrollably transformed. Against my will, the shift in the perception of others went from 'that cute blond-haired kid who ran marathons' to the oddity of the Ghost Boy. I felt as though, in some ways, I was no different than Leonel the 'lion-faced man', the leopard boy, or the Siamese Twins who were displayed in tents alongside some Carnival Row. This was not due simply to the increased social isolation, for as the haunting erupted from a seemed 'nothingness', strangers, acquaintances and friends alike, began searching for any unusual physical traits or characteristics that might present an underlying cause for my gift of 'seeing', and my curse of 'knowing'.

Above – Photograph from the October 14th, 1983 edition of The Lamron, the SUNY Geneseo college newspaper: Di Cesare racing against a runner from St. John Fisher.

It suddenly became a point of considered importance that my lower body was markedly more developed than my upper body. Was there the possibility of some physical DNA connection or progenitor template in terms of someone's unique musculature (ex. mesomorph, ectomorph, endomorph) in relation to psychic ability and/or paranormal experience? Had my countless hours spent dedicated to distance running, upwards of 70-80 miles a week, at my peak, somehow created a situation of endorphins now run amok? Could the established condition known as the 'runner's high' last far beyond (possibly for days) the cessation of strenuous activity?

It was also mentioned that I had an "unusually small and tight-fitting skull". That this condition might have led to additional – or excessive – pressure on select portions of my brain. Pressure that in turn might be the cause of whatever either had attracted the ghost to me, or allowed me to see it. After all, the brain does send messages back and forth via synapse, and the fast-moving electrical charges jump from synapse to synapse when we reason and think. If the distance between synapses was lessened or reduced, then perhaps the thought process or other faculties of the brain would be in some way quickened or enhanced?

Others looked inward, and away from my physicality.

To some who were present during the events of the haunting, I would be cast as an unlikely messenger sent from Above, preparing to reveal some previously hidden and Holy truth to the unsuspecting masses. One particularly unforgettable encounter began with a knock on my door and was accompanied by the whispered question: "So, if you are Jesus, then who am I? Am I Mary Magdalene?"

To another, I soon became an embodiment of the unrepentant sinner, whose past transgressions were now visiting upon us a terrible and unwanted fate: "I spoke to my priest last weekend, Chris, and he says that you need to repent if you want all of this to stop."

Aggressive statements like those stung the hardest, because they served to discount who I was.

In spite of the emotional anguish that remarks such as those may have caused, I tried to remind myself that they originated from a place of positivity, from people who were actively searching for ways to help me through. I recognized, quite early on, that it would feel far worse to be completely ignored.

When conversations eventually shifted to things such as the nature of the paranormal, cultural understandings, and family histories, I was able to breathe a bit more freely.

As frightening, odd, comical, or absurd, as some of these recollections might sound to a reader so many decades later, I feel that they do assist in demonstrating the complete confusion that had begun to envelope me, us, all of us. They also illustrate the lengths to which we strove in searching for some manner of understanding.

We had no clear solutions, thus no possibility did we dare to discount.

There were no support groups, no television shows, and no legal or practical remedies for our ever-worsening and shared affliction.

The haunting spread like a wildfire.

Worse for me, I was apparently the carrier.

While these reflections do offer some valuable background data, what I remember most vividly about those dark and confusing months was what occurred on Sunday, March 10th, 1985. Wherever I am, whoever I am with, I only need to close my eyes in order to see again:

I am face down, naked, shivering wet, and bleeding on the floor of the dormitory bathroom. At times the shadowy vision still feels more like some type of overwhelming dystopian dream, than an actual memory. How I wish that were true. My eyes are open but they are not focusing. The room's single light, which is fixed to the ceiling, is now far too bright for comfort. A numbing cold is creeping through my 19-year-old body, a body that has been relentlessly honed by training for – and racing in – nine 26.2 mile marathons. The source of the icy cold that races through my trembling form is not the tile-covered floor that presses up, uncomfortably, against the side of my face, my chest, and my thighs. Rather, the sensation is spreading from an area near the center of my back. An area where the wounds are: the scratches and the blood. My toes are cramped from the pressure of being forced unnaturally upwards by the floor since I fell, but I am too exhausted to shift my feet in order to relieve the pain. My breathing is weak and shallow. I fear that my body is beginning to shut down. My mouth remains open, slightly, just as it was at that precise moment when I had looked into the mirror, above the sink, and first saw those three 'impossible' scratches.

I am beginning to panic.

Death is here.

Less than an hour before, I had been running at a brisk (sub-6:00/mile) clip along the dirt roads that separated the local Western New York farming fields. The light blue sky was lined with wispy clouds of white that were hurried along by an unseen wind. Almost a month had passed since I was last able to stretch out my distance runner's legs like this.

Things were different now.

The priest, Father Charlie Manning, had performed his Holy Blessing, and the thing – that horrid thing – was gone. In the three and one-half days since he had raised up his cross, uttered his sacred prayers, and cleansed room C2D1, my life had returned to a healthy normalcy.

Approximately 3.5 miles out, I turned left onto Rt. 20A and headed back east, over the metal-railed bridge, and up the rolling hills to the waiting college campus.

The air inside the dorm was noticeably stale as I made my way up the stairs to the second floor. Still, it was better than the dread that had existed here less than 72 short hours prior.

Order had been restored.

I untied my left *Asics* running shoe when I reached my door and slid the room key off of the lace. Normally my roommate, Paul, would be inside sitting at his desk, his head bobbing back and forth as he listened to the local rock station wearing his thick, padded, head phones. But things had turned ugly in room C2D1, and Paul was now determined to spend most of his free time at home with his parents. I could not blame him. It would likely have been my course of action as well if I lived less than an hour away like he did. As it was not the case, I often became the lone human occupant, and I soon got into the habit of tying my room key onto my shoelaces, so that I could lock my door when I went out.

It was very important that the door remained locked!

Pulling off my shamrock green and white wool cap, I tossed it onto the old brown couch that kept watch in front of the room's lone window. Peeling off the layers of sweat-laced running clothes, I tossed them into the basket at the bottom of my closet and retrieved a small white towel, some shampoo, and a bar of soap.

The C2D Quad bathroom in Erie Hall, the site of the March 10th, 1985 shower attack on Chris Di Cesare. Above Left: Toilet stall. Center: Sliding bathroom door, sink and mirror. Above Right: Shower stall. Images: 2011, courtesy of Di Cesare.

The D-Quad bathroom was directly across from my bedroom and a heavy, two-inch thick, wooden door (on a floor-based roll track) guarded the bathroom entrance. It would rattle as it was slid open and closed, due perhaps to its sheer weight, which made passing in and out of the bathroom without notice impossible.

Entering, I had switched on the overhead light and proceeded to the lone shower stall. A cheaply made, largely ineffective, plastic shower curtain hung from a shiny metallic crossbar. The shower stall floor was clean, cool, and dry. It had not been used for several hours. The warming spray of shower water relaxed my tightened muscles as it washed away the dried salt from my pores. I lathered up my body and then began to shampoo my hair.

My peripheral vision caught sight of a minor fluctuation in the light that entered the shower stall, and an all-too-familiar sense of uneasiness crept over me. I glanced up towards the ceiling, and there – through the steady stream of shower water – I saw the dark, human-shaped, shadow. It was gazing, silently, down at me. My eyes squinted, watching as it swayed ever so slightly: shoulders, skull, a tilted neck.

Impossible!

The priest had arrived, just as he had promised, on Wednesday the 6th at 8 PM, with dark briefcase in hand. I had been there as he chased away the evil with his blessed water and his commanding presence.

Afterwards he spoke to me about the mysteries of God and I had made sure to ask him if the ghost could somehow 'get back in'.

"Only if you invite him back," he had answered without hesitation.

"*That's* not going to happen!" I guaranteed him.

For the truth was, that as the cleric packed away his belongings, I could state with an honest heart that there was no possible scenario in which I could ever imagine doing so.

"Call me if you need anything else," he had said as he strode out the door into the quiet hallway.

But there had been no need to call.

The strange closed-room breezes; the flashing clocks; the whispering voice that people heard calling my name; the empty creaking bedroom loft; the missing items; the cloudy white mists; the shadows washing across the walls; the cold finger tips touching my neck; the opening (while still-latched) closet door; the zones of cold that people claimed clung to their legs; the tug-of-war with an unseen adversary for my pillow; the self-activating tape recorder; the full-bodied apparition that would rise from Paul's stereo or hover over me as I slept, breathing my breath into its mouth; were all gone now.

Using both of my hands, I wiped the water from my eyes, only to see the shadow was still hovering near the room's ceiling. With the speed and reflexes that had recently contributed to a 2:09 half mile, I sprinted from the warm, misty, shower stall, and came to a sliding, bare-footed, halt in the center of the college dorm bathroom.

"Hello?"

I could feel my heart pounding inside my chest.

Ignoring my nakedness, as well as the immediate discomfort caused by the rapid drop in air temperature, I took a moment to check inside the toilet stall and to look underneath the sinks. My fingers clenched into fists, as pools of water began to form around my feet as it dripped down my legs.

It wasn't the ghost; the priest had sent him away.

Returning to the pleasing heat of the shower, I began washing the lathered shampoo from my hair, rationalizing that perhaps the shadow was nothing more than an 'afterimage' caused from inadvertently rubbing my eyes with my hands.

I watched as the steady stream of white shampoo bubbles quietly gathered around my toes, as they prepared to make their unavoidable journey down the shower drain into darkness; never to be seen again.

I shot a quick glance up to the ceiling.

The shadow was back. Now, suspended directly over me, the human-sized form seemed to have moved a bit closer, as though it were trying to get a better look.

A better look at me.

I darted – for a second time – out into the middle of the bathroom. This time nearly losing my footing in the puddles that I had inadvertently created just minutes earlier. The strength of my runner's legs prevented me from landing – with a 'thud' – on my posterior.

The bathroom was empty.

The heavy, wood, bathroom door had not been moved.

At this point my mind grasped something of significance: As I noted earlier, the bathroom's light (as is common) was located on the room's ceiling. By definition then, this meant that any shadow cast by its beam would be located on the *ground,* just as the sun's light casts shadows on the ground during daylight hours. Just as my own shadow now was. There could not be shadows on the ceiling unless there was an active, and continual, light source nearer the floor.

No. I wasn't ready to accept this. Everything had been fine for three and one-half days. The priest blessed the room.

"The hell with you!" I blurted out.

I trudged back, as defiantly as one can be in one's birthday suit, into the warming shower for a final rinse. When I turned off the water with my right hand, my left hand had remained free, but it didn't matter; there would be no time to react. There was no warning.

My eyes, perhaps instinctively, closed as my face connected with the hard shower wall. The wall tasted bitter, like soap powder. I was thankful that my top teeth did not feel damaged from the swift and sudden impact. Whoever — *whatever* — had just attacked me, on my back (just below my neck) used such force that my entire right foot was momentarily lifted off of the shower stall floor. I had a very real sense that the next action I took might well have been my last.

I wasn't a fighter by nature, but I decided that I was going to fight back. I was going to break someone's nose, even if it meant breaking my own hand (which it probably would) in order to do so. I reminded myself to protect my face, to make sure that if I was killed that there could be an open casket, having read - somewhere - that it was much better for emotional closure.

My mom would prefer that, I reason.

Plus, I had paged through a book on 'death masks' (impressions made of the recently deceased's face and kept for posterity) while in junior high, and seeing the contorted looks on so many of them, made me uneasy. Especially Julius Caesar's death mask. Legend held that he had been stabbed some twenty-three times. I had apparently been stabbed 'just' once, but Caesar's contorted face flashed through my mind, and it seemed uniquely relevant to the moment.

Initially, I had thought to pull the weapon out of my back, in order to use it against my attacker, but I was uncertain about the potential blood loss in attempting to do so.

Drawing in a deep breath with my runner's lungs, and with every ounce of strength that I could summon, I unleashed a powerful left-handed haymaker into the area where I estimated my assailant's head should be. I make sure to follow through with my motion. There can be no letting up, this was an important moment.

A sharp 'tearing' sound was followed by an odd, soft, flutter. My eyes verified that I had vanquished the nearest foe: The thin, still useless, shower curtain lay on the floor, near my trembling feet.

Damn.

The only audible sensation was the persistent soft tap of water dripping from the shower head directly behind me. No shoes, sneakers, or feet were visible in the toilet stall on the other side of the brightly lit room; the only possible hiding place.

The bathroom was empty.

Or was it?

Scornfully kicking the wet, plastic, shower curtain aside, I stepped out of the shower stall.

Without question the bathroom was colder still; too cold.

"*Who* are you?" I screamed, looking about frantically as I did so, "W*hat* are you? God? The devil? Show yourself, you *coward!*"

Total silence.

Even the repetitive drip of the water from the shower head stopped.

At that precise moment, the sheer lunacy of the situation gave me pause. I half-smiled to myself and considered that maybe *none* of this was actually happening. Maybe there was no shadow, no attacker … and no injury. Perhaps this was all some type of psychological flashback. Was it possible to simply 'disbelieve' everything?

It hadn't worked that way when the *thing* had first appeared in my room back on February 12th, or during the month since. But maybe, this time, it would.

Cautiously, I had turned my head towards the rectangular-shaped mirror which was fastened above the porcelain sink; the one nearest the shower. The uneasy hope that I might have been losing my grip on reality (in spite of the pages and pages of notes in Jeff's journal and the eerie ghost photographs that suggested otherwise) was still very much alive inside of me. Temporary 'madness' represented a treatable and uncomplicated way 'out' of this nightmare. The only acceptable course of action that I could see was this: *There is no wound … I am crazy.*

Damn. Damn. Damn!

There they were: three, long, roughly parallel, scratches! Their edges, cuts in my soft, human, skin, were already beading up with blood.

My blood.

This was clear enough proof that something had just viciously attacked me. It was proof that, priest or no priest, something dead was winning this battle. Most importantly: This was all *real.*

I gazed one more time at my reflection inside the mirror. I looked *so* sad, so young, so innocent, so pitiful. I felt sorry, for myself, as I weakly dropped to my knees, and then fell face down onto the bathroom floor.

It was March 10th, 1985. The digital clock in room C2D1 read 3:31 PM but I was not there to see it. I was lying face down, stark-naked, shivering wet, and bleeding on the floor of the bathroom some thirty feet away.

I was too busy dying.

2. Geneseo

Above – Sturges Hall, Geneseo from 35mm negative strip - J. Jeff Ungar in 1984.

I did not end up there by chance, I chose Geneseo.

I dutifully passed the college's three-year degree exam the spring of my senior year at high school, and I chose Speech Communications as my major course of study. Any notion of pre-law coursework was quickly dispensed as a result of my youthful impression that lawyers tended to be the type of people who spend hours arguing with each other over exactly how many leaves on a tree burned, rather than helping to put the fire out.

In spite of the tedious five-hour drive from my family's lower New York State home, I found Geneseo (which was an English translation of the Iroquois name for 'beautiful valley') to be a truly remarkable place. Main Street had a distinct 'small town' feel and looked to me like something out of the Andy Griffith TV show; a Jimmy Stewart movie; or a Norman Rockwell painting. There were local 'mom and pop' stores, an abundance of eateries, and elegantly aged Victorian homes lining the well-maintained thoroughfare. Some of the older men still wore overalls and brightly colored, potted, flowers adorned many of the wooden pane windows.

The personal computer had not yet made its mark on society, and most phones were still attached to the wall by a spiral cord and adorned with a rotary dial and a bell-toned ringer. "[Insert name here], it's for you! Telephone!" was as commonly a heard phrase as "Check your (cell) phone" is today. On evenings and weekends, I would journey up town and order a warm Italian sub at Aunt Cookie's, purchase the latest Billy Idol CD at Buzzo's Music, or take in a movie at the Riviera theater.

To the west, the Genesee Valley stretched out across the entire horizon and the view from any of the college dormitories was simply breathtaking. Growing up I had been to the theme parks in Orlando, Florida; had walked along the cultured sidewalks of Montreal; and run through seemingly endless golden cornfields in Kansas – but I could not recall having been to a more beautiful place than Geneseo, New York.

Over the years, no one has captured the aesthetic of Geneseo with more mastery than Keith Walters. His photography work is spellbinding, and well worth a look if you would like to get a more experiential understanding of the area's inherent beauty.

Although it initially felt as if I had gone back in time, non-academic college life was nothing like that. When class sessions ended, it tended to be more like a non-stop Mardi Gras celebration, especially on the weekends. Light blue-and-red neon beer signs in dormitory windows helped to light up the campus walkways, serving as beacons to legions of drunken co-eds staggering their way back home from a local fraternity house or social establishments like *The Vital Spot* or the *In Between*. That was life for many in college. Blue hair, green hair, spiked hair, no hair, beer pong, dance parties, I had never seen, nor come close to even imagining, anything like it. I was exposed to completely foreign lifestyles, many of which seemed to fly in the face of the very principles that had allowed me to gain access to college in the first place.

But, if I harbored any lingering doubts about my choice to attend SUNY Geneseo, they were dispelled once I experienced the professional way in which Coach Martin Kentner treated the members of his running team. Even when a runner fell short of a particular time or goal, he would look for something positive – a silver lining – to share with them.

He would stand with stop watch in outstretched hand, his Paul 'Bear' Bryant hat perched atop his head, wearing an ever-present suit jacket and yell: "Come on tigers! That's it! Good job! Finish up strong!"

It was while warming up for a race at historic Delaware Park in Buffalo, NY, on September 10th, 1983, I experienced my first déjà vu.

Typically, and unlike most of my teammates, I would do my warm-up for big races on my own, silently counting to ten in order to calm my nerves before the start, just like my maternal grandmother had taught me. But having never been to Buffalo, and feeling generally uncomfortable navigating alone through big cities, I felt it best to stick with the team.

As we began our first loop around the park, I asked aloud, "Hey, is there a white house up here on the right?"

No one seemed to know, or more likely, care. Even those who had run here many times in the past offered no reply.

"I'm pretty sure there is a white house up ahead on the right."

This time I included specific details (that I have long since forgotten) about the house along with some additional expectations about objects that might be in the yard that surrounded it. When we rounded a curve in the roadway several minutes later, the house that I had so dutifully described, was standing there, in exact detail.

A combination of confusion and exhilaration washed over my mind, and I felt slightly nauseated in considering the implications. Or maybe I was simply nervous before the race.

My prediction astounded some of my teammates, and freaked out some others. Not enough for them to disrespect or socially isolate me, I was still an important and valued part of the team, but enough that they started to shower a little further away in the gymnasium locker room.

Above — Coach Martin Kentner (front, left) with the 1985 Geneseo Cross Country Team. Chris Di Cesare is centered. Photograph from the 1986 Geneseo yearbook.

The following year, a teammate named Scott Ambrose (photo on page 17) - apparently having heard about the Buffalo incident from one of the other runners - confided in me that he had recently been visited by his grandmother's ghost, and was a bit frightened by it. As we jogged down a wooded dirt trail, he asked for my opinion on what it might mean. This was several months before the haunting would begin, and although he seemed quite sincere in both his affect and detail, I wasn't able to gauge how much stock to put into his testimony. Nor did I know how to answer his question if I had chosen to.

So, it would likely come as no surprise that to this day I do wonder how it must have been for so many of my friends back then. Friends who, realistically, could not have been sure how much stock to place in *my* words, yet who still worked diligently to help ensure that I was safe, and not left alone.

Never alone.

For all the talk today of the Ghost Boy of Geneseo, of that haunted college dorm room, and of the very existence of the ghost itself, no one today would know of these happenings, or of me, if not for their many selfless actions.

I suppose that's just the way things are.

History publicly lauds generals who have waged, and won, in war. Justly so. Yet washed away with time are the thousands of unsung, unpraised, often unrecognized heroes, who would pay the ultimate price. Heroes without whose efforts the fight would have surely been lost. Heroes who had names, and dreams, and families.

Walk through any military cemetery and start counting the headstones: One. Two. Three. Four. Five. Six. Seven...

Then you begin to understand.

3. The Eyes and Ears of the Campus

Above — "I wanted to capture moments, to preserve them." J. Jeff Ungar, self portrait

John Jeff Ungar arrived at SUNY Geneseo in the fall of 1983 from Webster, an affluent suburb of nearby Rochester, N.Y. His father was an accomplished architect who designed, among his many projects, the Margaret Woodbury Strong Museum. Known simply as 'Jeff' to his friends at that time, he was rooming with Edward S. in C2D2 when I first arrived at Erie Hall, the following year, on September 3rd, 1984.

He was extremely intelligent, keenly observant, and emotionally reserved. Wavy-haired, and more-often-than-not bearded, Jeff seemed to have an air of royalty about him, as though he might have been the inspiration for any one of the kings in the standard 52-card deck.

As to the makeup of his personality, my answer now would be no different than it was thirty years ago: precise, measured, and exacting.

To wit: "The power of doing anything with quickness is always prized much by the possessor, and often without any attention to the imperfection of the performance" – Mr. Darcy, *Pride and Prejudice*, Chapter 10.

I had the opportunity to visit Jeff's home in the spring of 1985, during the height of the haunting. Located on Drumm Road, it was actually an estate, crowned with a beautiful home and nestled amongst acres and acres of forestlands not very distant from the southern shore of Lake Ontario. It even had a name: Wolfern. It was named, I am told, after his dad's family's farmstead in the 'old country'.

Jeff himself resided in the basement. His 'room', which seemed large enough to me to ride horses in, was chock-full of ancient leather bound tomes of knowledge, with an assortment of smooth rocks, driftwood and far too many hand-blown glass bottles of varying color, shape and size to count. I was taken by the hundreds of small bubbles inside the hand-blown glass walls of the bottles, remnants of an earlier world.

The articles in Jeff's room caused me to wonder if he might have been an alchemist had he lived a few hundred years earlier. I could imagine him slaving diligently away, under dim candlelight, in some ivy-walled castle in the attempt to turn lead to gold.

What I could not imagine, however, was what I would witness in the hours just prior to our return to the college that weekend.

Jeff, after slightly cuffing the bottom of his blue jeans, had stepped into a fast-flowing stream on the property that was some fifteen feet across, and at random intervals ran as deep as three feet. Worried about the risk of getting pulled out into the frigid waters of the vast Great Lake at whose doorstep the mouth of the stream knocked, I remained safely on dry land, *terra firma*, as Jeff waded knee deep into the bitter flow.

"What are you doing," I remember asking him with what had to be a look of sincere concern on my face.

"I'm going to catch a fish."

"With what" I asked, seeing no fishing pole, net or bait.

He stopped for a moment, met my gaze and smiled: "With my hands."

Moments later he was stepping cautiously though the water, his hands raised just inches above the sparkling surface as though he was reading some type of invisible signal. With a startling suddenness, he plunged both of his hands into the dark water, focused for a moment, and extracted a large fish that seemed as shocked as I was in that moment!

Over the days and weeks following that visit, Jeff would claim to be in awe of my social skills, my running successes, and of the way that I could 'light up' a room (as he put it) or run naked through it. He would also claim to be in awe of my ability to see, and to speak with, the ghost.

Truth be told, I would have considered trading in all those things to be able to do what he had done in that rushing stream.

Jeff was cool. Cooler than the French Bayonet sword he purchased when he was ten years old, cooler than his collection of silver Peace Dollars (even the rare 1927 one, minted when Babe Ruth was hitting his record, 60 home runs in a season). Cooler than I was.

Above - It took J. Jeff Ungar less than two minutes to wade into a large stream, and catch an eight-pound steelhead trout with his bare hands. – Photograph C. Di Cesare

It turned out that Jeff was also a talented writer and photographer, and it is largely through his efforts in those areas (the 'C2D1 Journal Notes' and several 'ghost photographs' among the more notable examples) that there remains compelling physical evidence of the haunting today.

A creature of habit even in his formative college years, Jeff would rarely leave his room without his trusty 35mm camera, a notepad, and several writing utensils at his disposal. This would serve him well, as he would soon find himself acting as 'the eyes and ears' of the campus during the haunting.

I would meet Jeff a week or so into that fall semester inside Erie Hall.

My new roommate and I had walked into the D-Quad common room to find a group of boisterous collegians playing table football (the game with the spinning soccer players impaled on thin metal bars).

The second floor of Erie Hall, where the majority of the events covered by this book would occur, was comprised of a centrally-located common area, surrounded by four sections of dorm rooms called 'quads'. Each quad had a smaller common area, three bed rooms, and a bathroom. The D-Quad was where I found myself placed, with Paul A., by the college housing administration. Most of the other students were returnees from the prior 1983-84 school year.

Being that we were both approximately 5'6" and 130lbs, and baby-faced, the mistaken assumption was made that Paul and I were incoming freshmen, and that we might need to be 'schooled' in the ways of college.

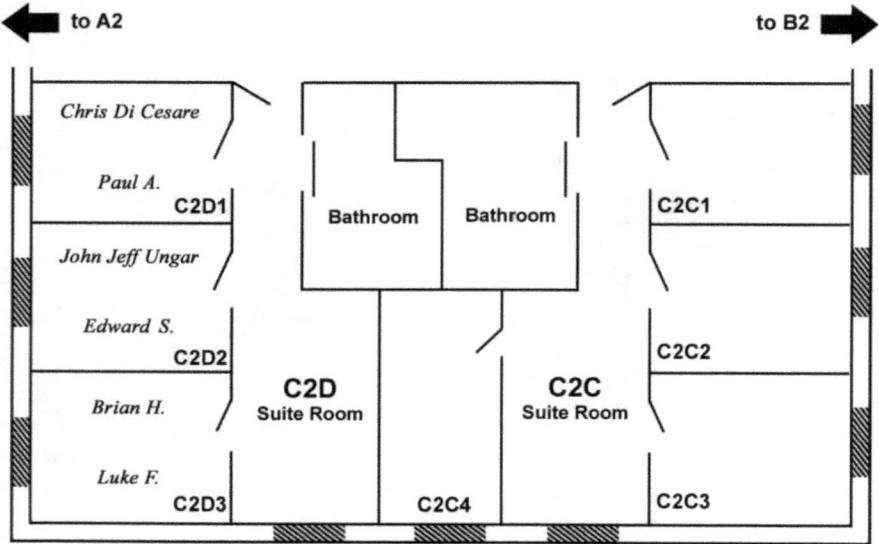

Above: A partial floor map of the second level of the C Building of Erie Hall.
Graphic by Mara Katria

Only two weeks prior I had completed my ninth 26.2-mile marathon at the Empire State Games in Baldwinsville, NY, and I probably knew a great deal more about life, and success, than these guys did. I just didn't go around bragging about it. I wasn't about to be dismissed away so casually.

Cutting through the smattering of laughter, I interjected that I was a Three-Year Baccalaureate Student, who – because I did so well on the multi-subject test (in the areas of humanities, natural sciences, and social sciences) – had received automatic credit for my entire freshman year. Thus, having essentially 'skipped over' an academic year (and saved thousands of dollars in the process), I was now technically beginning my junior year, and well ahead of all of them.

More aggravating guffaws and incredulous rejection followed my pronouncement, and Paul was now getting annoyed as well.

"This is stupid," he muttered under his breath.

He had no strong interest in socializing in the first place, it had been my idea. Seeing that half of the guys were obviously inebriated, he would have been just as happy turning around, heading back to our room, and listening to some classic rock on his state-of-the-art stereo system.

"I can vouch for him!" a sudden voice, from the corner of the room to my left, interjected.

The voice, one that I had not yet heard amongst the din, came from a student who was perched – not unlike a panther in the wild might be – on the back of a lone chair which was placed in the only quiet, dimly lit corner the room offered. Whoever this person was, he apparently had enough social heft to bring the room's activities to a sudden and grinding halt.

I liked that.

The Three-Year Degree at Geneseo
Source: *1985 Geneseo Brochure*

The three-year degree program was initiated at Geneseo with the assistance of a grant from the Carnegie Corporation. The program has evolved into a time-shortened honors program and, as such, provides a special opportunity for talented students. It is one of the most successful programs of its kind in the nation. All students in Geneseo's traditional four-year sequence of study, regardless of major, must complete … a core program. The core is comprised of selected courses from the five divisions of the curriculum (humanities, social sciences, natural sciences, critical reasoning, fine arts) and usually involves taking introductory courses in each of these areas. Students who qualify for the three-year degree program will be exempted from completing most of the core; thus, their total course requirement for the Bachelor's degree will be reduced 40 academic courses to 30.

Wearing blue jeans with a button-down shirt under a sleeveless vest that looked to me like it might have survived military maneuvers in Vietnam back in the 1960's, he hopped off of the chair backing and walked into the center of the room.

"I saw his name on the list."

It turned out that someone else in the room had taken the test as well.

Jeff walked over to me, permitted himself a close-mouthed smile in order to express an element of brief pleasure, and then shook my hand.

"Nice to meet you," he stated succinctly.

In what can only be defined as serendipitous, it was discovered that Jeff and I had taken the same exam (Three Year Baccalaureate) on the same day (June 30th), in the same room (Newton Lecture Hall, room 202), and at the same time (12:00 noon). We just did not know each other then. Jeff, in an effort to take his mind off of the multi-hour task ahead, had taken a moment to examine the list of student names beforehand. Apparently, my name was unique, or interesting, enough to attract his attention: Di Cesare.

It sounded Latin.

STATE UNIVERSITY COLLEGE OF ARTS AND SCIENCE, GENESEO, N.Y. 14454

EDUCATIONAL SERVICES
ORIENTATION PROGRAM
BEGINNINGS 1983

Wadsworth Auditorium
3:00 – 3:30 pm.

I have just received your card indicating that you are coming to orientation
and are interested in taking the three year degree examinations offered on
June *30*. The Educational Testing Service provides the examinations,
which last for about an hour each. The three general areas involved are
natural science, social science, and fine arts. A fee of $12 will be <u>charged</u>
<u>at the door</u> for test administration and scoring.

Because the three year tests are an addition to the regular orientation program
which begins at 3:30 p.m., you must arrive at <u>Ontario Hall</u> between 9:00 a.m.
and 11:30 a.m. on June *30*. The three year tests will begin promptly at
12:00 noon in the <u>Newton Lecture Hall</u>, Room 202.

If you live <u>more</u> <u>than</u> <u>five</u> <u>hours</u> <u>from</u> <u>campus</u>, we can allow you to check into
Ontario Hall between 7:00 – 10:00 p.m. the night before your scheduled date.
If you are interested in this option, please call (716) 245-5717 as soon as
possible, but no later than June 22, 1983. There will be no additional cost
for this arrangement. If either or both of your parents will be accompanying
you, they too, will be accommodated. Please remember to bring your own linen
and blanket.

We are really pleased with the quality of this year's Freshman Class and look
forward to meeting you at orientation.

Sincerely,

Dr. James L. Allan
Director of Orientation

Above – Exam information. Markings and notations by Christopher's mother.

These particular characteristics, Jeff's keen observational skills, and his
ability to project a sense of calm, even as events rapidly unfolded around
him, would leave a lasting and profound impression on me. It was an
impression that I would eventually choose to act on, and an impression
that would eventually change everything, for both of us.

We would develop a friendship over the next few months that was based
primarily upon our shared desire to understand the world around us, even
if we had differing approaches to getting there. We had a shared
appreciation for artistic achievement (I enjoyed drawing and he
photography), history, and the guilty pleasure of roleplaying in the form of
the classic dice game *Dungeons & Dragons*.

Controversial at the time due to the circumstances of a teen (James Dallas Egbert III) getting lost in 1979 in tunnels underneath Michigan University, and another teen committing suicide following a role-playing session in 1982, some media outlets began the attempt to link the practice to satanic cults and societies. The mother of the deceased teen, Patricia Pulling, sued his high school principal (in Richmond, Virginia) claiming that a D&D curse had been placed upon her son, but the law suit was quickly thrown out by the courts.

For Jeff and I, and the few others who would on occasion join us, it was simply an entertaining problem-solving exercise. One that allowed for risk-free application of concept to varied and challenging dilemmas.

```
15.   arcadia is a large town with a pop.of about 3,000.there are two
inns.the happy mans inn,and across the street the arcade,wh ich is
much larger and ornately decorated.a member,rn,spots a person who
he/she thinks is astrologer,going into the arcade.

16.   upon entering the inn,they will be approached by a small frail
old man,who looks very much like the horse salesman.he asks the party
if they would like to put thier horses in the adjacent stable,a gp/
horse.if asked if he knows the man who sold them the horses he will
say no.the clerk a large dark man will then call,is there a lord
valarian party here? message for a lenuvician party!when asked for
the note he will ask him for some proof.if he gets none he will tear
up the scroll.if it is pieced together the clerk will open the
door add allow the wind to scatter the paper about the room.if viol-
ence erupts and someone is severely hurt,astrologer will apear on
the scene and heal the wounded.when he is finished he will give a
strong glare to the leader of the group.then walk out the door,to
disappear into the crowd.
```

Above - A sample of the D&D role-playing notes used in the fall of 1984.

On occasion, we would role-play until the wee hours of the morning, and I could not help but to burst out laughing when, at approximately 2 A.M. one weekday morning, Jeff mournfully lamented that it seemed "Time's passage functioned proportionately converse to one's desires."

I also noticed early on in the friendship that there was no obvious ego guiding Jeff's visible actions. It was never about who won, or who was better at some task. Rather, he embraced the variations of interest, belief and accomplishment. He admired the achievements of others with the same honest passion that he held for his own. In fact, he would often take great inspiration from the success of those around him.

As an athlete, whose sole goal was often victory (or at the very least besting as many opponents as I could) this was a refreshing change of pace. I admired that his sense of self and happiness were not exclusively driven by accomplishment, and that he could quickly see value in efforts beyond his own. This helped in creating a cohesive dyadic relationship between us.

Jeff quickly became a trusted friend. And never lost on me was that he had voluntarily stepped up to assist Paul and I on that warm September night, as the summer's number one song (ironically) "Ghostbusters" echoed out through the college hallways above the reverie.

Above — J. Jeff Ungar at Fallbrook, near Geneseo 1984. Photograph by Di Cesare.

Mara Katria is the director of the feature-length docu-thriller *Please Talk with Me* that recreates the genuine story of the C2D1 Haunting. Ms. Katria was awarded Best Director for her work on the film at Wilson Horror Film Festival, and PTWM was awarded Best Feature at Spirit Quest Film Festival in 2014.

4. Friendship

The C2D1 Haunting recreated in the film *Please Talk with Me* is not a ghost story, not at its core; it is a story of humanity. While the paranormal was a catalyst for those students in 1985, it was the relationships that formed the breadth of the story and its uncanny tendency to impact people today. Trust was the key. Trust opened the door to understanding, then and now. Trust led the way to healing and resolution. Trust continues to light the path toward sharing and positive impact. The friendship between J. Jeff Ungar and Chris Di Cesare especially inspired me as a creator. Together they faced the darkness of the unknown — in the vulnerability of their humanity — with trust.

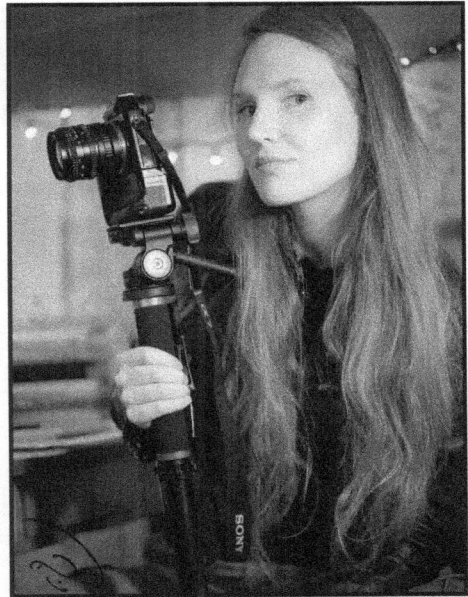

Most of us hold the details of our own stories close to the vest, don't we? We don't let just anyone see the faces we tenderly preserve behind our many masks. It's not overtly dishonest; it's careful. The more we live, the more evidence we have that things can go wrong when we open ourselves up to scrutiny, ambivalence, and betrayal. Furthermore, the deepest wounds often seem to be dealt by those we let closest to us. Why risk it? Ernest Hemingway said: "The best way to find out if you can trust somebody is to trust them"; but I certainly do not always walk that walk. As a film director I should only say this: there would be fewer great stories to tell without trust and risk. Learning about these two characters for the movie has ingrained that concept in me pointedly and poignantly.

Chris Di Cesare could have kept things internalized when his world was forever changed that winter. Telling Jeff could have damaged Chris' credibility in the eyes of his respected friend – especially in those days when the paranormal was much more of a taboo. Even if Jeff believed Chris, telling a person he'd only known for about a month could've led to Jeff spreading the story, thereby increasing the probability of mass panic. In kind, Jeff could have kept Chris at arm's length when his dorm-mate was pounding on his door with frightened reports of a ghost. Jeff could have theorized that emotional issues, overexertion, or drugs were to blame for the abnormal accounts which he hadn't yet personally witnessed. This was college after all. Jeff could've justifiably decided to safeguard his academic career instead of jumping down a potential rabbit hole in which "fancy stalks outside reason" – to quote Mr. Ungar (himself quoting Thomas Hardy).

Yes, it would have been understandable, perhaps even advisable, for Jeff and Chris *not* to engage with each other. It seems like the safer bet. Yet something told them that they could rely on one another, and because they took that gamble, we have the story of the C2D1 Haunting today. The artifacts they made and saved allowed some filmmakers to build an idea into a sturdy framework; their shared experiences formed the emotional substance for a screenplay and cast of actors; and their collaborative growth provided a robust purpose and platform for sharing what would become *Please Talk with Me*. It's a privilege now to reveal some details about what I've learned regarding the friendship of Chris and Jeff and how that inspired a team of people who themselves came together to share what happened to those kids in 1985.

When examining *Please Talk with Me* through the lens of the relationship between Chris and Jeff, it is quite interesting to first look back at pre-production and the very skeleton of the film. The phase I am referring to occurs before editing, before shooting, even before casting can take place. At this time dreams need to meet the reality of deadlines, business, and budget. It's crucial to have a scaffold from which to secure the complicated ligature of production requirements and build a safe structure where the movie ideas can live. Just such a scaffold was provided for us by virtue of the evidences and chronicles that Ungar and Di Cesare encouraged each other to record. Indeed, their solidarity is to thank for most, if not all, of the artifacts from Erie Hall that've been fundamental to producing countless radio programs, symposia, television episodes, and – of course – movies.

When PTWM was in pre-production, the "C2D1 Journal Notes" that Jeff wrote at Chris' request became specifically essential to getting the filmmaking rolling – in more ways than one. For example, long before we even began pre-production, our producer William J. Edwards (being a native of Western New York where the haunting took place) had received a photocopy of Ungar's writings about the ghost at Erie Hall. Bill and I discussed those notes at length when we were deciding whether this was a story we were going to try to tell. While the "C2D1 Journal Notes" had an effect on so many members of our cast and crew, this is now an opportunity to view them from my perspective. Reading the notes granted several insights, two I'd like to talk about for this missive: the voice of the writer, John Jeff Ungar, and impressions of a college-aged Chris Di Cesare.

Jeff's voice in the notes belies his young years. Veritably breathing off the page come the observations of his dignified approach, his instinct to remain unbiased when possible, his scientific process, and – most remarkably to me – his empathetic care. Jeff speaks about the occurrences in a way that does not seek to convince, excite, or incite an audience. It is clear he is taking on the experience of the haunting and the task of recording it, not only to enhance understanding in a little-known field of research, but also simply to help Chris who was in need of a trustworthy confidant. The lack of ego there is rare and so inspirational from the angle of a film director. Jeff loved the epic, the grand scale of fantasy, science fiction, and the arts. Yet he never propped up his own creations and viewpoints, which were and are extraordinary, as I know well. What a character to cast! And, as I mentioned, through the voice of Jeff I was also receiving insight into the friendship he had with Chris. As has been established, Jeff began writing the notes at Chris' urging after the first time the ghost appeared. Chris has stated that he wanted to have proper documentation in case he was going mad; he thought a recording could help diagnose the potential issue down the road. Jeff assented and began transcribing the astonishing supernatural horrors that swelled over the coming weeks and days. While the notes provide students of the paranormal with abundant examples, there are also many instances of exceptional decency, friendship, and compassion. On the sixth page, Jeff describes Chris' ordeal this way: "Wednesday was one of Chris' all-time worst days. The combination of three hours' sleep, a failed psychology test, [...] as well as the trauma of the hauntings had put Chris in an uncommonly black mood." We can see that Jeff, while fascinated by the phenomena, cares for Chris' well-being. We also see that Chris is known to be bright of mood and that the haunting is taking its toll. To underscore this, here is another excerpt from earlier that day when Chris needed time before telling Jeff of all the most recent incidences: "I was intrigued, but I respected his position and could do nothing but wait for him to decide whether to tell me or not. But damn was I curious!" Here now we see a mutual respect forming as well as a more comprehensive image of Chris as he was in 1985. This young man was not a person to divulge information arbitrarily. He was not looking for a reaction; it seems he wanted to think things through and cultivate his thoughts as not to create unneeded worry. It is heartening to consider that he was able to find and trust a person like Jeff who would listen, wait, and help when Chris was ready. Two good people, if I may say so.

The "C2D1 Journal Notes" could have me writing for pages and pages, but there is so much more to tell about the relationship between Di Cesare and Ungar that can be illustrated by my interviews and talks with them. I'd not yet met Jeff when first reading the notes, but I had the pleasure of speaking with Chris early in the production when delving into the journal and more. This was a unique opportunity to increase my understanding of these survivors and what went on during the haunting. Throughout this period, Chris generously provided numerous photographs from the college in 1985: snapshots of his track career and the campus, and photos taken by his friend J. Jeff Ungar. It was revealing and satisfying to be able to add pictures to the words I'd been reading. I could ascertain that Chris was a person of determination and great humor – with a mind excited by experimental thought. He had a desire to apply acquired knowledge actively about a wide range of subjects from the metaphysical to the political. I remember him telling me about the conversation he and Jeff engaged in after a recent presentation on campus given by the Warrens (well-known demonologists). Chris and Jeff spoke of whether or not it's likely that some humans could possess psychic abilities, and if so, what the moral implications might be. They expanded on the topic, challenged one another, and made each other laugh. They brought together minds that imagined from different perspectives but often arrived at the same conclusions. Though Jeff was a young man, he came across as eternally mature like the royal Dúnedain in Tolkien's Middle Earth. Meanwhile, Chris conveyed a character that seemed ever-youthful yet wise, like the immortal elves of Rivendell in that same imagined world. But I digress. I had already gathered that there must have been trust between them for the notes and story to exist as they did. Pairing that with the illuminating photos and Chris' descriptions of their times together additionally illustrated an obvious reverence between the two. Chris talked about Jeff with appreciation for his talents, bravery, and evident intellect. And, Jeff valued Chris' buoyant creativity and ability to improvise to outstanding effect. Notably as well, their shared penchant for philosophical discussion became a theme in our film.

Speaking of the movie proper, allow me here to interject that while rewarding, it's never easy making a motion picture or videogame, and the responsibility is greater when working with real subject matter and people rather than fantasy and fiction. The genuine items from C2D1 stoked the spark of creativity into tangible, reliable flame. Furthermore, such records can act as extremely helpful stepping stones which, in our case, we were able to lay on the path of the movie's narrative. For example, we needed to ask ourselves questions, like: how do we tell the story; how long will it be; how do we transition from one moment to the next. Such relics gave us meaningful answers to these questions and synchronously allowed us to craft a gift for the audience rich with examples and ephemerae, allowing viewers to feel immersed in the film. As a bonus, the artifacts (not to mention getting to meet the survivors on set, which I will point out soon) encouraged the cast and crew to treat the story with such excitement and gravitas – even to this day. Again, it's due to Jeff and Chris' bravery and co-creation that we have these items. Furthermore, it was the *way* in which they worked together, both throughout the haunting and contemporarily, that really got the cinematographic blaze going. This connects right back to my first interviews with Chris about C2D1 for the film. Conversing with Mr. Di Cesare along with studying the photos and writings provided me with more of the whole picture instead of just pieces to a puzzle. It was invaluable when, at our request, he signed on to adjust the script and give us his input as historical expert for PTWM – we wanted the film to be as authentic as possible. His feedback and support cannot be overvalued. Therefore, even then, we had Chris and Jeff working in tandem: Jeff's notes providing the backbone of the screenplay and Chris helping us hugely when fleshing out the story and characters. And, we did not stop there. It was time to reach out to this John Jeff Ungar.

I had already been researching C2D1 and Jeff's character for years when I first got to talk with him about the haunting. It was as though I was beholding a hero from legend stepping off the scrolls of history. He was just as Chris had described and as my reading of his notes suggested. I remember Chris saying to me that if I wanted to understand more about Jeff, I should listen to the song "I Melt with You" by the phenomenal post-punk band Modern English. John Jeff was the kind of American who holds himself so upright and measures his words so carefully that he might as well have an English accent. Rounded consonants, soft vowels, low timbre. It was providence when our production team asked Mr. Ungar if he would lend his fantastic voice to narrate our movie using excerpts from his notes. What could be more authentic? That he agreed was a massive boon to our film and to my creative enthusiasm, which was already exceedingly high.

Even with all of the research I had done and the intensive preparations we'd collectively made, nothing could prepare me for the sheer fun of seeing Chris and Jeff actually together for the first time in years.

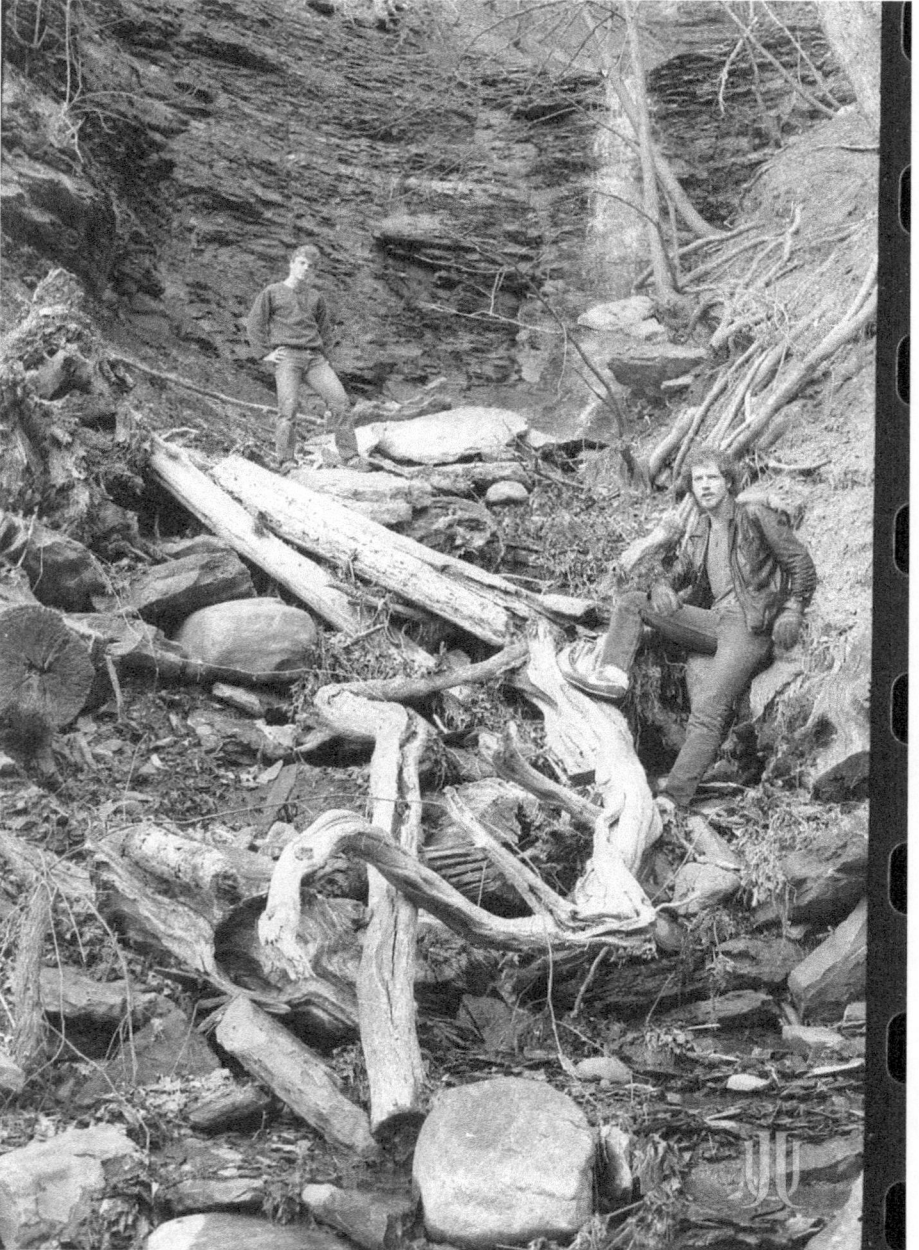

Above – Friends Di Cesare and Ungar at Fallbrook Park on April 26ᵗʰ, 1985.

Let me paint you a picture. A team of dedicated individuals build a film set in painstaking detail, reconstructing the 1985 college dorm room C2D1. The dorm set is replete with the appropriate posters, plush toys, books, art, pictures, and furniture. The producer William Edwards himself brings the lofts beds in from Western New York. A cast of outstanding actors and actresses is assembled. They've been carefully vetted based, not only on their sincerely wonderful talent, but on their ability to portray the real Geneseo students with essential veracity. They're dressed in 80s regalia, ready to reenact a proper dorm party that'd taken place in C2D1 during the first month of the haunting. Now, picture two great friends, 'battle buddies,' who survived the darkness of an extreme haunting a quarter century previous. Picture them as they quietly move into the back of the room – back into their own recreated past. The scene is about to start. "Cameras rolling," reports cinematographer Kerry Lyon, "quiet on set." As director, I state: "Action!" Aaron Katter is in the role of John Jeff Ungar and delivers a staggeringly accurate performance, full of just the right amount of concentration and social reservation as he plays a keyboard synthesizer in the corner. Dawn Sobolewski and Clara Heller (deftly playing the actual fellow Geneseo alumnae Linda Kalasinski and Beth Kinsman respectively) direct their exuberant lines to actor Kyle Shea who is vibrantly portraying Chris Di Cesare on the 'neg zone' couch. Kyle looks up at the loft for a moment as if he can sense the ghost (eerily depicted in PTWM by Nicholas Pearl). The chill in the air, the lights, and the mood all feel real; the room is a veritable time-machine. Amongst the merriment of the party scene, the second camera pans over while you hear the ladies' voices say "Chris!" And, from the back of the room you hear, "Yeah?" It's the voice of the real Chris! "Cut!" I call out, and the room reverberates with laughter. We all come to realize that what we're creating is so real that Chris and Jeff feel like they are home again. Who says you can never go back? I look over and see Chris laughing right next to Jeff who is, of course, covertly recording intermittently with a discreet video device. Classic.

Gratifying. That's how it felt in that moment. That is how it felt again and again on set, at wrap parties, at premieres and showings, as well as on the follow-up symposia tour and radio shows. At some of these events, the feeling has had the added dimension of certain other Erie Hall survivors like Linda Kalasinski and Craig Norris, as well as the person who actually blessed the room in 1985, Charles Manning. It was the feeling I had when I watched two friends walk, side by side, down a nondescript road in the falling snow. Part of that feeling is the lasting, positive impact of trusting others and, *importantly*, behaving in ways that are worthy of that trust.

Instead of making what could have been a thriller about a ghost – loosely based on true events – Jeff and Chris provided the inspiration to create a film about the human experience and relationships. The ghost was a catalyst, but it was Jeff and Chris' actions and choices that defined the story. They continue to mold it with their generosity, trust, and giving. From their example, we were able to unite to share a moving narrative that is utterly authentic and allows each audience member to step into that situation and ask themself "what would I do?"

I'd like to end with a selection from one of my earlier interviews with Ungar and Di Cesare recorded in late 2010. I asked them: "What role do you think the friendship between the two of you played in making it through the events?" Chris responded first: "I trusted him; I trusted him because I saw what he did. I watched his actions, he didn't hurt anybody. He didn't assail anybody. He was reliable. He had integrity. He was a nice, nice person." Jeff emphasized the point immediately stating: "I can say the same about Chris. He genuinely cared about people. When he was listening to you, he really wanted to know your answer, to hear your input, and he wanted to share what he could with you." "It sounds like there was a mutual respect there," I offered, "perhaps providing a grounding stone during those times of upheaval." Chris took a brief pause and replied with frank conviction: "I ran to him. When things started to happen, when the voices began, when the ghost started to appear, I ran literally *to him*. I could have gone to the police; I could have gone home; I could have gone to a professor; I could have gone anywhere. I ran to him, who I knew for all of a few weeks or a month tops. I ran to him instinctively. When you're in a panic mode where it's fight or flight, you do what you feel is natural without even thinking about it. So my subconscious was telling me instinctively: trust him. That underscores the trust I had in him as a person." "That's the takeaway from all of this," Jeff added with fervency, "it's that experiential quality about these events that brings out the person." Chris and Jeff shook hands after the interview. They hugged before they went home. I've been lucky enough to see the phenomenon of their friendship often since then, even just this winter 2019, almost thirty-five years after the haunting. I don't expect that bond will ever diminish. That gives me hope. My thanks to all of the survivors and witnesses; to the entire cast and crew; to you, dear reader; and always to J. Jeff Ungar and Chris Di Cesare.

5. Heart of Darkness

Above – 35mm contact sheet. Geneseo Landscapes, J. Jeff Ungar.

It is March 10th, 1985 – and I need saving.

It has been a good ten minutes since I had ambled into our quad bathroom for a hot shower. Now, I am lying face down on the chilled tile floor, bleeding, and not doing very well.

I can still feel the sting of the three cuts that run vertically down my tightened back. My feet and toes continue to ache because of the way I landed when I collapsed onto the floor.

Summoning what strength that I have, and with great difficulty, I turn my head to the left, taking the ever-increasing pressure off of my chin and neck. With my head now tilting down, I attempt to focus my eyes.

There is a fairly large, unmoving, white mass near my feet that soon comes together in my vision as the shower curtain that I had torn off of its bar while trying to defend myself. An inch or so from the curtain, I notice that the toes on my left foot are bent upwards and are very pale from an apparent lack of circulation. My carefully trimmed nails, a distance running necessity, are pressed deep into the meat of my toes.

I concentrate for a moment, and then signal my left thigh to 'lift'.

My running teammates often marveled at the musculature of my legs. It was time to put this vaunted attribute to use, but not for another trophy or medal.

This was more important.

A slow, deliberate command travels from my brain, down my spine, and into my limb. I can see the outline of my thigh muscle as it tenses up beneath my skin which is flecked with fine platinum hairs. I am relieved that it is responding properly. The movement creates enough space, enough opportunity, for my foot to spring quickly back into its natural position, and allow my toes to relax.

Yes!

The effort pays off beyond my initial expectations and I find that my entire body has now shifted just a bit. I am lying, partially, on my right side. This allows for the opportunity to continue my physical inspection, much like an auto mechanic might do. To 'check under the hood' of a car to see if it was still able to run. I wish that I was back on my run. I wish I hadn't stopped and returned here ...

My straining gaze makes its way from a now thankful, but still aching, foot and travels up the length of my runner's legs. I pause every few seconds to protect my neck from the difficult bend that it is currently making. I do *not* want to lose consciousness; the *thing* is probably still in here watching me as I lie helpless.

Waiting and planning.

A full month has now passed since 'it' had arrived, uninvited and unexpected. I still have no idea what it actually wants, other than to cause me to suffer.

I notice that a barely audible 'sigh' of relief escapes my increasingly dry mouth as I confirm that there is no (visible) damage to my legs. The 'meal tickets', the key to any future road racing success, remain intact. Though I have already established that I have little control over them.

That's likely going to pose a problem.

Shimmering lines of water cover the side of my stomach up to where my left arm now obstructs the rest of my view. It is bent at the elbow, and there is a throbbing pain here as well. It is the result of my flexed bicep being pushing uncomfortably into my forearm. The fingers on my hand, which are trembling uncontrollably, are fully extended; much like a bug's legs on the water's surface.

Are you kidding me, God? Why is this happening? Where are you?

It is a very selfish plea, and I should have known better than to make it.

How many of the millions of Jews had their prayers answered at places like Auschwitz or Buchenwald?

I am no better than them, no more deserving.

Lying there, I recall the stark, black and white WWII concentration camp photos from my history classes; stacks of unclad and emaciated corpses piled dozens high. A sickening recognition brings my thoughts to a halt: They were killed in the showers.

In the showers.

The bathroom is misty, and oppressive, and still.

My eyes fix upon a single droplet of water, and I begin to examine this suddenly intriguing, nearly-transparent, physical construct of two-parts hydrogen and one-part oxygen.

It hangs down, perilously, from the underside of my left wrist, which is located close to my face. It looks almost pear-shaped, and seems to be holding on for dear life; just like I am. I can see the inverted image of the bathroom floor being reflected in its bulb-shaped base.

It is mesmerizing.

Refraction.

That's the word that I'm searching for. That's why the image of the room is upturned inside the water droplet.

But the Universe is constantly moving and changing, and I watch as the droplet falls without a sound, just as I had only moments earlier, and flattens against the unyielding floor.

Gravity.

I am saddened until I notice that the droplet's wetness has darkened the grout between two of the bathroom tiles nearest my hand; the natural result of liquid hitting the porous grout.

Moisture.

It is a compelling awareness: that I am literally 'observing' my mind putting itself back together.

Metacognition.

Without actually making a conscious choice to do so, I am also experiencing a slow, steady, restoration of who I am and what I know.

The sheer weight of this effort quickly leads again to despair with the understanding that I will never have the cerebral strength required to do this, again and again. The *thing* is going to wear me down; it's going to kill me. Because no matter how fascinating the process is, I cannot put my mind back together each time it moves to destroy me.

It is a losing proposition.

I want to give up.

I want to go to sleep on a large, round, smooth, rock in some primeval forest. I want the crows to knead my skin with their sharp claws; to heat my ears with the breath from their pointed beaks; to carry my tired eyes away. Shutting my eyes, again, I wait for the crows.

They do not arrive, but *something* does: The sharp squealing of the door's metal wheels rolling on the metal track is almost deafening in my current state. A wave of much warmer and drier air arrives. I feel it pass over the back of my tired heels and up my trembling calves. I hear sounds, someone is speaking. The voice is nervous and unsure, but not panicked. I want to trust it.

"Chris! Chris! Are you all right?"

I am able to blurt out a soft "mmm …" but not any words.

Now there is a flutter of movement, the noise of sneaker bottoms starting and stopping on a wet bathroom floor. There is also the sound of nervous breathing, but it's not *my* breath.

I open my eyes when I sense I am being pulled up by two hands that are clasped together near the middle of my chest. They successfully pull me up onto my knees, but the arms attached to the hands seem to be trembling a bit from the strain.

They cannot do this alone.

There is a quality of friendly determination to them, I trust them. I command my legs to stand. They refuse, but the effort shifts my balance enough that the arms are now able to prop me up against the wooden door which rattles angrily as I lean into it.

"Chris, can you *hear* me? You're bleeding, what happened?"

A dry towel – perhaps my own - is wrapped, very tightly, about my waist. The warmth that it creates around my lower half is welcome.

I mumble out a weak: "Thanksssss."

"No problem. Are you OK to walk? Here, just lean on me."

I follow the words to Jeff's face, and I can see that he has worry etched deeply across it. Seeing him now, assisting me in this manner, makes me regret that I was willing to accept the crows only moments beforehand.

I never want that to happen again.

Jeff navigates me across the quiet hallway into the safety of his room, C2D2. His roommate, Ed, is standing as we enter, his expression implies that he is concerned. I am shivering uncontrollably from the cold, or the fear, or the exhaustion; maybe all of these things.

"And ...?"

Ed queried, raising both of his eyebrows in expectation.

"He was attacked, in the bathroom."

As Jeff carefully sits me down at the foot of his bed, my cold and wet feet leaving imprints on the tiled floor, Ed apparently catches his first glimpse of the cuts.

"Oh, my God ... Oh, my *God*!"

There is a pause.

Then he continues: "All of this is *real*, isn't it?"

Mark Keyes, a retired State Police Detective, currently working as Private Investigator, is the Director of the Pennsylvania Paranormal Association and author of *Chasing Shadows, A Criminal Investigator's Look into the Paranormal.* Mark has appeared on many television series due to his expertise in identifying and resolving hauntings and has served as an author's consultant on a variety of paranormal topics.

6. Analyzing an Urban Legend

I first learned of the C2D1 haunting when a colleague contacted me regarding attending a symposium with her at Penn State University in State College, PA in 2011. The subject of the symposium was 'The C2D1 Haunting'. Although I was unable to attend that symposium, it did peek my interest in learning more about the haunting and those who claimed to witness it. I reached out to, and connected with, Christopher Di Cesare who was the alleged focus of the events, via social media. I immediately found him to be very personable and quite accommodating to my inquiries about his experience. "Chris", as he asked me to call him, personally invited me to the symposium but I explained that I had a prior commitment but would have otherwise loved to attend. After hearing a little about his experiences in enduring what seemed like a very negative haunting, to the point where he was being physically attacked, I asked Chris if he would be a guest on an AM/FM talk radio show that I hosted in the Scranton/Wilkes-Barre area to discuss his experience. This was the type of show that offered the opportunity to many people from all aspects of the supernatural or metaphysical world to share their personal stories or to enlighten listeners on their specific interest in the paranormal and to provide a better understanding of our world from varying perspectives. Chris immediately accepted, and we arranged for him to come on the show on a date that was convenient for him. This would mark the start of a wonderful professional and personal relationship

between Chris and I that allowed me to learn much about Chris, both as a person and as a victim of a malevolent ghost.

I was very impressed with the great amount of personal detail that Chris shared during our radio interview. Fifteen or twenty years ago it was very rare that someone would share such intimate details, even with close friends, for fear of being ridiculed. Many people have been called crazy for sharing a story that was far out of the ordinary, stories such as seeing ghosts or believing that their house was haunted. With the onslaught of paranormal-related TV shows that have hit the airwaves, it has become more acceptable to talk about such topics, but Chris went into considerable and notable detail, and shared some very personal information in terms of what he experienced. I was impressed by his sincerity and the clarity of detail he still had for events that had happened so many (twenty-six) years before. Although, if this had happened to me, I don't suppose it would have been so easy for me to forget either. Sitting inside the studio listening to Chris recall his story took me to a very interesting place: I slipped into a weird state of mind, as though I was once again at work, as a detective that investigated major crimes, and listening to a victim describe an assault. I have heard testimony from many victims. The difference in this case was that the assailant was dead. The situation provided me with a very unique and interesting perspective. I was a detective trained to look at incidents objectively from many different angles, while at the same time acting as a radio show host who questions guests in a way that keeps the conversation flowing in order to keep the listening audience interested. The detective in me was starting to take over, and although I filtered my questions as not to get too personal or interrogative, but there were many, many questions that I wanted to ask Chris. I had begun to look at Chris' 1985 college dorm at SUNY Geneseo as a crime scene. The continuing list and descriptions of alleged incidents during the haunting had now produced other victims and provided me with potential first-hand witnesses to the activity. This was something that many serious assaults and other type of crimes often don't have. I wanted to know more!

Apart from my career as a Pennsylvania State Police Detective, I have been a paranormal investigator for many years. I put together a team of professional people with the intent and resources to respond to reported hauntings when the victims were not comfortable with the level of activity and wanted it stopped. Our goals were to identify what the original cause of the haunting was, find evidence not only of a haunting but also who the culprit was behind the haunting, uncover the intent behind the type of activity that was occurring, and in the end, resolve the haunting and stop the activity on behalf of the living. The assembled team investigates these types of hauntings just as we would a crime scene: with the utmost respect to the living, and to the departed, in order to objectively get to the bottom of what is happening. In many cases we found that what the family was initially perceiving was often different from what was actually occurring. But this particular case was both complex and detailed, encompassing many different viewpoints from the various people involved, both within and exterior to the dorm itself. My curiosity as a detective and paranormal investigator wanted to determine if the events that purportedly occurred years ago could actually have been a credible haunting, or if the information that was now being reported - years later - was just a bunch of college kids misinterpreting a series of events. Events that made them believe that they were experiencing a haunting, which often happens in cases that I investigate. This possibility was something that I kept to myself, but it certainly kept me motivated to learn much more about the events that were said to have taken place, as well as the people involved in them.

After inviting Chris onto the radio show and keeping in occasional contact with him, he asked me to MC another symposium that he would be speaking at, this one at the college in Geneseo, N.Y. I was hesitant to do this at first because I was not comfortable speaking in front of people at that time in my life. But recognizing that it was another opportunity to hear more about the haunting and see if the information presented was consistent with what Chris had told me, I graciously accepted. Plus, Chris was just such a kind and likable person, I wouldn't have said 'no' anyway so as not to disappoint him. One thing that became prevalent right away, once Chris began to speak, was that he was definitely a master storyteller. His passion and flare to present information to people was far beyond what I was capable of, which made me question for a second whether this was all just a story or an act that he was putting on, but his sincerity was so obvious that I soon dismissed any thoughts of this being just an act. Then, when I found out that he was a teacher, all doubt left my mind and I totally understood why he was so good speaking in front of people: That's what he does! But that was the never-ending skeptical mind of a detective continually trying to look at all options and corroborate information over and over again. It has always helped me get to the truth in both criminal and paranormal investigations.

I enjoyed the symposium even more than having Chris on the radio show and had a chance to meet Mara Katria, the Director of the soon to be released independent film, *Please Talk with Me*, which highlighted the human side of the effects of the haunting Chris endured. J. Jeff Ungar, Chris' college dormmate, who helped Chris through this difficult period in his life and who documented daily events of the haunting with strict detail, was also present and someone who I had the pleasure of meeting.

Above – Di Cesare in screen captures from a VHS tape recorded with J. Jeff Ungar. Keyes was determined to analyze both the strength and accuracy of Chris' ghost tale.

Speaking with Mara and "Jeff" as he invited me to call him, gave me additional insight into the haunting and added more credibility to the information that Chris related to me. Both, without hesitation, fully endorsed all the information being released about the haunting and Jeff was one of the first-hand witnesses to many events that Chris was reporting. One thing that stood out to me was that these were all very intelligent people in their adult lives, so I had to weigh that against what they were like in college. They did not strike me as the type of people who could misinterpret events that were happening, and they definitely did not seem the type to fabricate a story, but it was many years ago and they were now relying on a recollection based on memory and notes taken by J. Jeff Ungar at the time of the event. Although Mara was not present during the time of the haunting, she was in total agreement that Chris and Jeff were sincere in what they were reporting to her. I was able to take a lot away from this symposium. Chris seemed to have a great desire to share his experience so that others who may be going through something similar would know that they were not alone in their struggles, and that they understood that there are other people who might understand what they are going though. This stood out to me because as part of my paranormal resolution work I created a network for victims of a haunting to connect with each other. I found that was very important to help some people recover from their experiences. This was also the first time that I heard from Jeff and got to see some of the notes that he recorded in college as to the day to day experiences that were taking place. What I didn't know at the time was that based on the mutual respect that had developed between Chris and myself, was that I would soon be able to get a first-hand look at much of the evidence and an opportunity to speak with Chris and Jeff in much more detail about the haunting.

One day, unexpectedly, I received a phone call from Chris. He informed me that EIA Productions had been quietly working on a follow-up docudrama film that would present a type of, "What if?" scenario to the audience about how his haunting experience would unfold if it had taken place in a more modern era. It would be partially fictional in that it would give an alternate course of interaction between people who had heard about the haunting. The producers were calling on Chris, as part of the story, to be interviewed by a paranormal investigator who, initially, wanted to research the claims and then try to debunk the haunting. This is something that paranormal investigators will sometimes do in real life to get to the bottom of what is perceived as paranormal activity and dismiss anything with a reasonable explanation. Chris, taking into consideration my background as both a serious paranormal investigator and as someone who interviews people for a living, gave me an extremely great complement by telling me that, if he was going to go through this process, which was for the most part going to be unscripted, he wanted me to be the one to conduct the interview and asked if I would consider doing it and to appear in the film. I graciously accepted and was asked to get together with the film's director, Mara Katria, for more information on how she, and the producers, wanted me to be involved. I was very excited to be a part of this project because it would give me an opportunity to take a first-hand look at much of the evidence and notes that were collected during the period the haunting took place and to ask a lot more questions that I really didn't get to ask Chris during our radio interview.

Once I had spoken with Mara Katria, it really struck me how much flexibility they were giving me to interview Chris (in my own style) and just how intense they wanted the interview to be. In fact, Mara told me that they did not want to interfere with the interview of Chris in any way and asked if I would come up with a list of questions for Chris myself rather than have them provide questions to me to use. Mara related that although the film is scripted, she wanted the interview to be authentic and did not want Chris to know what I would be asking him so she could get raw reactions from Chris while they were filming. I agreed, and Mara advised me that she would furnish me with a copy of the journal notes that J. Jeff Ungar had written throughout the haunting and other physical evidence that they collected for me to analyze. I had already viewed the film, *Please Talk with Me* and heard Chris speak in-person and during interviews on several radio shows so I had a pretty good foundation to start my list of questions. If you ask Chris now, he would probably agree that I did not hold back.

When I started preparing for my line of inquiry, I had initially created a list of over 100 questions for Chris. Once I presented this to the film's director, she asked if we could work together to narrow the list to the most pertinent questions for time's sake. If we got through those questions quick enough, I could go to the secondary list, but the initial list really proved to be sufficient for the time I had been given and the intended purpose that I set out to achieve. Mara had asked me not to hold back on Chris and to conduct the interview just as I would as a detective with a suspect at work, with an edge of being more like an interrogation rather than an interview, which normally would be a little tougher on a person being interviewed. After all, my part in the film was that of a skeptical detective and seasoned paranormal investigator trying to debunk the story. When I thought about how I was going to conduct the interview I had mixed feelings because I knew Chris to be such a nice guy with a lot of integrity. It's tough to be hard on people that you like and I wasn't sure how he was going to react to the manner in which I was questioning him, or understand why it seemed like I did not believe what he was saying due to the type of questions I would be asking him. This was really pushing me beyond my comfort zone. To do this to someone I considered a friend at this point would be difficult, but as I do with criminal and paranormal investigations, I was going to be tough, try to trip him up on something, and be objective through the process to see where it all went.

The day finally came when I was to film my part in the docudrama. It required a limited amount of acting that I would attempt to do, and then conduct Chris' "interrogation". I was much more prepared for the interrogation as it would require no acting skills. The introduction between the two characters Chris and I played in the film that would set the stage for the interview and subsequent post interview interaction between us was the challenging part for me. Never having acted in anything before I felt very uncomfortable the entire time, so I wasn't very upset when those parts were completed. The interview, however, I was very much looking forward to. Since I was asked to be tough on Chris, I thought I'd have a little fun with this and see just how solid his story really was. As far as my work as a paranormal investigator, I pride myself at relentlessly analyzing evidence our investigators present to me. I typically find the actual physical or natural cause for whatever it was that happened. Many events that, at first glance, look paranormal often have a very normal cause to them. I debunked so much 'evidence' gathered by the team that the members started calling me "The Ruiner". This was my goal with the claims and saved evidence from this reported haunting as well. Not to ruin anything, but to take a very objective look at all the events, claims, and evidence and see if I could dismiss some of it as misidentified paranormal activity, or perhaps, verify that it was legitimate based on the information that I had to work with.

Above Left – J. Jeff Ungar photographing Chris Di Cesare and teammates during a 10K race on the SUNY Geneseo campus. Above right – Ungar's photograph.

The scene for the interview was set at a small table in the dining room of the Shanley Hotel in Napanoch, New York. This is where many of the events and scenes in the film took place. For those not familiar with the Shanley Hotel, it is reportedly a very active haunted location itself and a great place to film a story about a haunting. One of the very first things I noticed, just prior to the interview, after explaining to Chris my intentions and expectations of the interview, is that Chris appeared very outwardly confident and showed no signs of nervousness. Obviously, Chris was not under criminal investigation, so he would not likely show extreme signs of nervousness that someone in trouble would. But knowing that I was going to be digging into his story pretty deeply, he did not seem concerned that I would expose anything that he did not want me to know. Chris maintained this same composure for the length of the interview, enduring in-depth questioning about his life before the event; his time at school and with his friends during and after the period the haunting took place; his emotional state; his perceptions of the haunting and feelings of victimization; the fact that he agreed to assist in making a film about the events of the haunting; why he was now going public with his story; and many other questions related to the evidence that he and his friend, J. Jeff Ungar collected during that time period. Some questions were asked multiple times, and in various ways, to see if Chris would be consistent with his answers. Some were meant to make him feel uncomfortable to see how he would respond. Other questions were just for my own understanding about particular events that took place or why Chris did certain things during the haunting, this so that I could use those answers as a comparison with other potential people that I might interview in the future. As the interview concluded, Chris commented that he really enjoyed speaking with me because the questions that I asked were bringing out a lot of old memories that he had forgotten about, some good, some bad. That the memories helped give him more perspective on what he had gone through and where he was now in his life. Even though I was blunt with Chris, and fairly tough on him during the interview, he personally found value in it for himself and was pleased with the outcome.

Some of my initial impressions following the interview were that Chris either had an incredible memory and paid very close attention to detail when I was speaking or that he was being completely honest. Chris' answers were very consistent throughout the entire interview and gave me no concern that he was making up anything about his story. Many of the questions that I had asked specifically about the evidence collected during the haunting seemed to have appropriate answers for a typical haunting case and I do believe that Chris went through a period of having to deal with post-traumatic stress. My team often finds this in victims of extreme hauntings. Nothing Chris was reporting was out of the norm for an authentic haunting, nor did he make me think that he was exaggerating events. The evidence, as presented and explained by Chris, appeared to be legitimate based on Chris' account of how it was collected, but I did have some lingering questions about the process that was used to collect it and analyze it. I wanted to follow-up my concerns by interviewing J. Jeff

Ungar. Being that he was the one who recorded the extensive notes on the events that took place, he was the next logical person to speak with. As far as the interview with Chris, there was nothing that came out of it that concerned me at this point and nothing changed from my earlier impressions of Chris: He remained very sincere about what happened and legitimately seemed interested in helping others who may be going through similar events by sharing his story. One thing that started to stand out to me though, was that Chris may have been very sensitive to spirit energy, in a psychic sort of way. As a side note, the interview was so intense, people who later watched it on film whole heartedly believed that I was a jerk just trying to dismiss Chris' story and thought the whole encounter was a bit 'too real'.

A decision was later made by Mara Katria to have me interview J. Jeff Ungar. This was done on another date and at a different location. I would use the same interview strategy that I used with Chris and, for the most part, many of the questions would be the same to look for consistencies or differences in Jeff's answers when compared to Chris'. This is the fun part of interviewing: Often where one person's story starts to fall apart when the information doesn't match. Much of my questioning of Jeff was regarding the daily events of the people involved leading up to and during the haunting. But my true focus with Jeff was directed more to his interaction with Chris, the way that he documented what was happening, and how he collected what they considered evidence for the haunting itself. In particular, one of their main pieces of evidence was a 'whispery' voice captured on an audio recorder within room C2D1. One of my greatest concerns was that the way Jeff collected audio was probably not done properly, with controls set in place and steps taken, to reduce ambient noise that could have appeared on the audio recordings. After all, these were just college kids who had never been trained to investigate hauntings and would not likely consider outside contamination as a possible cause for the voice that was recorded within room C2D1. This is something that many modern-day ghost hunters fail to do and they mistakenly authenticate human voices for paranormal evidence because they either forgot hearing something or didn't account for outside contamination that a recorder can pick up even if their own ears didn't hear it. What I learned from Jeff is that he took into account that there would be students outside of the building or, at least outside of the dorm room, so he put the proper controls into place and made sure the area was free from noise and that the recorder would only pick up voices from inside the room. I was very impressed that Jeff had the foresight to do this at a time when there were very few paranormal investigators and no TV shows to at least mimic. This may initially seem like a small detail, but more times than not investigators believe they have found authentic ghost voices on recordings but when compared against other control recorders, the voice was just contamination from a living person speaking somewhere else. Jeff Ungar had accounted for this.

Above – The Circle of Trust. 1984-85 Erie Hall residents (left to right): J. Jeff Ungar; Judy Y., Beth Kinsman; Linda (Fox) Kalasinski; and Ungar's C2D2 roommate Ed S. – Photograph by the Chris Di Cesare. As private investigator Keyes noted during his investigation of the C2D1 Haunting, a large number of former Geneseo college students have come forward to verify significant portions of the oft-compelling collection of memories and details provided by Di Cesare and Ungar. Kinsman recalled seeing the "three scratches" on Di Cesare's back, and was present when Ungar shared the 'skeletal image' photo for the first time, Kalasinski also recalled the 'shower attack' and the change in Chris' personality after it. Ed S. was present when Di Cesare fled his room screaming after he first saw the ghost, and for portions of the Valentine's Day photo investigation during which some of the most iconic images of the haunting were captured.

Another piece of evidence that I was sure I was going to trip Jeff up on was the photograph that was taken in C2D1 - of a skeletal image - at the time that Chris said he was seeing a ghost. Although I must admit, it would have been quite a coincidence for Chris to point to the spot where he was seeing a ghost, to take a picture, and then what looks like a human skeleton in the very same spot appear in that picture. But I have been fooled before, crazy coincidences do happen. One of the possibilities that I pointed out to Jeff was that because the left half of the skeletal image appeared over a poster hanging on the wall, and posters are known to have wrinkles and creases in them, should someone take a picture with a flash, it was possible that the deformities in the poster could have caused a reflection of light onto the wall, essentially mirroring what was on the poster. Jeff acknowledged that could be a possibility if the poster was wrinkled. He told me that the poster was something they had checked at the time of the occurrence and he was certain that the poster was completely flat when the picture was taken (on February 14th, 1985). Again, I was very impressed that they followed up and considered these factors at that age and with no training. But what I had anticipated tripping Jeff up on was the fact that, although the image looked like a skeleton, it was being looked at by a group of college kids, during the time of the haunting, or even untrained adults now, all these years later. I asked Jeff if he, or anyone, ever had anyone with expertise, such as a forensic biologist or anthropologist, look at the image to compare it with actual human bones. Much to my surprise, he had. Rather than take the image at face value, Jeff and Chris had someone with a science/anatomy background at the college compare the image with a human skeleton and the findings appeared to be a relative match: a male human skeleton, facing away from the camera. Again, I was impressed that they took the extra step to validate what they believe was evidence of a haunting. Jeff's journal notes, documenting events that spanned the entire course of the haunting, were so comprehensive that I could only compliment him on the amount of detail that he had included. Many physical occurrences were noted in the journal, such as cold spots, physical manifestations, and other witness accounts of 'voices' and things that were not documented by audio or video means at the time but that remained pertinent to the overall collection of evidence in the form of witness accounts. I commented to Jeff as we neared the end of the interview, that given the level of investigative skill he possessed, even back then in college, I would not have hesitated in adding him to my team. For a bunch of college kids with no training or experience in paranormal investigation, they did an amazing job at documenting and validating the events. Jeff came across as truthful in his responses, and corroborated the information that Chris had given me with no discrepancies noted between them.

My interview with Jeff complete, the final part of my process was to look at all the factors including: witness statements (either by those I spoke with directly or observed speaking at one of many public events), documented evidence, methods of collecting and validating evidence, the other participants that were involved in the haunting (directly or indirectly) and then to come to a formal conclusion. I wanted to take an impartial, objective look at the entirety of the events to see if anything stood out as inconsistent with what I know of hauntings, and to offer an opinion on whether I found the haunting to be authentic in nature. One of the most prominent factors that stood out in my mind when considering if there was any fabrication in regards to this haunting actually taking place, was that so many people (over a dozen) were involved who were willing to collectively come out in a public fashion and tell their part of the story.

They were able to consistently recall many intimate details of the events that they stated took place, and many claimed to witness first-hand what Chris was going through. There were just too many people involved for this to have been faked. I can confidently state that I do not think that there was any misinterpretation of events by Chris, Jeff or anyone else involved. If Chris, Jeff, and the numerous other people are all truthful in their accounts, as I believe they are, I do feel that Chris Di Cesare (sometimes referred to as 'The Ghost Boy of Geneseo') did indeed endure a very negative haunting. As to the fact that he emotionally and physically struggled through the evolution of the haunting, I stand by my initial impression that Chris was psychically sensitive, and that he, out of several hundred students who attended the college with no issue of a haunting, was chosen to help a very troubled ghost who was reaching out for help in perhaps the only way he knew how. This lost soul was likely desperate to get Chris' attention and assistance and in cases like this, we tend to find extreme activity. Over time, I believe Chris came to realize this and received some personal validation in the way of discovering who the ghost likely was and their possible connection to each other. Through the strong bond that Chris had with his friends, I believe, they together were able to finally embolden Chris to confront this ghost head on, which ended up giving the ghost, and Chris, the peace that they both needed from this entangled relationship that they found themselves in.

7. The Twins

Above - Paul A. and Di Cesare stand in front of the newly-erected loft in room C2D1 on September 3rd, 1984. They were quickly dubbed 'The Twins' by their suitemates who noticed their many similarities. Photo by: Patricia Di Cesare

Once in a while, a heart-warming story surfaces about a person, who while sharing a photograph from their youth, discovers — ten, twenty, even thirty years later — that their future spouse, or boss or teammate unknowingly appears in the same photo. It offers us a comforting sense of inevitability, of 'meant to be', of divine providence.

The point here is that you may not always know when something first begins, or recognize a particular moment for what it will later come to represent.

Paul A. (as of this printing, permission has not been received to share his full name) and I had met the previous spring, both of us circling around the indoor track above the college ice rink. We found ourselves running lap after lap talking about everything and anything under the sun as we did so. He spoke of a local rock band that I had yet to hear of named 'Rush' and of his severe disdain for the quality of much of the college food, while I shared with him the (likely boring) details of the marathon courses that I had run and the importance of consistency in training.

In a matter of weeks, a friendship was struck and his family invited me out to their home near Geneva, in the Finger Lakes region of New York state. It was late April and we hiked through some woods not far from the shore of one of the lakes. Paul's mother prepared an excellent home cooked meal, and as I left, I offered to have Paul come down my way as well. Paul agreed to do so.

That summer, just before the Olympic Games were held, Paul came to visit my family. When he arrived, I invited several of my friends from high school to join us. It wasn't lost on me as we swam lap after lap in the pool, and as we hit the volleyball back and forth over the net, that both Paul and I both thrived on exercise. The mere act of movement provided us with satisfaction and purpose. Understanding that we had a great many shared interests and habits, we made a mutual decision right then to room together at Geneseo in the fall of 1984.

As I was deep into the summer road racing circuit (often racing four times a week) and would be busy training for the Empire State Games Marathon in August, Paul agreed to contact the college on our behalf. We were assigned room C2D1 in Erie Hall, and it looked to be a fresh new start for both of us.

On the day that we moved in, September 3rd, 1984, Paul and his dad brought with them a large wooden loft. I had never seen anything remotely like it. Once assembled, it reminded me of an indoor tree house. The thought of being perched (relatively) high above the floor's surface with little danger, or effort, was appealing to me.

More importantly, however, was that it provided some much-needed space in the typically compact college room. By having our mattresses raised up five feet in the air, we had increased our floor space quite considerably, which created the effect of having both an 'upstairs' and a 'downstairs'. It also allowed for additional privacy should we need it.

After we had tacked the prerequisite half-naked girl posters onto the barren dormitory walls, my new roommate added several strands of Christmas lights to the beams on the underside of the loft, which served to give the entire 'downstairs' area a decidedly festive look. The final decorative touch was a light brown fishing net, replete with dried starfish and other 'beach-type' ornamentation.

C2D1 was now an intriguing amalgam of childhood wonderment and night club desire.

Perfect.

I had never gotten along so well with anyone outside of my tight circle of neighborhood friends and relatives as quickly as I did with Paul. In fact, within a few weeks we had, perhaps unsurprisingly, been nicknamed 'The Twins' by the other students on our floor. We were, after all, the same height, had similar builds and were nearly inseparable in the early weeks of the semester. Paul with his matching dark brown eyes and hair, and slightly more serious demeanor, was labeled the 'Dark Twin' by our suitemates. I was dubbed the 'Light Twin', owing to my fair complexion, and more upbeat (perhaps frenetic) persona. Although we never called each other by those names, neither of us seemed to mind them.

For my part, 'Light Twin' was still preferable to what I had been nicknamed in the past, everything from 'Goldilocks' and 'Blondie', to 'Stretch Armstrong' (don't ask), and much more recently, 'Krill' by my first college roommate after my name had been misspelled in the college newspapers' sports section. How do you misspell 'Chris'?

Without question, Paul and I were as close as two friends, who still barely knew each other, could be.

Our skills and interests worked well together. What I lacked in 'streets smarts' was easily compensated for by Paul's expansive knowledge of both the local social scene and of various upstate customs (putting hot sauce on chicken wings), and where Paul felt that he needed to push too hard in order to win a 'decent' girl's attention, I tended to have them surrounding me. So much so, that Paul began referring to me as 'Romeo' instead of Chris.

So, tell me Romeo, how many girlfriends are you seeing now? Have you gotten in touch with that cute girl from Geneseo? I hope you get all the soft bodies you can, then I'll enter you in the book of records.

Above - Excerpt of a letter sent to Di Cesare by Paul during the summer of 1984.

This type of attention was something new for me. What made matters difficult for me was that I wasn't someone who was good at saying 'no'; at least, not since *Paula*.

Paula Perrera was a tiny little girl with a huge personality.

We had been friends since junior high when we ran modified track together. When we reached high school, she decided that she wanted to be more than friends. Her best friend at that time, Barbara Emery, confirmed (as recently as 2014) that Paula had developed some type of noticeable infatuation for me.

But all of this would come to a screeching halt when she decided to ask me out, publicly, on the sports bus one Friday at around 4:30 PM after an exhausting Winter Track practice. I had become exasperated with her relentlessness and had finally built up the courage to let her know that I would not go out with her, no matter *how* many times she asked.

The truth of the matter was that she already had a boyfriend, and we both knew that.

Paula grew visibly upset by my refusals and walked off the sports bus, against the driver's orders. The last thing she said to me, as she exited the dimly lit bus, was "You *should* have said 'yes'." She was hitchhiking home.

I never saw her again.

She would be found, after being picked up while hitchhiking – battered, raped, strangled, and left for dead – in a swampy area off Rt. 211 in Montgomery, N.Y. on March 1st, 1982; a few hundred yards from her home; she was sixteen.

When I left for Geneseo, a year and a half later, I brought with me a picture that Paula had given to me shortly before she was taken from us. I hid it inside of a metal-framed photograph of my young cousin that I kept on top of my dresser inside of room C2D1. No one knew of it, until several months later, when the ghost – or someone, or something – would tear open the picture frame as Paul and I slept, and leave the photo (along with the broken frame) sitting, smack in the middle of my desktop and several feet away, the following morning.

You should have said 'yes'.

For almost twenty years her murder went unsolved. During some of those days I couldn't help but wonder what would have happened, and how her life might have changed for the better, if I simply lied to her.

If I had just said, 'Yes'.

Above - Paula Perrera points at Chris, age 12, after he had set the 7th grade half mile school record of 2:30 in Middletown, N.Y. A few short years later, she was gone.

Eventually, Michael Bruce Ross, nicknamed the 'The Egg Man' (he had grown up on an egg farm) and 'The Roadside Strangler', was charged with Paula's murder through collected DNA evidence. A serial killer, Ross had apparently victimized eight young women, ages 14 to 25, all via strangulation between 1981 and 1984. Most of them had been sexually assaulted.

He was executed by the state of Connecticut via lethal injection on May 13th, 2005, the first in that state in forty-five years.

A book written by a former Columbia School of Journalism, professor Martha Elliot (*The Man in the Monster: An Intimate Portrait of a Serial Killer*, Penguin Press, 2014) serves to detail much of Ross' activities and his eventual execution.

Not lost on me, after Paula's murder, was the likelihood that for every young man like myself, who made a concerted effort not to use, or hurt, someone for self-benefit, there was somebody whose desire was clearly the opposite. To my mind, the world certainly had its share of gray areas, but this, clearly, was not one.

I wanted to stay as pure as I could.

Thus, I would continually find myself sitting on the edge of some girl's bed, trying to keep things as innocent as possible; or politely focusing on my, ever-cooling, dining hall meal as someone attempted to create a more 'personal' connection. Whatever it took, I wanted to try my best to 'save' myself for marriage.

My favorite quote, at the time, was from an elite Japanese Olympian, a marathon runner named Toshihiko Seko. He said: "The marathon is my only girlfriend; I give her everything I have."

At one point, I did approach Geneseo's top female distance runner in order to see if there was any interest, on her end, in starting up a 'friendship'. A friendship that, if projected out to the point of absurdity, might have led to us breeding an entire team of little 'super runners'.

As Jeff's journal notes would soon point out, I probably shouldn't have shared *that* part with her.

Like most roommates, Paul and I would have some very interesting conversations.

Although Paul claimed that he wasn't at all religious, or spiritual, he decided to confide in me, and eventually in Jeff, that he was being plagued by a series of 'prophetic dreams', multiple incidents of déjà vu.

In fact, by November 14th of that year, he had begun warning both Jeff and I that something "very bad," perhaps even catastrophic, was going to happen!

Hearing all of this, Jeff decided that it would be best to write down the information Paul was sharing inside one of his trusty notebooks. We did not know it yet, but this would soon become a very important pattern in our own friendship.

I watched as Jeff, writing implement in hand, began to create a series of what looked to be 'decorative swishes' on the lined pages of his trusty notebook. He looked more like a painter than a scribe.

Paul revealed to us that his dreams occurred "just between the wakeful and sleeping state" and although he seemed to be able to distinguish between which dreams would and would not come true, he often lacked specific details such as exactly when, or who, might be affected.

What alarmed him the most, however, was the certainty in his mind at this time, that if 'the situation' (whatever it was) wasn't addressed properly that he, or somebody else, might end up in a casket, surrounded by their family.

I glanced nervously over at Jeff, trying to get a read on his reaction.

Just a week or two earlier I had spotted the latest issue of *Discover* magazine (November 1984) in the racks at the stationary store uptown. It contained a special report on 'The Hudson Valley UFO Mystery'. I stopped in my tracks when I saw it.

It must be a different Hudson Valley, I thought to myself, not *my* Hudson Valley in New York state.

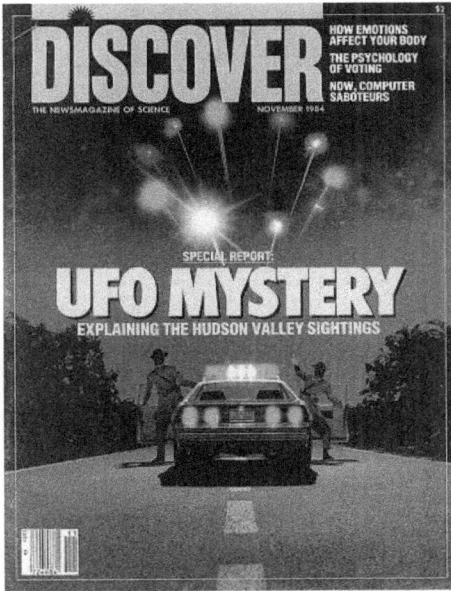

As I paged through the issue, I was amazed to learn that the area I was born and raised in was, said by some to be, a UFO hot spot.

One initial possibility that ran through my head was that the lights were likely from some type of covert military operation being originating the airport (Stewart International), just one mile from my home.

But as would be reported some fifteen years later (1998) in the book *Night Siege* by authors Hynek, Inbrogno and Pratt, the airport confirmed that none of those huge C-5a carriers had been flying in or out of the airport when the sightings began on March 24th, 1983.

In spite of the fact that I figured there must be some logical explanation regarding the phenomena being reported so close to my home (maybe a new stealth vehicle), the notion that there just *might* be alien craft flitting around in the skies above my home was disconcerting. Now this.

Jeff, meanwhile, was betraying no emotion, other than the obvious: an interest in the information being shared with him.

Paul had been in a very serious mood over the past few days, but I thought it was due to the fact that his relationship with Beth, an energetic and attractive brunette he had been seeing, had recently gone south.

Shifting in my chair, I leaned forward and tried to take a look at what Jeff was drawing. There was no drawing. Rather, what I mistook for the beginnings of a sketch was simply the artistic flourish with which Jeff wrote his words. It was a style of writing that would eventually be used to capture events that would transform my *own* life forever.

Apparently, my investment in what Jeff was writing must have allowed Paul to feel comfortable enough to bring me into the conversation in a more active way: "Romeo, you remember what happened the other day?"

I had no desire to recall what he was referring to. But soon as he had said it, my mind raced to a place where the memory had been stored.

"It happened just the other night. I was talking with Paul about how I wasn't sure if I was going to run winter track this year, when all of a sudden this look came over his face, it was spontaneous. Then after about ten seconds he blinked his eyes, started to hold his head in his hands and said:

'Wow, I saw this, years ago.'"

"Saw *what* years ago?" asked Jeff with a marked intensity, "What did you see?"

Paul pursed his lips for a moment. He was obviously debating whether he wanted to say anything. He looked over at me, glanced toward the ceiling, turned to Jeff, and then replied: "Let's just say that what Romeo was talking about, has something to do with it. That's what I'm worried about."

Paul stood up, clapped his hands together once, and then grabbed his bathroom supplies, signaling that the discussion was now over.

While the actual conversation had come to an end, the lasting impact of this conversation was just beginning to take root, and in less than three months, we were all going to pay a price.

John Jeff Ungar
November 14, 1984
Geneseo, Erie Hall c2d2

    I just had a most fascinating conversation with my suitemate Christopher V. DeCeasre' revolving around the topic of paul A█████, his roomate, whose nature of late sparked our interest. Paul has been quite moody lately, and from discussions previously, the cause of his strange moods seem to be "dreams or premonitions" of impending happenings. He has talked to me briefly about dreams he has had, that have come true; small occurrences remembered in episodes of De ja vu'. However, he feels quite strongly that things are happening and will happen very shortly which shall change or effect his entire life as he views it now. He is unable to say whether his life will be changed for good or bad, but he is noticeably upset. He seems to internalize all his fear, and except for brief revalations to myself or Chris, he refuses to talk about it. He claims that these things that are happening, the string of de ja vu's which are occurring more frequently, are leading up to some major event, and ominously asumes ists to be a catastrophe. Whatever he fears, he says it will manifest within two weeks, he will say no more to me although he assures me he will tell me afterwards if anything has happened. He will not write anything down and he is emphatic about not writing anything down. He feels its predetermined anyway. I hope for his sake that he survives this ordeal. All in all, though, he is not in control of

At left – The original notes of Jeff's conversations with Paul and Chris have not been found, but this type-written copy was found in 2016.

It was typed up in the fall of 1985 as part of an ongoing effort to analyze what had transpired just seven months earlier inside of Erie Hall.

Also mentioned in this packet were: the involvement of both Father Charles Manning and Dr. Casler. The ghost was referred to as 'the apparition'.

8. Dancing in the Dark'

Above - A block of photographs taken with J. Jeff Ungar's 35mm camera during the January 1985 Erie Hall Toga Party. Clockwise: Craig Norris (top right), J. Jeff Ungar (bottom right) and Chris Di Cesare (bottom left).

The entire first floor lobby of the C-Building had been filled with partygoers. Initially it was meant only for residents of Erie Hall and their friends, but by the time the cacophony of dance music, drunken laughter, clanking beer glasses, and bad pickup lines had wafted up the staircase into C2D, it was overflowing with dozens of party crashers.

I was aware, well in advance, that there was going to be a party on January 26th and that it was going to be 'themed' but I had not planned on going as the theme selected was 'The Toga Party'. I had only walked out of one movie: *National Lampoon's Animal House*. It seemed to me that this was precisely what we were going to get.

One of my suitemates, a talented guitar player named Luke F., (who looked a lot like Rick Ocasek, lead singer for The Cars) knocked on my half-opened door as he was passing by on the way to the party. He was wearing only a bed sheet and an expensive-looking red neck tie.

"You're going to the party, right?" he asked in a manner that suggested that I would regret it if I did not.

"I dunno', Paul isn't here so ..."

Luke didn't seem to dwell on the weakness of my excuse, and simply replied: "I think Jeff is going."

He was gone from my doorway, and headed off to the party, before he had the chance to watch my mouth drop open in overdramatized shock.

Jeff was going? Jeff? Jeff didn't even like it when the 'yahoos', as he called them, threw down a few beers over a quick game of poker. 'Yahoo', a term used to describe the brutes in *Gulliver's Travels,* was one that Jeff had been quick to employ and with regularity.

I hopped down the loft's ladder and scampered quickly out my door to room C2D2, just two feet from my own.

There he was. The man who never seemed to go anywhere without accessorizing two or three layers of clothing, was now standing in his room and wearing a sheet and holding aloft his trusty 35mm camera. I realized that it was the first time I'd ever seen his feet.

"Jeff, you're going to the toga party?" I asked in near shock, "With all of the drinking and cursing ... and the *yahoos?*"

He gave me a sheepish smile and then admitted, "I think I can capture some interesting photos."

Now I understood it! Jeff wasn't going down to the party to *participate* in it; he was going to *observe* it, to *record* it, to *memorialize* it.

I let out a healthy laugh of relief.

There could be no arguing the fact that John Jeff Ungar had truly become 'the eyes and the ears of the campus'. He was an extraordinary photographer, and was probably correct in his assumption, that if he went, he would certainly get some memorable shots; shots memorable enough to overcome even his well-established disdain for all things 'unaesthetic'. Without skipping a beat, I made a beeline back to my room. After all, if Jeff was going ...

I was pleasantly surprised as Jeff and I emerged from the staircase and gazed out upon the undulating mass of bodies moving to "Two Tribes", by the band Frankie Goes to Hollywood. Everyone seemed full of life, so happy and energized. Jeff set himself up in a corner not far from the main lobby entrance, his camera poised.

As I waded into the energetic crowd I realized that I knew very few of the revelers. Perhaps expecting that this might be the case for many of us, the party organizers were distributing name tags to help break the ice. Jeff politely refused to take one, informing the confused organizer that he preferred to remain 'anonymous'.

I too, would have foregone the nametag, but I didn't want her to feel as though she, or her efforts, were being marginalized.

As a joke, I wrote the name: "Apollo".

The reflections of the dancers on the insides of the windows soon caught my eye. The pitch black of the night sky served to create a strong contrast to the reflections of the flashing colored lights, the honey-colored drinks, and the bright white togas.

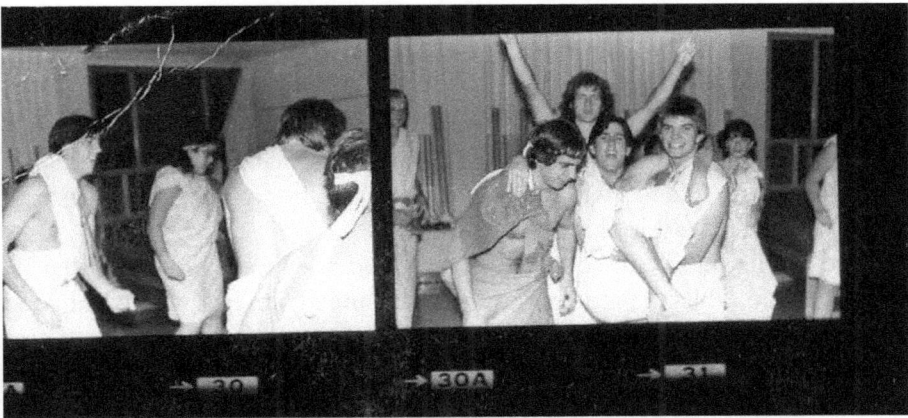

Above – Neither Di Cesare nor Ungar were a fan of wild social gatherings or the laxity of social norms, but the Toga Party provided both with enduring and distinct memories.

Normally parties tend to spill outdoors, onto sidewalks and into a bush or two. But on this cold evening, I could make out just one lone person on the outside looking in. It was difficult, at first, but I did see him. He was standing about twenty feet from the southernmost windows – on the edge of the darkness – and was almost remarkably still.

"Chris?"

I turned to see one of the girls from my Speech Communications class standing behind me, beer-filled cup in hand, looking resplendent in her makeshift toga. I felt bad that I couldn't remember her name, and the fact that I saw her on a daily basis made it far too awkward to ask her.

"What are you looking at?"

"Nothing really. Just some guy out there. He's staring at something. Hopefully he's okay. Do *you* see him?"

I pointed to where he was standing.

The girl carefully pulled her long, sandy brown hair back, and then pressed her face against the window.

"I don't see anyone," she whispers to me, "is he still there?"

At that precise moment, there was a loud 'BANG!' on the window just inches away, and the entire pane trembled from the surprisingly powerful impact. The girl screamed in abject terror - her beer spilling out onto her dress front - as she nervously grabbed my arm to stabilize herself.

On the other side of the window there was now a tall, skinny, dark-haired college student, completely stripped of his clothing, being pressed up against the glass. He was being held in place, against his will, by two massively built guys who were restraining him from behind. They were laughing, and he too seemed to be laughing, even as he struggled to break free of their combined grasp. Soon most of the hundred-plus partygoers were laughing as they too watched the strange scene play out.

"Crap, *that* was scary! Was that him? Was that the guy you saw outside?" my unnamed acquaintance asked, waiting for my reaction.

"No." I responded, recalling the characteristics of the unusual person that I had seen. "He wasn't as tall, or as thin, and he was definitely wearing clothes; darkish, odd-looking clothes."

His clothing had been so strange, and his demeanor so intense, that he looked to me a bit like a meandering, unbalanced, stalker. He had glared with an intensity as though we had been dancing on his grave.

There was a slight tingling sensation in my extremities as I considered that thought, the kind you get when you are home alone and the family pet begins to react strongly to something that you cannot discern.

"This is going to make me sound very weird," I shared with her, "but I don't think that he *wanted* to be seen."

"You don't sound weird," she offered. Her glasses did little to conceal the vivid blue and green hues of her irises.

The two boisterous, muscular dudes carried the cold, bare-skinned kid inside the dorm lobby atop their shoulders. A large portion of the crowd erupted with drunken cheers; alcohol cups and containers being raised in the air. The shivering student was quickly given a towel (which lead me to believe they had planned on embarrassing him) and he began walking over to an area near where the girl and I were standing.

I recognized him as he moved closer, and under the lights of the main lounge. He was an Erie Hall resident, an Irish kid from Long Island; Thomas something. O'Sullivan. O'Connell. O'Connor.

A short, heavy-set, darkly-bearded guy, with a pony tail wearing a red, plaid, wool shirt over his wrinkled toga made a disparaging remark about the kid's body. The Irish kid thinks that I made the withering remark.

He yelled at me to "Shut the f**k up!"

For me, using such vulgar terminology was no different than blowing cigarette smoke into someone face. In that instance, it was my face.

"Don't curse at me," I yelled, as I stepped forward into his personal space, "I didn't say *anything* to you."

Although the Long Islander's reach was significantly longer than mine, his arms were bony and reed-thin. I knew that he would 'break' much faster than me in a fight. I also understood that if we did fight, that it would probably hurt - just like the day after a marathon does – a lot.

Perhaps the Irish kid noticed the look in my eyes. Maybe he had seen my picture in the Sports section of the college paper, and knew that I was an athlete. Or maybe, just like me, he wasn't much of a fighter.

Whatever the underlying factor, he took a step back, and in a soft tone apologized to me. I was relieved, because even if I *had* succeeded in taking him down, his many friends might not have let go that unanswered.

I unclenched my fists.

None of this had dulled the girl's interest in me.

"I have to go," I offered, "I have to get ready for a big track meet."

I neglected to tell her that the big track meet was actually still several weeks off.

She was a bit saddened, but I was confident that she understood this was not a rejection; just an inopportune time. We kissed each other on the cheek, and I began my slow serpentine retreat through the noisy throng.

Jeff, for his part, was keeping a watchful eye out for what he hoped would be some notable photos. His initial take on the evening's catch was somewhat cursory and tepid: "The lighting isn't that good in here, so I'm hoping that I've got the exposure timed properly. At least my flash appears to be working right now."

At some point over the last half hour, he had acquiesced and was now wearing a name tag of his own; just like the rest of us 'yahoos'. Recalling the reaction of the girl when he initially refused, I liked that he was now wearing one. He noticed my approval and afforded himself a slight smile.

A quick Reagan-like 'thumbs up' later, and I was heading back up to the friendly confines of room C2D1.

I eagerly threw myself onto the old, soft, brown couch, and gazed up at the underside of the loft. As we had set it up in September, it remained adorned with multiple strands of large, colorful, Christmas lights along its perimeter and had a large, purely decorative, fishing net hanging down from its center. My ears were still desensitized from the loud music, and as my body began to relax, I wondered where the factories that had produced the lights and the net above me were located. How was it that all these objects had, to a positive effect, come together there and then?

I felt lonely. It was then that I remembered: Genesee Hall. The girl from the party lived in Genesee Hall. It would be a simple thing to go over and talk with her for a while.

Then, the thought of the strange-looking man, who had been staring into the party from the darkness, crept back into my mind. There was clearly something 'wrong' or 'unbalanced' about him.

Days later, I would share my concern with Jeff. When pressed, I described him as some type of 'crazy person', like an 'Eastern European gypsy' due to his strange clothing and pale complexion. Jeff found the whole situation oddly compelling.

Not wanting to risk a chance encounter with some lunatic (or worse) I decided to get some much-needed rest instead.

When Jeff developed the film a few days after the party, there were quite a few memorable shots. There is the picture that I had taken of Jeff standing like the great Roman orator Cicero. I can imagine him amongst the patrician senators declaring: "The life given us, by nature is short; but the memory of a well-spent life is eternal."

Craig's appearance echoes the marble statue of Augustus Caesar in Prima Porta, albeit with a cup of alcohol replacing the consular baton.

I laugh out loud when I see the photo that Jeff has taken of me (see page 71). Had I just climbed out of a Salvation Army dumpster?

Then I remembered, that early on in the party Jeff had succeeded in convincing me to return to my room to add some additional layers of clothing (a cap, coat, clip-on tie, sneakers, etc.). He had noticed that several girls had 'cornered' me by the north wall of the lobby. To the rhythm of Madonna's 'Lucky Star', they were trying to tear my toga off.

"You *know* what always happens when they (girls) get around you," he sternly warned me, "you don't want to take any chances, Chris."

Jeff understood my goals, and I dutifully complied with his suggestion. Though someone did manage to move my 'Apollo' name tag down to my groin area before I was able to make my hasty retreat.

Well played, whomever.

Eventually the images would become notable because of what they would come represent: The last images of us, before the ghost came.

9. An Echo from Amityville

2 - The LAMRON - February 8, 1985

The Warrens' Ain't Afra

by Susan Connelly
LAMRON Staff Writer

Excitement filled the air as the Real-life Ghostbusters Ed and Lorraine Warren, kept the crownd waiting in Wadsworth Auditorium. "Do you believe in ghosts?" was the most popular question being thrown back and forth amongst the members of the audience. This sweet, grandparent type couple, has been hunting ghosts for thirty-seven years; in that time-span they have dealt with approximately three thousand cases of exorcism.

Their interst began before the couple met. Ed Warren grew up in a house that was haunted, while his wife has been a psychic since her childhood. Ironically, both wre raised in strict Catholic settings.

The Warrens work closely with priest and ministers of all denominations. They are highly knowledgable on the power of God and the deceits of the devil. Although the Warrens firmly believe in all of this psychic phenomena, they admit that seeing and experiencing these occurences often depends on being in the right place at the right time.

The Warrens' goal was to prove, beyond a shadow of a doubt, that these things actually occur. They were very convincing. Slides,

ghost is seen only by an individual. Ghost syndromes are most commonly created because of tragedies. When a person dies, they refust to accept the fact that they have passed out of their physical

Douglas Dean - the incident from which the exorcist originated.

Other strange phenominon depicted ranged in a wide variety. Religious statues spouting ancient human blood and shedding genuine

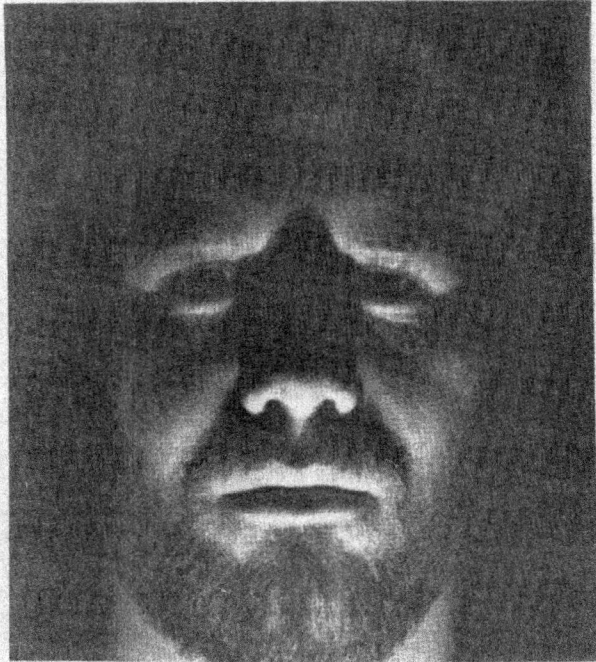

Above - The newspaper article about the Ed and Lorraine Warren's visit to Geneseo that appeared in the SUNY Geneseo college newspaper on February 8th, 1985.

In 1977, Jay Anson wrote *The Amityville Horror* (Prentice Hall). What it held in its pages would serve as the inspiration for numerous films, television shows, and magazine articles, including the now cult classic movie of the same name in 1979, starring James Brolin and Margot Kidder (who gained greater recognition as the character of Lois Lane in four Superman movies).

In his book Anson shares with the reader the purported events that surrounded the Lutz family, events that would occur in a short time span, between December, 18th, 1975 and January 14th, 1976; a mere 28 days. Yet, in that 201-page collection of written material and witness statements, George and Kathleen Lutz (both of whom spoke on behalf of the young children) would lay out a series of events so traumatizing, that they felt forced to flee their home at 112 Ocean Avenue.

It became the stuff of legend.

In the book's afterward, Anson offers the following in regard to the book's authenticity: To the extent that I can verify them, all the events in this book are true. His confidence was derived in part from the fact that George and Kathleen created an 'oral diary', an 'exhaustive and frequently painful' (45-hour) reconstruction of the events spoken into a tape recorder, from their combined memory. The testimony of witnesses was also considered, but the greatest 'proof' for Anson was found in the urgency and turbulence of their flight out of the home that had so terrorized them.

It had moved them to action.

Over the years many events recorded in the book, have been called into question. From inconvenient facts such as that there are no records of police contact made as described in the book, to the potentially embarrassing gaffe that the priest who was supposedly driven out by the malevolent forces in the house would later claim that he saw nothing when he was there. Then there are the questions surrounding the ghastly photograph of the 'Amityville Ghost Boy', which was allegedly a demon, or perhaps, the restless spirit of one of the young DeFeo children killed in the home years earlier. It is the one tangible piece of evidence that is known to exist. However, recent research has suggested that the figure in that photograph might have been that of Paul Bartz, an investigator who was working on the case alongside noted demonologists Ed and Lorraine Warren. He was photographed wearing a similar plaid shirt in the time period during which the 'Ghost Boy' photograph was captured.

Although I was alive during the time of the alleged events (ten years of age, and living a only 90 miles away) I knew almost nothing about them. In truth, I cannot recall ever discussing, or *wanting* to discuss anything about them until my days at college, in Geneseo NY, nine years later.

When questioned on the topic by Jeff Ungar, I was able to recall only "something about red eyes in a fireplace", which may or may not have been a part of the actual lore.

I had not heard of Ed or Lorraine Warren, but Jeff had, and they were coming to the college on some type of paranormal 'barnstorming tour'.

The date was January 30th, 1985, one day before Lorraine's 38th birthday.

Jeff and I approached the double wooden doors of the towering, ivy-covered, brick structure where the presentation was to take place. It was the kind of clear, chilled, night that called you to look up at the shining stars in the heavens above. I glanced around, through the steam of my own breath, at the high level of enthusiasm etched onto the faces of the crowd that was entering the building around me.

Once inside, Jeff led the way to a series of seats on the left side of the large room. About halfway down, he stopped, assessed, and then sat us next to the aisle. As I sank down into the red-clothed theater seat, Jeff was deftly twirling a no. 2 pencil through his moving fingers.

The auditorium reverberated with the sounds of excited voices and people exchanging greetings as Jeff began jotting down some words.

In gliders, they came, the 12, offspring of the Pleiades, there silver ships.

A few weeks earlier, Jeff and I had decided to collaborate on a science fiction based comic strip (dealing with intelligent design) named "Operation Overlord" that had been submitted for inclusion in the college newspaper. Jeff's written statement, about the 'gliders', had been an underlying concept for the strip. It had been my task to properly illustrate it.

Above - Operation Overlord comic strip (one of three), written by J. Jeff Ungar and illustrated by the Chris Di Cesare. The project drew its inspiration from the theory that God might have been some form of advanced extraterrestrial being.

I had even harnessed the once unthinkable courage to use my own sketched bare form in that particular strip; still unsure if a good Catholic should be doing that sort of thing.

Excepting the fact that the comic's story background caption had been taped on crookedly (most likely by me), I liked the result. Jeff and I seemed to have an almost effortless creative knack when we worked together. If the haunting hadn't soon consumed the majority of our time and energy, it would have fun to see where could have taken the project.

I offered a positive 'thumbs up' gesture, and Jeff handed both his journal and his pencil over to me, perhaps expecting me to add my own creative thoughts to the mix. Instead I simply jotted down what was about to take place: *Contemporary Forum Presents: the Warrens,* along with the date.

Jeff exhibited some mild disappointment over my lack of assistance.

As the theater lights dimmed, esoteric background music could be heard. A large screen hanging near the back of the stage featured the identical image of the two demonologists who Jeff pointed out to me on a flyer at Letchworth Dining Hall just hours earlier.

"Those are the individuals who investigated that Amityville Horror House" Jeff whispered with confidence, "they're well known."

I draw in a deep breath.

Here we go.

The Warrens' presentation was rich with what was purported to be both photographic and audio evidence. Ed reminded me of a modern-day P.T. Barnum, strong-voiced, commanding, and direct. There was no hint of hesitancy in his voice, or his mannerisms, as he facilitated the show; sharing with all gathered dreams made of spirits and mist. When he shared with the audience that 3A.M. was commonly called 'the witching hour', as it was an insult to the Holy Trinity, many in the crowd gasped at the mere sound of it.

I soon discovered that it was not Ed, but his regal wife, Lorraine, who claimed to be psychic; someone able to see 'behind the veil', the thin spiritual fabric that was said to separate the living and the dead.

They spoke of the Jackson Homestead; of the Brown Lady of Raynham Hall; of recorded cases of spontaneous human combustion; of multiple bleeding statues of Christ; and of the Borley Rectory which was said to be the most haunted house in all of England.

Most startling to me, was that they also offered a chilling account of an older woman who was photographed sitting in the backseat of a car ... at her own funeral.

That thought, that very possibility, frightened me to my core.

Jeff would find out why, in detail, later that evening.

In gliders they came... The 12, offspring of
the Pleides, there silver ships

Contemporary Forum Presents: 1/30/85.
The Warrens

psychokinesis - ghosts draw peoples/rooms
heat and appear — on infrared film.
smoke
president   laws of attraction—ghosts attracted to
ex on stage compassionate or sympathetic people.

- mother-in-law - 2 wrecks died in back of car
- Boy/dog — elderly woman staring at puppy
        curtains in windows

                                        laws of
- man standing at bookcase -(color)   attraction

usually alone   - telepathic image explains
                why some people see things while
                others don't
3:00 witches hour — insult to trinity.

psychic energy drawn from you— beads of light
from you — shot about— basketball size
image forms

        photomania— weight → died
psychic paralysis   cannot move.

*Above - The first page of notes recorded by J. Jeff Ungar during the Warren's lecture on
January 30th, 1985.*

Sir Arthur Crookes

- Katy King materialized — ectoplasm
  1874 — also recently Spain France
  Time and distance mean nothing in
  spiritual world

spirit guide — each has at least one

- Jackson homestead — lady / youth
- Vietnam shot
- Bio luminescence (child polaroid shot)
- Girl / Brother on tricycle drowned
  30 years before
  Earth bound - death - people
  do not believe they
  are dead - confused
  as though sedated.

curses —

Soldier, girl in churchyard - Hollybush Benz turned
1920   recognitions
  — Sour graves considered
  if they were lovers

- Brown Lady of Rainim Hall
  Coincidence of inn
  meeting
  records of Brown lady
Hall House — exorcism
  House burned down —

Above - The second page of notes recorded by J. Jeff Ungar during the Warren's lecture on January 30th, 1985.

records would have been lost if not
for coincidences.

— "woman/baby - in Interstate house
table in back   calamine

— SHC — spontaneous human combustion

— 2 young man in pickup st intersection
10 years apart to the day.

— The Exorcist 1949 — actual case
Demonology
                  non-levitate - vomit material
Bleeding Christ - Penn.
         Afternoon 3! — wafers appear
near statue

    Bernadet Subaru — Lady of Lourdes
         130 years — "uncorruptable"
                  never deteriorated.

    Globus castle - Scotland — 1/2 dozen spectres
         astral projection while tortured
                            in dungeons
                  believing they are in
         real body.

Above - The third page of notes recorded by J. Jeff Ungar during the Warren's lecture on January 30th, 1985.

Lorraine was truly elegant. She presented with an air of sincerity as she related their many experiences set all over the globe. I found her to be brave, very brave. I could never see myself being as brave as she was in that moment, standing on some large stage under the heat of the bright lights, speaking about things as controversial as bioluminescent forms, or levitation, or 'Christ Lights'.

But I also knew that life had a funny way of repeating itself, and when Mrs. Warren appeared to look in my direction as she said, "There is a Law of Attraction. Ghosts are attracted to compassionate or sympathetic people.", I paid very close attention.

Yet, as fascinating as all these concepts were, nothing in any book I had read allowed me to put full stock in the things that she, and her husband, have shared on this night.

Sure, Ed sounded genuine, perhaps even credible, when he listed the 'five steps' in a manifestation (encroachment, infestation, oppression, possession, and death) and when he offered that Ouija Boards were merely a 'distracting tool', that it was a person's *intent* to summon that was the true danger needing to be addressed. But come on.

I was certainly open-minded enough at the age of nineteen to accept that there were things that were too miniscule in scale or at too far a distance away for the human eye to see (germs and microbes, planets and asteroids). But over the ensuing centuries, humanity had developed the tools necessary to verify their existence. Tools such as microscopes and telescopes that served to amplify humankind's natural sight.

Yet while we could now see objects millions of miles from Earth, there was still, interestingly enough, no tool that demonstrated ghosts existed.

I scribbled a question into Jeff's notes: 'If ghosts exist than how come we can't prove it?'

It was an intentional effort to protect myself from being coerced into acquiring information that I would never be able to use, or into a belief system that might get in the way of potential successes in a career, a marriage, or a healthy social life.

The normally boisterous college crowd remained unusually respectful, having been quickly drawn into what was a fascinating presentation.

As the Warren's presentation came to a close, audience members were invited to approach the stage to meet, briefly, with the two famed demonologists.

An expansive line formed immediately, and Jeff excitedly signaled that he would like to speak with Ed and Lorraine, maybe even take this rare opportunity to ask them a few pertinent questions. Jeff was very well read (dozens of books could be found, scattered about his desk, at any given time) as well as a connoisseur of multivariate thought. So, the prospect of speaking with two paranormal icons, such as the Warrens, was not to be passed up!

Initially Jeff had been ahead of me in the greeting line, but in an effort to buy himself a few extra moments (in order to more effectively compose his thoughts) he asked me to move ahead of him.

For my part, I had no clue as to why I had even gotten on the line in the first place, except perhaps to accompany Jeff.

Or maybe just to be polite.

The line moved much faster than either Jeff or I had anticipated, and I suddenly found myself walking up the steps to the stage. I was about to come face-to-face with 'The Amityville Horror' folks.

"There is a Law of Attraction. Ghosts are attracted to compassionate or sympathetic people." – Lorraine Warren

I make direct eye contact with Lorraine. My left sneaker lifts from the final step, and I moved up onto the large, wooden, stage.

Then, time seems to slow.

I watched as her eyes began to focus squarely on me, as she drew back both of her shoulders slightly, and as she glanced nervously towards her husband, who, somehow, was already beginning to approach me.

Ed quickly moved in to block me, to prevent me from getting too close to his wife. He did so with a practiced ease and effectiveness that I would have normally associated with a veteran law enforcement officer, or someone with some military training.

Jeff's research, a few days later, would reveal that Ed Warren was indeed a World War II United States Navy veteran, *and* a former police officer.

In the midst of this commotion, as I was being forced off of the stage, one thing will stay with me forever: Lorraine Warren said to me: "I won't shake your hand, I don't want to know my future."

I was beleaguered by what had just occurred at the conclusion of the Warren's presentation.

Jeff had the opportunity to join the Warrens on a campus ghost hunt, immediately following the demonologists' lecture. A large amount of the audience was taking part. Instead, he had opted to sit, and talk with me, in my dorm room, C2D1 of Erie Hall. To assist me in making some sense out of what had just happened.

"Did you make any faces, any strange gestures?" he asked, his pencil scribbling furiously, trying to accurately record the events of the last half hour.

"Jeff, this is my face," I replied jokingly, "this is how I look."

As he shifted a bit in Paul's desk chair, Jeff mulled over the many possibilities now traversing through his active mind. He speculated that I might actually have a 'gift', something genetic perhaps, that Lorraine Warren had picked up on.

He asked if any of my family members had spoken about strange or fascinating events in their lives.

I uncomfortably detailed all that I could remember hearing:

- My 82-year-old great grandmother, on my father's side, once claimed to have seen the "Virgin Mary", who she said appeared at the foot of her bed, stared at her, then disappeared. She didn't like to speak of the occurrence, that had apparently happened some 15-20 years prior. She remained an avid churchgoer.

- According to my mother, her grandmother was said to have heard her brother, Michael Connaughton, calling out her name, while entertaining some friends and relatives at her home in NY. She repeatedly went outdoors, informing the others that she heard her brother calling her. They all claimed to hear nothing. What made the story truly frightening was that they found out, a few days later, that he had died on the RMS Titanic the very day that she had heard him calling for her! The story goes that he was coming back home to the states, after having failed to persuade his father to leave Ireland, and see America for himself. Since his father would not return with him, he exchanged his two tickets for one, on 'the big, new, ship.'

- My mother had a strange accuracy for guessing the gender of an unborn baby. I, myself, had curiously observed her guess accurately in 20 of 21 attempts to that point in time.

Twenty-five years later - I was obviously unable to share this with Jeff at the time - my paternal grandmother, Grace, would tell me about how her grandmother (my great-great-grandmother Maria Antoinette Ricciuti Fracasse) had been a seer, and a fortune teller. That she had brought with her, from Limosano, Italy, a set of very large, ornate reading (tarot) cards.

At left – The Fortune Teller. Maria Antionette Ricciuti Fracasse, Christopher Di Cesare's great-great-grandmother.

"I was living with my grandmother when I was around 7 or 8 years old. People would come, from all over, to talk to my grandmother. They came from New York City, from New Jersey, from Chicago even. How they knew about her, I had no clue. It was all kept very quiet. She would tell me to go out and play."

Well, like any curious child, one day my grandmother Grace found a 'door' in the headboard of her grandmother's bed. Inside she found all sorts of items from the reading cards to what she claims were actual 'lobster eyes'. She claimed to often wonder about these things, and that she decided at that tender young age she too would conduct some readings herself, once she got a little older.

At left – Elvira Fracasse Barrar, Chris' great-grandmother. A snake charmer in a traveling circus, she was killed in an automobile accident (while pregnant with a son) when Di Cesare's grandmother, Grace, was still a young child. Grace was then placed with her own grandmother in Newburgh, NY.

Eventually her grandmother became gravely ill, and she lay in her bed in a coma-like state. The doctor advised the family that she would soon pass on.

Friends and relatives gathered

by her bed to pay their last respects.

But one day became two, and then three, and then four.

At right – Chris Di Cesare, age 9, standing with his grandmother, Grace Di Cesare, at Cronomer Hill Park in 1974.

"We tried everything to make her comfortable, opening windows, adjusting her covers. Then, I said to my Aunt Margie, 'I know what to do!'"

When she had the opportunity, Grace retrieved the tarot cards, and with her worried Aunt by her side, threw the entire deck into the furnace of the Newburgh, NY home.

"And wouldn't you know it, Christopher," she said "the death card turned face up! Aunt Margie would be able to verify this, too, but she's gone now."

Grace and Margie went back upstairs, and at midnight, just two hours after the cards were burned, her grandmother was gone.

"Some people believe, and some don't," she offered, "but you know the flash of information when it comes to you. I don't know where it comes from, maybe God, but I've felt it."

I did have one story of my own to share with Jeff on that night, and was anxious to hear it.

In fact, it had occurred on January 29th, 1983, almost exactly two years earlier, to the day.

Sacred Heart Church, Newburgh.

My family and I had arrived to church ten minutes late (which seemed to have been our unintentional custom) and thus were forced to stand in the back of the church, so as not to interrupt the priest while he shared his homily with the congregation.

The sole benefit of this inconvenience, to a young boy, was that we were the closest to the church doors. This meant that when the mass was completed we would be among the first to be able to make it out the front door and back to our cars.

Victory!

However, to my obvious dismay, on this particular day my father mentioned to us that he had seen some of our relatives during the service, and he wanted to wait and say 'hello' to them before we left.

I stood on the marble steps of the church, and watched as parishioner after parishioner shook the priest's hand, and then filed around me to the sidewalk that rang alongside Route 9W.

Among the last to straggle out of the church was my great-great-uncle Johnny Rotundo (his sister being my great-grandmother Mary who had claimed to have seen the Virgin Mary image at the foot of her bed) and his wife Betty. Both were in their late sixties at that time. When he saw me, Johnny walked over and began to shake my hand in an unusually energetic manner.

"It's great to see you, Chris," he smiled.

While I certainly appreciated this newfound interest, I was perplexed by the sudden intensity of it. He was behaving as though he hadn't seen me for several years, when in fact I had seen him just two weeks prior.

Dementia?

Then, it happened.

A 'look' came into his eyes, a kind of look that, to me, indicated: I know something that you do not, but that you will know soon enough.

In that moment, I swore that I could see something swirling around his head, like a thin, white, animated mist. A mist that, upon reflection, looked an awful lot like the gold circles that were painted in those old religious paintings.

Then everything noticeably decelerated.

"Howwww arrrre youuuu?"

The words rolled ever-so-slowly out of his mouth, as the world seemed to came close to a full stop all around us; then kicked back – accelerating - into gear.

Johnny nodded to me, and then proceeded on to greet the other members of my family, as though absolutely nothing unusual had just occurred.

I looked around – frantically – to see if anyone else was reacting to what had just occurred.

I was completely alone in the crowd. It was a feeling that I would eventually experience with great regularity, one that I would have to learn to accept.

Five minutes later, as we walked back to our parked car near the bustling football field, I felt compelled to ask: "Did anyone else see what happened with Uncle Johnny, on the church steps?"

Silence.

"You know, the whole 'mist around his head thing' and the slow-motion way that he was talking to me?"

Their expressions told me all that I needed to know.

My father chuckled a bit and suggested that I might be 'reading too many comic books'. My mom wore a worried expression, her mind considering my words. My two younger sisters, well, they just stared at me.

But that was normal.

Eighteen days later, on Ash Wednesday, my uncle Johnny was dead.

IN LOVING MEMORY OF

JOHN A. ROTUNDO
Entered Into Rest
February 16, 1983

RESURRECTION PRAYER

Most merciful Father, we commend ou departed into your hands. We are fillec with the sure hope that our departed wil rise again on the Last Day with all whe have died in Christ. We thank you fo all the good things you have giver during our departed's earthly life.

O Father, in your great mercy, accep our prayer that the Gates of Paradis may be opened for your servant. In ou turn, may we too be comforted by th words of faith until we greet Christ ii glory and are united with you and ou departed.

Through Christ our Lord.　Amen

COLONI FUNERAL HOME
New Windsor, New York

Jeff's summary on that night read as follows: It seems that both (sides of the family) have genetic ability to use untapped parts of the human brain, and Chris has received from them an even greater capacity.

Lorraine Warren could not have known *any* of this, yet somehow, she absolutely did.

10. A Voice from the Darkness

Above – The loft as it appeared in room C2D1 in late September, 1984. 'Upstairs': Paul's mattress is on the left, Chris' (partially obscured) is on the right. By the time the haunting began, Di Cesare had replaced the generic hot air balloon poster with one of marathon runner Bill Rodgers, that would appear in the 'skeletal image' photo.

It was Monday, February 11th, 1985, and I was walking back to Erie Hall in an aggravated mood. It was 26°F and my nose felt frozen. A thin layer of crystallized ice was forming underneath my jogging suit; sweat from an intense track workout that was now freezing as I trudged my way across the windy winter campus.

Normally, after the track team workout, we would all hit the showers and clean ourselves up a bit.

In fact, we were *expected* to shower. We were also required to dress in a way that properly represented the college on our frequent trips across the state: formally. Walking into a fine dining establishment wearing muddy running shoes, and with salt residue on one's face, was not going to fly!

Making the adjustment to showering, often elbow-to-elbow, with my college teammates was not as difficult as I had imagined it might be. In part because I noticed, early on, that those commonly joked about male stereotypes (regarding one's shoe size, or height, or ethnic background) were typically off base; which worked in my favor.

Ultimately, the experience of the communal shower was not much different than the contrast between the shock of changing a baby's dirty diaper for the very first time, and raising several children over the years:

You quickly get used to it. Besides, whatever our physical, cultural, or political differences, we were all trying to do the same exact thing: run as fast and as far as we could.

However, now that I had grown accustomed to the new-found luxury of using the showers inside the athletic center, they had apparently stopped working.

A considerate-minded hockey player (the sound of unseen workers banging away on some pipes behind him) informed me that the showers were not operational. Some of the water pipes had frozen.

That is why I was now walking back to Erie Hall … chilled, tired, and more than mildly aggravated.

C2D1 is dark and quiet.

The large brown 'care package' that my parents had sent me, in advance of Valentine's Day, sits quietly at the foot of my desk, unopened.

As I switch on the standing floor lamp beside the window, the heavy wooden loft above me emits a loud creak. I have never heard it make such a loud sound before, and my first reaction is to bolt out from under the loft, so that it will not collapse on top of me.

I watch the objects on my desk for movement, and look for evidence, perhaps, of a minor earthquake. They were quite uncommon on the east coast, but did occur from time to time. I rule that possibility out, as there is no commotion echoing through the dorm hallways, and because my trusty Ulster County Pentathlon pen holder is not rocking as it characteristically did, from even the slightest of vibrations.

Paul and I, combined, weighed almost three hundred pounds, and the loft had never so much as even 'squeaked' or 'clicked' before.

This was unusual.

Glancing up into the darkened area by the ceiling that contained our mattresses, I call out: "Paul?"

There is no motion, or sound.

Moving over to the nearest of four support beams, I attempt to give it a good shake. It does not budge, and there are no discernable signs of cracked wood or chipped paint that would indicate some type of damage.

Perplexed, I take a seat on the edge of the couch.

The loft emits another noise. Only this time, it is the sound of someone crawling across the top of it!

Yikes!

My new conclusion is that Paul has decided to play a sick joke on me. There was no precedent for this, but I accepted it as the most likely possibility under the circumstances.

Well, *two* can play that game!

I carefully slide off my running sneakers, in order to reduce the sound any walking would make, and, as silently as I could, I creep out across to the quad bathroom.

The large wooden door had been left open, so I am able to quietly fill one of my plastic cups with cold water from the sink faucet and then creep back to the room.

My plan is a simple one: slide up the ladder, locate Paul, and then douse him with the water. Thus, a taste of his own medicine.

Everything proceeds effortlessly, and according to plan, with one significant exception. When I climb up the loft's ladder, no one is there!

What the ...?

I squish up my face in confusion, decide to drink the water, and then return 'downstairs'.

My mind races back to something earlier in the day that had been just as bizarre, and just as unexplainable.

I had been working on a college paper, my fingers typing away in synchronized fashion, when I heard someone call out my name.

"Chrissss!"

But I was not about to have my workflow impeded, so without glancing up from my work, I nonchalantly replied, "Come in."

There was no answer, and nobody entered the room.

Fair enough, I preferred that. Whoever it was that had called my name had evidently moved on to bother someone else; someone who wasn't as busy as I was.

I returned to my pile of reading material. A minute or two later I heard the voice again.

"Chrissss!"

This time it sounded louder and closer and stronger.

Confused by its proximity, I decided to get up out of my chair to see who it was. It wouldn't be too difficult a task to let the person know that I was too busy to engage in a conversation right now.

I opened the door of C2D1 and glanced in both directions down the empty hallway.

"Hello?"

No one was in sight, in either direction.

"If this is a joke, it is not funny," I declared to no one.

Fittingly, no one answered.

My mind, now markedly muddled, I shut the door and then, ducking under the loft, made my way over to the second-floor window. I looked down at the sidewalk below, no one down there either, not a single soul.

This had to be some type of practical joke, I decided. What else could it be? As funny or entertaining as it might be to someone else, right now I was not about to be part of it. I still had an academic deadline to keep and a paper to type.

In order to rid myself of any further bother, I powered up Paul's stereo and inserted his Sammy Hagar, *Voice of America,* CD. The hard rock CD had just been released the previous July and Paul loved listening to it.

Above — The area below the loft as it appeared in room C2D1 in late September, 1984. Paul's stereo is visible to the left, as are the Christmas lights and fish net on the loft's underside. The poster, from the 1983 film 'Flashdance', was also Paul's.

Fitting the large, cushioned, headphones over my ears, I settled back into my desk chair to return to the task at hand.

The first song to play was *I Can't Drive 55.* The song had initially offended my sensibilities. Why would a public figure willfully advocate for a violation of the speed limit? But for my current purpose, it was ideal. The loud, fast-paced rock anthem would easily be able to drown out the sounds of anyone who might continue to pester me. Especially with Paul's headphones fitted securely over my flattened-against-my-head ears.

Barely a minute into the song, it arrived. Inside the headphones, *over* the loud music, I again heard:

"Chrissss!"

In a state of severe panic, I had thrown the headphones on the floor, turned the stereo off, and quickly fled the room; eventually making my way to track practice.

That had been three hours prior.

Now confronted by the additional turmoil of the broken gym showers and the strangely creaking loft, I just wanted the madness to stop. I wanted to take my shower.

The sweat that had frozen on my body on the walk from the gym is now warming into cold droplets of water that, at uncomfortable and unpredictable intervals, race their way down the center of my back and into the waistband of my running shorts, giving me the shivers.

When I open my closet door to get my shower supplies I am startled by a frigid blast of air that pushes past me and out into the open room.

Things have become downright eerie in Erie Hall.

I move my hands around the darkened closet space in search of a partially-used ice pack, or anything else that might have caused this intense drop in room temperature. A sleeve, from one of the running shirts that hangs in the closet, drops lightly onto the back of my neck. I jump up and leap back from the closet. Taking a moment to catch my breath, my eyes note the gently swaying garment, and I laugh out loud; "Stupid shirt."

I decide to close my closet door.

Turning towards my dresser; I feel a sharp tug on my right Gore-Tex sweat pant leg. This was odd, because there was currently nothing near me that it could have gotten caught on. Looking down, I notice that the ankle snap has now 'popped' open.

On any other day, and in any other place, I would not have noticed this. But on *this* day, it is all that I can concentrate on.

I bend at the knees, and work the snap with my fingers: snap – unsnap – snap – unsnap.

The structure is sound.

I rally around the notion that I simply had not snapped it completely closed before my run, or perhaps, that I had partially loosened it prior to being told that the gym showers were not functioning.

Amid all the other chaos, this was certainly possible.

The left ankle snap opens.

Still, I counsel myself, I *had* been bending forward, and the flexing of my calf muscle might have placed added pressure on the fabric around the metal clasp.

This was all logical enough.

Then the snap by my neck, accompanied by a notably icy draft, opens.

Not so logical or likely.

I stand back up, and can feel the few microscopic hairs on the back of my neck rise in fear as I watch - my latched - closet door slowly open.

There is now a visible two-inch gap between the folding door's edge and the door frame.

The air in C2D1 is dry and cool, and the latch might not have caught properly when last I closed it. Reaching over, I make sure that I latch the closet door properly this time.

I give it a quick tug.

Again.

It remains latched.

For some reason, I now have a slight ringing in my ears. I want it to go away. Rubbing a hand across my forehead, I feel some of the built-up pressure begin to leave my eyes. I need to stretch out my muscles.

The dried particles of salty sweat on my fingertips remind me that I still need to take a shower as well.

I strip off my wet, soggy, clothes.

Moving to the exact spot in the room, where Jeff would later take the famous photograph of me 'calling' the ghost, I stretch out up onto my toes, reaching up with arms extended towards the roughly textured, spackled ceiling. My arches, my calves, my shoulders, and my biceps are now warmed by the flow of blood into them as they expand. Letting my head drop back a bit, allows my neck to release some additional tension.

I close my eyes.

I try to clear my mind.

Relax.

I take a few moments to knead my wrists and palms and fingers to reduce the tenseness in them. I lower myself into a sitting position and extend my legs out in front of me. The back of my knees feel the calming pull and leaning forward, I grab my feet and begin to pull them back towards me. My hands pull with a constant pressure until my toes can bend upwards no more

This was a pre-workout exercise that the entire cross country team completed at the start of each workout. I was never a big fan of stretching before a run, allowing that my legs would gradually 'kick into gear' by themselves, but I am now fearing that some type of nervous breakdown might be occurring. I had seen some athletes fall to pieces (crying, yelling, throwing things) as an important race was about to start due to stress. I know enough to recognize that seeing and hearing things that are not actually there is a *major* problem.

Turning my head, I notice that Paul's silver and black headphones are still lying on the floor. I had thrown them off of my head earlier in the day after hearing the strange voice calling out my name.

They sit there in silence, not far from me, looking out of place.

Lifting myself up off the rug, I place them carefully atop his stereo.

Turning away from the stereo I am alarmed by the fact that the closet door has, somehow, opened again.

I stand absolutely motionless.

There is something very, very *wrong* about all of this.

An unknown fear washes over me as unseen waves of ice cold move around and about my uncovered feet, calves and thighs. My body, perhaps instinctively, tightens, and I squeeze my hands into fists.

Some*thing* is in that darkened closet.

Total and absolute panic sets in.

I sprint past the partially open closet, casting my bathroom towel behind my head and down over my back, and like a young child who is deathly afraid of the sound of thunder, I make a mad dash into the bathroom.

My arm muscles flex with extreme effort as I feverishly slide the heavy wood door back across its track in order to close it; to keep whatever that thing is from following me.

Leaning my full body weight up against the door in order to keep it closed, I look at my heaving, frightened reflection in the mirror. I am not looking very happy right now, more like a six-point buck draped over a hunter's roof rack.

I have absolutely no idea what the *hell* is going on, but I do know one thing: I am going to take my shower!

I can't.

Tremors of fear shoot through my body from the 'imagined' terror, and as I stand under the shower head, I cannot bring myself to turn the water on.

Whatever has gotten into my mind has now become dangerous. I am still confident that, with the passage of enough time, the creaking loft, the disembodied voice, and the unlatched closet door would be logically explained away. But that unknown length of time certainly has not yet passed, and for me to cover my eyes and ears with running water would be nothing less than foolish. How would I hear it, or see it, if it decided to come after me?

A part of me, the disciplined and organized runner, is now actively and forcefully judging my fear: Are you *kidding me,* seriously? Do you actually believe that there is some *boogey man* in the closet? *Turn the damn water on!*

Fear wins out.

I stand, in this shower stall, for at least twenty minutes; possibly as many as forty. For the life of me, I can't ever remember being this cold before. The air temperature in the building is at least 65°F, yet my finger nails, my lips, and any other place that does not produce melanin now retains a slight blue tint.

'I'm a blue blood, I'm royalty," I joke silently to myself as I shiver uncontrollably in the shower stall. Yet nothing about this situation is even remotely funny. I cross my arms in the failed attempt to reduce the aggravating shivering, to hold myself still. If the *thing* should come for me, I need a plan, and that plan requires a body guard; there is safety in numbers

One arrives.

Paul enters the quad. He is whistling a familiar tune, and I can hear him as he walks past the heavy wood bathroom door and into C2D1.

This is amazing luck!

After he has a few moments to 'settle in' from his long day of classes, I will call him into the bathroom and then create a conversation – about anything under the sun – in order to keep him nearby.

This does not happen.

For as I formulate my plan - one that would involve me running towards the right into the main hall area, and not to the left into a dead end - I hear Paul screaming in what sounds like abject fear: "Holy shit! Holy *shit!*"

Before I have the opportunity to call out to him, the wooden door to the bathroom screeches open, and Paul, looking like he has just seen the family dog run over by a truck, is gasping for air, bent over slightly, with both hands on his knees.

He looks terrified.

"Paul?"

Against my intent, I scare him badly. He jumps back with a look of sheer fright etched on his face. He had not been aware that I was in here, as I had been hiding, silently, behind the flimsy shower curtain.

"What's the matter with you?!" he yells while trying to catch his breath. "Why are you trying to scare the crap out me?"

"Sorry," I replied in mock complaint, "I was about to take my shower, what's the matter?"

His big brown eyes are still wide with fear, and I can tell that he is deliberating whether or not he should tell me. Given the day's events, I can certainly empathize.

"You won't believe me," he says, between pained and apprehensive glances over his shoulder into our room.

"Tell you what," I offer with my hand literally extended outward for effect, "Why don't you just hang out here for a bit. When I'm done cleaning up we can go back to the room together, and you can decide if you want to tell me then."

He glances once more over his shoulder, and then gazes directly into my eyes. There is a moment's hesitation. Like me, he is in uncharted territory. He slowly nods his head in the affirmative.

I have my guard.

Above — Geneseo negatives by J. Jeff Ungar. The once-friendly college environment was viewed in a different light by Di Cesare and his roommate as soon as the haunting began.

I can only imagine what thoughts are running wildly through Paul's mind as we walk into C2D1. He gives me a minute to get dressed and then, in the most honest face I can imagine says:

"There is something in here!"

I shoot a quick glimpse over at my closet door, which remains open a few inches, and I hope that Paul doesn't notice.

"What do you mean?" I ask trying my best to calm the queasiness that is growing in my stomach.

Paul blinks his eyes a few times, almost as if he was holding back tears, and says, "You aren't going to believe this. I know this is some crazy shit, but ..."

He takes a few steps over to his desk and then with his back turned to me, he begins to recreate the events that led up to his frantic sprint into the bathroom area.

"I came into the room," he says retracing his steps, "put my books and my room key down, and then I heard someone say your name:

"Chrissss!"

His eyes look worried as he turns to me, "But no one was here. The voice was *this* close," he adds putting about a foot between his ear and his extended hand which now gestured towards my side of the room. "I'm telling you, I swear, there was no one in here! It called your name, twice! I freaked!"

Paul paces back and forth a few times, and then repeats his words and his actions: "The voice was *this* close!"

There is not much that I can say right now.

I am still wrestling with my own doubts and fears. I still haven't ruled out that this is one elaborate, and epic, prank.

But the threads of my courage have already started to fray. That Paul had heard the 'bodiless voice' is at once frightening *and* comforting to me. Frightening in that something freaky is going on in the place where we work, talk, and sleep, comforting in that I can now be slightly more confident that I am not having a nervous breakdown or losing my mind.

But overriding all of this was a growing dread. The realization that this was all aimed at me.

Paul may have been terrified by the unexplained phenomena, but he hadn't heard *his* name called. And if this were a practical joke, the hoaxers would have called *his* name when he had entered, not *mine*."

I feel a bit light-headed, and the tops of my ears feel icy cold. There is no way that I am going to share what had happened to me earlier in the day, not right now anyway. I don't want to add any element of hysteria. Feeling a bit deceptive, all I say to Paul is: "That *is* pretty weird."

He is carefully considering my muted reaction; I know that he expects more of a response, that he *needs* more of a response. I just can't give it to him right now.

I'm so sorry.

11. He is Here

I send my Love to you, and keep warm when you go to bed Honey. you sleep good every body send there Love to you and God bless you dear, from your dearly your Great Grand ma and God bless you, Mary R Di' Cesare.

Above - A cropped section of the letter that Chris was reading on the night in February when the full-bodied apparition first appeared inside room C2D1. His great-grandmother, Mary, also claimed to have seen an apparition, many years before.

By 8PM, Paul and I are settled into our nightly homework routines, both of us are sitting at our desks, quietly working. Paul now has his headphones on. They seem to be functioning properly in spite of my frantically tossing them across the room earlier in the day.

I work on my assignments for about 40 minutes, and then allow myself a break. The October 1984 issue of *Runner* magazine, which covers the prior summer's Los Angeles Olympics results, is my reading choice for this evening. There is an article by Eric Olson entitled: "A Race Hot with Mystery" that provides a detailed review of the men's Marathon.

I am poring over the article, and its many photographs, looking for quiet clues as to how the race was won and lost by the world's eighty-four fastest runners, when Paul abruptly commands me to: "Stop it!"

I smile as I look up, assuming that he is simply trying to get a rise out of me, but he hasn't even lifted his head from his studies. It was likely that he was complaining because some annoying radio deejay had been talking through the introduction of a song that he enjoyed listening to.

I quickly return myself to my running magazine.

In the higher the level of competition, the more the mental aspect came into play: One single split-second decision can have a lasting effect on a two-hour race.

That is what I loved most about competitive running.

"CUT THE SHIT! I don't want to play these games!"

I am harshly rattled back into the moment. Paul has yelled a second time, and even though is he still facing away, I am fairly sure now that he is directing his comments towards me. He is flailing his arms, almost wildly, above his head.

This is no joke.

"Stop, I told you to stop!"

I decide to intervene.

"Paul!"

I yell loudly enough so that he would be able to hear my voice over his headphones.

It works.

He turns, an angry expression on his face, and pulls his headphones above his ears. His body language hints that he is about to yell back, until a look of pure confusion washes across his face. He asks: "How did you get back to your desk so fast?"

"What are you *talking* about," I reply with an annoyed expression, "I've been sitting here reading, I haven't left my chair!"

"You keep blocking my light," he fires back, "You keep making shadows across my desk; it's blocking my light!"

In an attempt to tone the conversation down, I ask Paul: "And just how exactly can I do that if I am ten feet away from you? It's not like I am Mr. Fantastic (of Marvel Comics' *Fantastic Four*) where I can stretch my arms across the room; am I right?"

Paul is now considering my statement. I can tell that he thinks it is reasonable enough. The problem was though, if it wasn't me, then it was someone, or some*thing*, else.

I see it in his face as his mood darkens. This is just too much. I can't blame him; it has certainly too much for me as well.

"That's it!" he yells as he stands up and throws his head phones down onto his book-covered desk, "I'm going out for a while. This place is getting f**king crazy!"

Paul pushes out of the room at a brisk pace, slamming the door behind him. I get up from my chair to lock the door behind him.

I need some quiet time to help me figure out just what the heck is scrambling the entire structure of my life. Maybe someone has put some type of drug in our food?

That might explain some of this craziness.

But that doesn't make any sense. I didn't eat lunch with Paul, and we had different meals at dinner.

Perhaps it was a gas leak that is causing the hallucinations in Paul and me, but I can smell no gas, and the college has carbon monoxide alarms that would alert us if that were actually the case.

When I lived in Genesee Hall my freshman year, I had watched as a purported hypnotist appeared to 'control' the minds of some of my dormmates. Was it possible that I had been, inadvertently, hypnotized as well? Had that the 'trigger' word only now been uttered?

Eh, more nonsense.

Even if that were the case, it wouldn't be affecting Paul now, as he wasn't there.

Left – Genesee Hall during a snowstorm in December 1983. Photograph by Chris Di Cesare.

In any event, I am not going to let one freakish day threaten the stability of my entire personal foundation. The care package that my mother had sent was still sitting on the floor close to my desk.

Written very neatly on the outside of the parcel are the words: "Do not open until Valentine's Day."

I double check my calendar, it is still two days away, but I am in dire need of something to 'ground' me, and a care package from my family seems the perfect remedy.

Using a pair of scissors, I slice a neat opening in the box.

A hand-written letter from my 82-year-old great-grandmother is carefully placed atop the assorted goodies. She wants me to stay warm.

I love her.

There are humorous individual letters from my two sisters, Nicole and Melissa; a full-length letter from my mom; and some money from my dad with the latest dart league stats on green and white striped computer paper. At the very bottom of the carton is a thin red box of *Hot Tamales*, chewy, hot, cinnamon candies.

I hold the box up into the air over my desk with, perhaps, as much reverence as I've ever seen a priest hold the communion wafers above the altar.

Pouring several of the candies into my mouth, in order to maximize the excellent flavor, I re-read the letter from my great-grandmother. I know that she will not be 'with us' all that much longer, just doing the math, and I want to take in every word that she has written to me.

When she was born, there were no automobiles, no televisions, and no air conditioners. Women could not vote. I wonder what it must have been like to have lived through the beginnings of the communication age.

She witnessed the 'Roaring Twenties', survived the Great Depression and then cried as her son, my grandfather, went off to fight in World War II.

I wonder what she was thinking when Neil Armstrong stepped onto the moon, or what thoughts went through her mind when President John F. Kennedy (the son of the man who almost had her husband killed while he was bootlegging alcohol during prohibition) was shot.

Even though I had seen her, almost every week, from the time I was born until the time I left for college, there was so much more that I wanted to know.

My great-grandfather, who she was married to for over 50 years, once told me that life was quieter in the 'old days', that there was less noise, fewer people, and the skies weren't crowded with wires or cables or airplanes. He said that people were more polite; that they said 'hello' to one another on the street. That when the actor from the movie *Gone with the Wind* said: "Frankly Scarlett, I don't give a damn!" many folks considered that profane.

He had seen Babe Ruth bash colossal home runs; Lou Gehrig shoot scorching line drives into the outfield; Mel Ott dominate at the Polo Grounds; and Ty Cobb hit .400; and said that it was expected that you 'dressed up' when you went to a ball game, as it was a special event.

I lean back into the support that my brown, sturdy, wooden chair provides as I reminisce.

I miss my great-grandfather.

He had passed away over seven years ago, and I was still saddened that the last time I 'saw' him I did not properly express my respect or love.

At the age of eighty year, he collapsed in his home.

He was lying in a bed at St. Luke's Hospital, tubes in his arm, a black patch over one eye the last time that I saw him alive. The man who once had the strength to swim across the Hudson River was now tired, and frail, and fading.

My intentions were simple: Let him know that I loved him, and that I was proud that he was my great-grandfather. But there was a sickly smell throughout the ward, and as he made a determined effort to look over at me – for the last time – I was wrinkling up my nose, sticking my tongue out, and complaining: "Ugh, what's that *smell?*"

Pasquale DiCesare

NEWBURGH — Pasquale 'Patsy' DiCesare, 80, died Tuesday in St. Luke's Hospital, Newburgh.

The son of Vito and Mary Casioni DiCesare, he was born Sept. 13, 1897 in Naples, Italy.

He is survived by his wife, Mary Rotundo DiCesare at home; two sons, Vito and Joseph, both of Newburgh; one brother, Louis of Glen Falls; two sisters, Mrs. Laura Eanni of Newburgh, and Mrs. Mary Montabello of Wappingers Falls; seven grandchildren; and eleven great-grandchildren.

A funeral mass will be said at 9:30 a.m. Friday at the Sacred Heart R.C. Church in Newburgh.

Friends may call from 2 to 4 p.m. and 7 to 9 p.m. today at the Coloni Funeral Home, Route 9W, New Windsor.

Burial will be in Calvary Cemetery, New Windsor.

My dad nudged me and said: "Stop that."

My great-grandfather looked sad. Shame.

I walked away a few feet, dejected and worried, and leaned against the shiny beige wall that held an old metal fire extinguisher upon it. I watched other people, for a clue as to how they behaved in these kinds of moments.

A few quick minutes later we were leaving.

On the way home in the darkness, as the pattern of the city of Newburgh streetlights on Broadway intermittently lit my wet face, I cried silently, my mouth moving to the words, "I'm sorry grandpa. I'm so sorry."

I can't remember his funeral.

I place my great-grandmother's letter back down onto my desk. My eyes are wet. I am relieved that Paul has left the room and that my door is locked, I don't want anyone to see that I have been crying.

Tossing a few more pieces of the cinnamon candy into my mouth, I decide to offer some to whoever it is that is now standing behind me, over my right shoulder …

I am sitting as still as I can. Muscles that have spent thousands upon thousands of hours training my body move as fast and as far as they could, were now being called upon to keep it perfectly and absolutely still. If my senses are functioning properly, the impossible is occurring: *something* is standing behind me.

There is no doubt that whatever 'it' is; it is shaped like a person.

My peripheral vision, whether through slight fluctuations in light or color, holds it in place. Even as an out-of-focus mass, standing by the stereo, it resembles a human figure.

Here is the problem with this: Only Paul and I had been in the room that night; only Paul and I had been given door keys to the room; and when Paul stormed out, complaining of shadows circling all around him while he tried to work, I had immediately locked the door behind him.

The only other entrance into the room is through the second story window, which is a good eighteen to twenty feet from the ground. It is also locked.

There is no possible way for someone to be there.

I close my eyes, then I will start counting to ten.

Tossing two more tamales into my mouth, I clear my mind, and as the technique had been successfully reinforced in race after race, I start counting.

One.

My brain is working hard to understand.

Two.

My breathing rate has increased.

Three.

I can now feel the pulse in my neck.

Four.

Every part of my body begins to tighten.

Five.

There is a ringing in my ears.

Six.

I think I might vomit.

Seven.

I need to look.

Just to make sure.

I'm not sure that I can trust my senses anymore.

At 'seven' I open my eyes and turn my head, slowly, to the right. I am now looking at Paul's desk. The quiet familiarity of his headphones on its flat surface, his poster of a wolf on the wall, and the sports drawing that hangs just above, allow my entire body to breathe a sigh of relief.

That is, until I see the pale, bluish face, with the slightly opened mouth, and a tilting head, about a foot to the right.

My chest heaves.

The head and face, almost as if they are only loosely connected to the body, seem to float an inch or two closer my way.

It is the damaged thing from the closet! It wants to see me up close!

My neck muscles twitch and it becomes hard to swallow my saliva. I try to say "no," but I cannot speak a word.

There is no *way that this is actually happening,* I am thinking as my mind races to understand.

As quietly and steadily as I can, I stand up. I am not even sure if I am effectively breathing right now, and my legs have a slight tremble to them.

The almost holographic head shifts and glides back into its original location, atop what looks to be a blue and yellow striped shirt.

I think it is a shirt, it resembles a shirt.

Next, its torso seems to slide, unnaturally, forward a bit from its hips; the dark blue-covered legs are half in front of, and half *inside* of Paul's stereo!

Not knowing what else to do, I *literally* pinch the side of my own left thigh with my thumb and forefinger in order to make sure that I am awake.

I hope, dearly, that I am not.

I attempt to concentrate on what exactly it is that I am seeing, trying to make some kind of sense out of it all. My visual and mental focuses are working together in the attempt to define this absolutely impossible object.

The thing's eyes, appear uniformly light gray, with the barest hint of blue, like a pinhead, in their centers. They seem to be moving loosely and unnaturally, in their sockets. It looks at me with a unique intensity that I cannot compare to anything else that I have ever experienced.

I stand petrified.

My mind is continuously reminding me that I am not supposed to be seeing this, that I should not be seeing this; that it simply cannot be real.

The mouth forms a slight smile, the loose corners lifting ever so slightly.

Or maybe it is a pained expression; I cannot discern.

The thing looks 'wicked' to me.

Wicked and terrifying.

I know, with perhaps more certainty than I've ever known anything before, that I will never be the same.

Not after this.

My entire torso convulses from an intense and unexpected chill that creeps its way up my spine, causing both of my arms to fly momentarily upward. The box of cinnamon candy flying out of my suddenly useless right hand into the noticeably chilled air of room C2D1.

I scream.

I scream loudly.

I scream uncontrollably.

I continue to scream as I bang my knee against the sharp, hard, edge of my desk and begin my mad dash towards the door, towards safety.

Out into the hallway I dart.

My lungs, regularly strengthened through the thousands of training runs, drawing in as much air as they can through my opened mouth that is now yelling: "Help, please, help me!"

I am banging on Jeff's door.

He is not there.

Above – Di Cesare, a Speech Communications student, in happier times: His first day at Erie Hall, Monday, September 3rd, 1984. Photograph by Patricia Di Cesare.

12. Madness

Above - Erie Hall stairwell. – Photograph by J. Jeff Ungar, 35mm, Spring 1984.

No one is answering!

I can hear movement behind the door that leads into C2D2, but for some reason no one is opening the door! I increase both the rate and the force of my fist pounding.

"Help, I'm in TROUBLE!"

The terror that drives my fear leaves my hands numb to a pain that would normally be coursing through them for having banged so vehemently on the solid, unmoving door.

I don't understand why they won't open the door.

Can't they hear my voice? It's me, Chris!

"OPEN THE DOOR!"

Only the Hawaiian-shirt-wearing dog on the beer poster in the hallway is able to notice me in this state, and he is no help.

Being forced from my own college dorm room was bad enough, but having no safe place to go seems worse.

"HELP ME, PLEASE! PLEASE!"

I bang some more, until I hear some nervous mumbling behind the door. I watch as the copper-hued door knob moves slightly as though it is being unlocked from the inside.

I stop my shouting and attempt to catch my breath.

As the knob begins to turn, I am still hoping that I am actually asleep in my bed, simply trying to work my way through a vivid and nonsensical nightmare.

No doubt, I will awake safely in the morning with the sun's light gingerly peeking through the blinds. By the time that I walk to the bathroom in order to shower and brush my teeth, I will have forgotten all but the most trivial aspects of this darkest of dreams.

That's what is happening right now, I am sure of it.

My hopeful delusion is short lived, and replaced by a bizarre reality as a very worried looking Ed S. (Jeff's roommate) opens the door to C2D2.

At that moment, I realize that I am still out in the hallway with some impossible specter of death hovering in my room behind me.

Ed's eyes halt for a moment, as he takes stock of who is at his door, and then cranes his neck to look behind me for signs of anyone else. I fear that the *thing* will be there, so I do not look back.

The alarm in his voice, which refocuses me back into the urgency of the moment, is sincere when he asks: "Are you all right, what the *blazes* is going on?"

"I need to come in, please. Something *horrible* just happened!"

Ed steps to the side so that I can enter the room, and asks in a concerned tone with both arms raised:

"What, Chris? *What* just happened?"

I look at him closely.

He is clearly confused and exasperated.

It dawns on me, in that moment, that I wasn't truly sure myself what had just happened, except for what I had just done: panicked.

I had panicked.

It is common knowledge for those who follow horse racing that when a thoroughbred race horse breaks its stride; the race for them is over.

Likewise, a successful athlete must never panic.

They needed to be able to fully trust in their conditioning, in their strategy, and in their ability to problem solve through even the worst situations.

I had panicked.

Whatever that thing was, my fear of its very existence was greater than my ability to control my emotions. When you lose control of your environment, and you lose the race.

Apparently, I had just lost the race for my own sanity.

This understanding is devastating.

Race horses are oftentimes equipped with blinders. When they race, the blinders keep them focused on what lies ahead, keeping distractions from 'spooking' them.

Moving forward, I decide, I will need to find my own set of blinders if I am to retain any sense of sanity.

But I am still trying to catch my breath as Jeff rushes in through the door behind me.

I feel dizzy, and nauseated, and freezing cold.

Glancing rapidly about the room, my eyes are drawn to, and then focus upon, a black and white image taped onto the wall.

It is of a young girl, both of her hands are placed on a static-filled TV screen, and the caption reads: "They're here."

I clench my hands together, and I wondered why the poster had never bothered me before. Because now I am quite sure that it *should* have bothered me. Because, well, something *was* here!

Jeff leans in towards me and puts a hand on my shoulder. His eyes, which are protected by a pair of wire-rimmed reading glasses, are actively seeking clues, searching for information.

"Chris, look at me," he states with an affect that suggests to me that he has experience with people going through emotional crisis. My eyes meet his and I can tell – in an instant – that the sheer terror in mine has struck home with him.

He has never seen someone this scared before.

A feeling of guilt now compounds my shivering terror.

I don't want him or Ed to suffer because of me. I should be back in my own room, taking care of this myself. But I can't go back there. I am too afraid of whatever that *thing* is in there, and too afraid of what its continued presence might do to my mind.

Above - J. Jeff Ungar sketching at his desk in room C2D2. The Poltergeist movie advertisement on the wall in C2D2 was likely a coincidence, but had Di Cesare wondering if the haunting in Erie Hall had been inevitable. Ungar, erring on the side of compassion and safety, would take the image down.

I don't want to be broken.

I don't want to panic again.

"Chris, you need to tell me what's wrong."

Jeff's choice to invest in my well-being, to ask about *me* and not about *it*, encourages me to take a risk.

It is a potentially dangerous risk, but I need to tell him the truth.

I need to let somebody know.

This is more than I can handle on my own.

"I panicked, Jeff! I can't believe I panicked! It was horrible! The head was tilted! It looked at me, Jeff, right at me! I panicked! I can't believe I panicked! It kept looking at me!"

"I don't understand, Chris. You're not making any sense; w*hat* looked at you?"

"The ghost, Jeff! The ghost!"

13. The C2D1 Journal Notes

A special note of gratitude to J. Jeff Ungar for allowing his first journal to be shared, printed in its entirety, for the very first time.

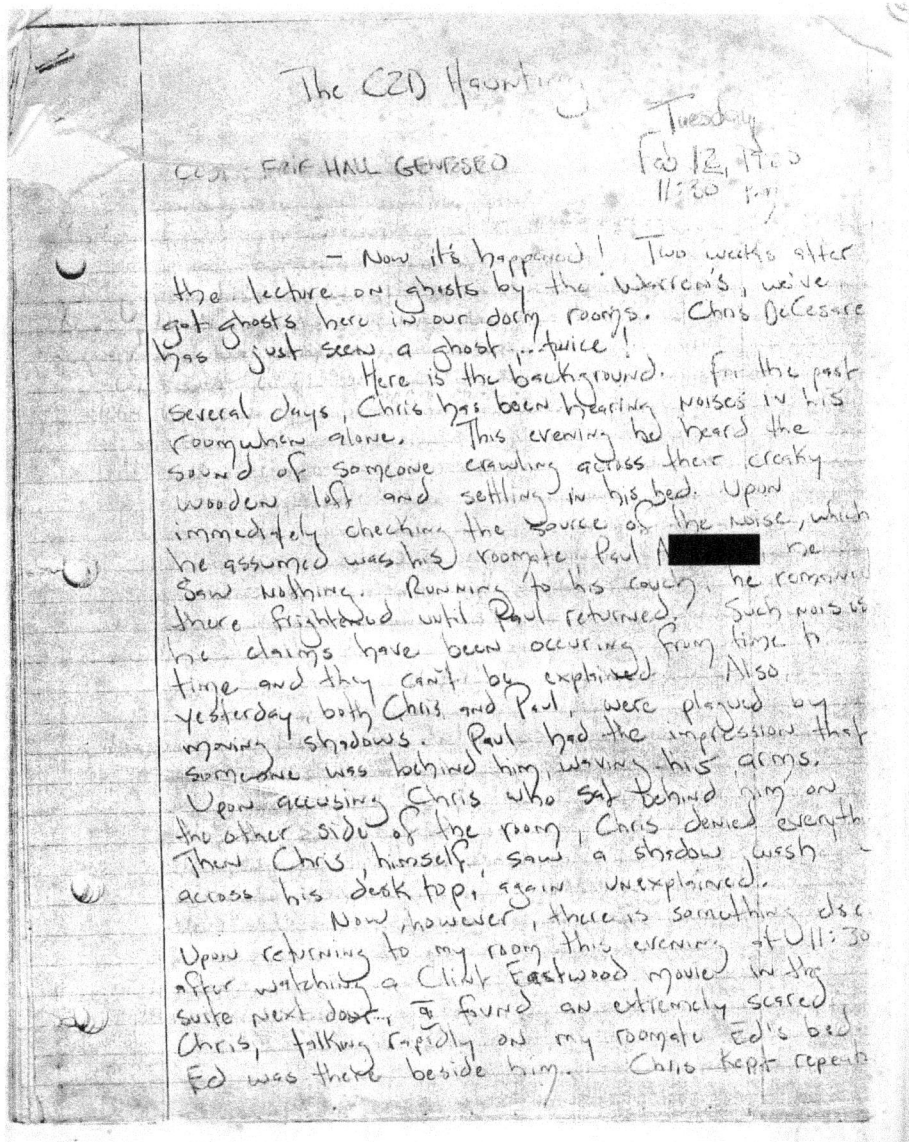

Above — Originally Jeff's notes made reference to the 'Cd2 Haunting', as it was not yet clear that the ghost was focused primarily on one room - C2D1; and primarily on one of its occupants: Christopher Di Cesare.

②

that he had just seen a [ghost in] 12 or 13 year old, brown-haired boy with a yellow and blue striped shirt and navy blue sweatpants, hunched over looking at him from ~~his~~ ~~the~~ Paul's [near] desk across from him. He ~~near~~ kept saying "I can't believe I panicked?" This is doubly odd since over the weekend, while playing D&D — we happened to discuss how we would react in such a situation. (must explain D&D game) Chris said if it was an adult, he wouldn't panic and if it was a child, he was unsure. The truth of the matter is that he did panic. Upon seeing the youth staring at him, he quickly averted his eyes and sprinted toward the door to mine and Ed's room, next door. He was quite scared, eyes watering, voice near hysterical, shivering. Even now ½ hour later he is still nervous, which is understandable. * (P.A. 1)

At the news of this sighting, I was much intrigued as well as almost equally terrified — This was too close to home! Anyway, I accompanied him ~~back~~ into his room. He described the scene, the positioning and the reaction several times, I tried to relate this to what the Warren's said. ~~The~~ Ghost's are sometimes attracted to certain sensitive individuals, which I am positive Chris is — maybe this is the explanation — The room was not cold, which is one sign of manifestation.

Above — Di Cesare repeated, over and over again, "I can't believe I panicked!" He would later remark that his own reaction over having seen the ghost (in his dorm room) was actually worse than the possible presence of the ghost itself. "When you panic, you lose control of your environment, often when it is the very worst time to do so."

(3.)

Anyhow, while we were talking, Chris was
through the motions, he went ~~through~~ before —
fumbling with the candy "Hot Tamales" box he had
been trying to open — when suddenly he stopped,
uttered something and averted his eyes claiming
that its there. I looked but saw nothing neither
did Ed. What ever Chris saw, it appeared only
to him.   * ? maybe a repeat description

Now he was really upset, claiming that
the "Hot Tamales" box was the cause. After this
second sighting he ~~said~~ said he was never going
to stay in that room again whereupon he got
up came in ours. Trying to block the incident
from his mind, he worked on his homework, but
as I was writing this, he reacted as if he
saw it again but refused to say anything.
                    *

I find this all most odd. I asked
Chris if he knew anyone like that but he said he
didn't stick around to notice details. ~~——————~~

~~————————————~~ (removed by request)

I don't know what to think — Now, he
is whimpering about going to bed "there", which
he is attempting to do — but he is noticing
all these objects moved about: The granola bars
(2) he was going to offer Ed are completely gone
an apple has suddenly appeared in his closet; the
Tamale Box has moved — I don't know what to
say, but he has thrown everything out ⟶

Above — Page three of the notes remains the most troubling for Di Cesare. On it he frantically wonders if the candy had been the cause of the haunting, and he asks Jeff to scratch out part of the notes dealing with the ghost's appearance. It does, however, give one a window into what the sheer terror of the encounter had done to his faculties.

116

Strangely, however, this relates to the
hauntings in our room, Craig and I
experienced last semester — Craig
continually had pages of his letter he
was writing disappear — only to be
found crinkled in the waste basket — Also
the closet doors continually opened by
themselves — and my pretzels disappeared
from a locked room —
                    What can I say —
We thought our hauntings only strange
coincidences, nothing more, but now ?!

          As I end this, I
hear Chris in his room — "Oh my God, Paul,
I was standing where it was! It's near me, I know
it is." — and Paul is teasing him — I
    wonder if things are really back to
normal.. One things for sure however,
Eric Hall, sure deserves it's name...

                              John Jeff Ungar

*Above – J. Jeff Ungar's quick sketch of room C2D1 (on page 4 of his journal notes)
was the only visual representation of the room's layout shared for many years. Those
studying the haunting would rely on this visual representation for their understanding
until the 'Skeletal Image', and other photographs, began appearing on the internet in
the early 1990's.*

Haunting II:

February 13, 1992
Erie Hall (2?)
GENESEO

And you thought last night's episode was scary; that was just the beginning! As I went to bed at 12:45 last night, listening to the worried shouts of Chris begging Paul to turn on the lights, I hoped the worst was over. I guess I was trying to comfort myself that Chris' sighting was a freak occurence — Chris' panic next door was certainly understandable! — and I didn't want anything like that spreading to my room! I even began hoping that Chris had simply imagined everything, much to his own misfortune, and that since no one else saw anything, it was not real. But that was an ignorant thought for I could not have been more wrong! On my message board this — morning I found scrawled a message from Chris, which read. "Have I got a story for you!"

I had gotten up around 10:15 and the message had been scribbled over, apparently Chris had changed his mind about telling me after he had written it. I was intrigued but I respected his position and could do nothing but wait for him to decide whether to tell me or not. But damn, was I curious!

As the day progressed, my hopes began to fade about Chris ever revealing what happened last night. He had hinted at one point that it was the most frightening experience of his life, even compared to the three foot black creature in his hall at home — // But today,

(delete)

Above — The emotional intensity of the haunting, with Chris begging Paul to turn the lights on in room C2D1, is captured here. The notes were not conceived of as a way to gain public notoriety, but rather, as a means of understanding what was occurring all around them.

(2.)

Wednesday, was one of Chris' all-time worst days. The combination of three hours sleep, a failed psychology test and seeing his desired girlfriend with another guy ███████████, as well as the trauma of the hauntings had put Chris in an uncommonly black mood. It wasn't until after dinner while complaining of developing an ulcer overnight that he chose to tell me the story.

Standing in the bathroom with a cup of alka-seltzer he swore me to silence (I could write about it) but he did not want me to tell anyone until at least after this semester — The reason is that Paul, his roomate, was involved and Paul wants nothing to do with these sorts of things nor does he often tell people of his own experiences. Anyway, he told Chris about what he saw last night only under an oath of secrecy. If Paul finds out Chris told me, their strained relations will be over along with Paul's confidence in him. I don't know why Chris told me, but he knows I am extremely interested and I am glad he did.

Well, this is it; the moment of confession — Chris admitted that he saw it again (he calls it Tommy now as Paul jokingly

Above — Di Cesare's request of Ungar not 'to tell anyone until at least after the semester' serves to back up his oft stated comments that he did not want the haunting, or his own involvement in it, to be known. He did not want his reputation or his relationships, particularly with Paul, to be adversely affected.

(3.)

referred to it) He saw it four times last night between 1:00 and 3:00 Am, and not only did "Tommy"—— move objects in the room, but Paul saw him also. This fact eliminated all doubts I had entertained of Chris' emotional state and I am almost glad Paul saw him, for Chris' sake. It is interesting to note here that Paul saw Tommy. // I have written before of Paul's psychic experiences which would logically make him sensitive to such apparitions like Chris, who himself has had plenty of psychic experiences. Also, a link which ties both Chris and Paul is an experience Chris related to me last week. Upon waking in the middle of the night, he half-wondered if Paul was awake, whereupon Paul murmured while asleep, "Yes". Chris repeated his telepathic question twice more with the same response from Paul. This is quite extraordinary. No wonder Paul has been seeing Tommy.

together at least psychic similar psychic levels

Anyway, Chris told me that upon going to bed last night (reluctantly, that i. Paul turned off the light whereupon Chris immediately became aware of Tommy's presence next to him. *Turning to his side with the blanket over his head facing Paul, he watched a shadowy head-shape.

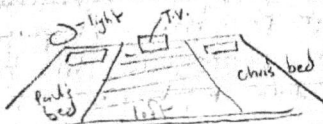

Above — Specific details of the haunting are now being shared for the very first time. By now, Chris apparently feels that he can trust Jeff enough to share to a fuller extent. Ungar speculates on the possibility of psychic potential not just in Chris, but in his Chris' roommate, Paul, as well.

(4)

recline inches away next to him. Petrified,
he called for Paul to turn on the light (which
I overheard next door) There was nothing
there when the light was turned on. *
       Chris, then at this point, didn't
know what to do. Paul suggested he turn
the desk light on, but as Chris
leaned over the edge of the loft, reaching
for the light, Paul jokingly switched off

the light which naturally upset Chris more
than a little. Chris jumped back up
and lay still for some time before
he got up the courage to turn on the
desk light. Getting up, he reached over

the edge, flicked the switch and was
lying down again somewhat relieved
when just like in a B-horror movie, he
saw Tommy inches away from him on his
left near the wall — * Tommy was smiling
his lower body phasing through the
loft boards. To get some idea of Tommy's
expression the night before, Chris showed
me the expression of Jennifer Beals
on a poster that Paul had. Anyway,
Chris pulled the covers over his head
and tried to endure it, knowing that Paul

Above — Added here are the relevant details of what J. Jeff Ungar had heard though his walls (in C2D2) the night prior: Chris begging Paul to turn the lights on inside of room C2D1. Also provided is Di Cesare's apparent observation that the ghost's lower body was 'phasing' through the loft boards, not dissimilar to the earlier report of it phasing through Paul's stereo on the night it was first seen.

(5)

did not want to hear it.

After some time again, Chris heard a hissing sound down below, and, wondering what it was, looked around, but discovered nothing. Determined, he decided to get his Bible which was down below. He hopped down and retrieved it from a pile of books behind his desk, —— beside the couch. Bible in hand, he was just about to mount the chair and climb onto the loft when right where he had just been, by the pile of books, was Tommy, hunched slightly looking at him. Chris immediately jumped into the loft and sat there with the bible. Then, tired and somewhat comforted by the
extremely
bible, he resolved to go to sleep, so he quickly turned off the desk-light and leaned back. Then, as an after-thought, he decided to get the blue pillow with the picture of Christ on it that his mother had made for him for Christmas which was on the couch below. — Reaching over the back edge of the loft — (There is a 4-5" space in back, away from the) wall. — He grabbed the pillow and had just settled down with it firmly beneath his head, when the really scary thing happened: His two other pillows were slowly dragged out from under him and toward the space in back! Grabbing the pillows with two hands he struggled with

Above — As noted here, neither Chris nor Paul initially knew what the 'hissing' sound that they both heard was. They would later discover it was the sound of a cassette recorder that had somehow been activated. Also mentioned here is the blue pillow that Chris would soon have a 'tug of war' with the ghost over. It was one of the indelible moments of the C2D1 Haunting that Paul A. would recall with clarity, some nine years later, when speaking with early researcher Alan Lewis.

(6.)

them for about two minutes before Tommy gave up. Chris during this whole struggle kept shouting "Leave my pillows alone! their mine! Go away and leave my *@!*! pillows alone!" He was quite upset. Immediately after this, Chris called out "In the name of Jesus Christ I command you to go back to where you came from", as the Warren's had suggested if such an encounter should befall. Upon saying this, Chris was immediately at peace and fell directly asleep. . . .

I must comment here. The scene just described I find most interesting. According to the Warren's, most ghosts are people who do not realize they are dead. In this case, Tommy could simply be such a spirit who, confused, has found Chris, a focus, a light in the darkness. As this relates to the pillow conflict, Tommy thinking himself alive, acts like he is still alive. Chris claims that he often occupies his bed during the day and during the night, it was as if Tommy "played" with them until they were asleep! Now, consider that either Tommy was playing by dragging away the pillows or he was upset about Chris' taking away "his" pillow; The pillow he was using down below on the

---

Above — This page of the Ungar's journal notes has proven quite meaningful for those who have an interest in legendary demonologists Ed and Lorraine Warren. On it we find that, although Di Cesare might have had some doubts over their conclusions, he attempts to follow their instructions to the letter when he encounters the unknown. The, almost immediate, influence of their words on Chris could not be overstated.

(7)

(neglied)

couch, which we call the "Neg Zone" because it is so comfortable. I don't know, my narrative is rather confusing here, but Tommy has been getting bolder as Paul's story will explain. One more note about Tommy — he likes granola bars and pretzels. This morning Chris was sure he had two granola bars left in his closet (This is significant as I'll explain) sure enough to even offer them to Ed, but when he went for them, they were gone, and a bag of pretzels was open. My pretzels disappeared last semester, as well as a pair of sweatpants; Chris has lost his favorite pair of shorts within the last few days. Now, about the closet, the far one. It continually opens by itself, not much, but it does open. I just returned with Chris from examining his room and sure enough, the closet he closed on the way out is now open. Chris thinks Tommy is trying to trick him, by hiding in the closet because ½ hour ago, when Chris went in the room, he saw his bed and blankets move and heard a sigh; Tommy was on his bed; but Tommy heard us coming this time and jumped into the closet. (Tommy heard us coming) (Yea, this is real stuff)

— Last semester, as I stated before, Craig was alone in the room writing letters when over

(I messed up with this)

Above — In what would become his primary lament over the journal notes, Ungar would eventually learn that one of his hungry dormmates inside Erie Hall was the actual culprit in many of the instances of missing snack foods. Jeff's dedication towards recounting every conversation, event, and potentiality adds to the value of his efforts.

(6.)

I hope Tommy doesn't ... this in the middle of the night...

the course of two hours, our closet continually opened at least 1 foot 4 or 5 times. Craig was most annoyed and his letters kept disappearing only to be found crumpled in the waste basket. Craig seems to have noticed a correlation between the instances of the closet opening, himself turning to close it, and the disappearance of his pages. Chris however, doubts that it is Tommy for Tammy does not seem to be that intelligent. I don't know... Chris was extremely scared that day we discussed it and was extremely skiddish of a particular corner of our room — the far closet corner ???

Now. For Paul's tale. After Chris fell asleep last night (Oh no, something just happened, I'll explain later!)

→ Paul was treated to several strange manifestations. It is important to remember that up until this point, Chris was the only one who had actually witnessed anything. But now, Paul heard at one point the sound of his desk chair below him, being rattled against the sides of the desk and pulled across the rug into the middle of the room. Sure enough, the next morning. That is where the chair

Above — Here we find that Paul, too, has begun to experience a visual component to the haunting. The apparent anomalies inside of room C2D1 are now being seen by two people, independently. This would reduce, in those around him, the quiet fear that Chris was in the throes of some type of severe mental breakdown.

(9.)

was found. Also, at another time during the night, Paul glanced over at Chris' sleeping form only to see a ball of light about 6" in diameter hovering near the wall immediately behind Chris. I believe the color of the light was gold or yellow, but it was definitely a seperate entity, not attached to Chris. I must add here that Chris was once approached by a student here who told him after a speech, that Chris did well and had a nice "golden" aura. Maybe there is a correlation here, I don't know. We've even tried to find our aura last semester through an experiment we found in an occult book in the library. I didn't see anything but Craig and Beth, both claimed that Chris had a "golden yellow" aura — Make of this what you will.

Anyway, Paul now had seen something confirming Chris' story. The worst sighting for Paul however, occurred a short time later. Upon awaking around 3:00, he glimpsed a shadowy form standing on the chair at the end of the loft looking at both him and Chris. I like to entertain the idea that "Tommy" was checking to see if they where still asleep. So there's Paul's side of the hauntings.

Oh, yeah, I almost forgot about another sighting Chris had. Before the Bible scene, he himself forgets exactly when, he saw a

Above — Here Paul mentions the appearance of a 6" ball of light 'hovering' over Chris' head while he slept. Chris claimed that he would often wake to the sight of the ghost's face, just inches from his own. Could that sphere of energy have been a feature of the ghost? Or was it possibly some aspect of Chris' 'gold aura' as described by his communications classmate, Dean B., and supposedly later 'verified' by his friends?

(10.)

dark silhouetted figure on his closet door. Thinking (hoping, rather) at first that it was just a dresser and his salamander tank casting the shadow, He experimented by putting his hand in the light source...but it cast a shadow in a completely different direction! You can imagine what Chris thought!

So, that is the night Chris told me about. Pretty intense, huh! As I'm writing this, Chris and I are in my room. He is extremely reluctant to be alone in his room, especially at night, the "witching hour" when fancy stalks outside reason and malignant possibilities stand rock firm as facts" (Thomas Hardy, Tess). Sorry! Anyway, Paul and Ed went out so I'm keeping Chris company, periodically checking up on the ghost. Oh, by the way, Tom, just moved the closet door again. Chris is taking things more calmly though his stomach hurts. He is even joking about Tommy, a form of masochistic solace as he readily admits. Going into the room he just said, "Tommy, come out and play, Tommy..." I don't think he should

Above — Detailed is Chris' attempt at validating possible causes for the dark shadow they had seen, and is representative of his statements that he wanted to find 'natural causes' for the strange phenomena. His father, Vito, had impressed upon him from an early age, the value of empiricism: that Knowledge and understanding should be derived from sense-experience rather than one's imagination or emotional state.

(11.)

have said that for apparently Tommy just answered. I mentioned before that something just happened. Well, Chris and I went into the room where Chris said what I just told you, when suddenly leaning near the couch to check for draft from the windows, Chris heard a low harsh voice, gurgle his name as though beside him. Chris jumped and ran towards me, but I had heard nothing. This has caused Chris to panic again — the voice resembled those on the Warren's demon tape. Chris seems to be able to feel Tommy's presence now. Anyway, Chris is lying on Ed's bed now and he just asked me what I'd do if I saw my mattress indent, the blankets move and heard the sound of someone sighing. Would I sleep in my bed ever again? I said probably not whereupon, he told me that upon a solo venture to his room a little while ago, he saw exactly that! Oh, Hell! This was before Tommy hid from us in the closet as I described earlier.

But now let me finish yester-night's happenings before I begin tonight's. At this rate I'll never catch up! This—

Above — Unsure of the proper course of action, we read of Chris asking Jeff what he would do if he saw his mattress 'indent', the blankets 'move', and then heard an audible 'sigh' from that same area. Chris had initially thought that his roommate Paul was up on the loft, possibly attempting to play a 'prank' on him. Upon actual inspection, Chris discovered that no one there.

(12.)

morning, Chris noticed some remnants or
reminders, of last night's incidents! Other than
the moved chair, Chris noticed a
framed picture of his baby cousin pulled
apart on his desk, and his alarm
clock which had been been set so he
could attend an 8:10 class was reset
or 8:30?

at 9:16! But Tommy, didn't stop
there, in fact he was still there! As
Chris dressed, he noticed that in the
course of a few seconds, three small
splotches of a white "slimy" material had
appeared on his pant leg. Could this be
ectoplasm? And the incident which lends
support to this hypothesis is the fact that
moments later, while attempting to button the
cuffs on his shirt, he meticulously watched as
they were immediately unbuttoned. Buttoning
one sleeve, he would turn to the next,
when the other would open itself.
Finally, Chris had to go into the bathroom
to put on his shirt. It seems Tommy
would have him stay.

After, Chris told me all this earlier
this evening, we went into his room. There

Above — *Questioned in 2014, Chris was unable to recall the report of the ectoplasm, but was able to provide a detailed recounting of the 'un-snapping' of his jogging suit. The incident regarding the dissembling of the photograph frame was proof positive for Chris that the ghost was able to 'know' things that it should not have been able to. A photo of Paula Perrera, killed four years prior, had been hidden in the frame by Chris.*

(13.)

he redescribed all the incidents in detail and going through the motions several times. While in there, however, I felt nothing... except for a rather chill draft that had not always been there. I was sitting at Chris' desk and Chris was on the Neg Zone - He was really cold. The Warrens had said that ghosts use energy, including heat energy to manifest themselves.

Chris claims that, sure enough, the periodic draft has only been around for about two weeks and that every time he saw Tommy clearly opaque, all the lights in the room had been on, including the Christmas lights, (how ironic!). Needless to say, he keeps as few lights as possible on now. Sort of defeats the purpose don't it.

There has already been much talk about who Tommy is and where he came from, but by far my favorite idea is that he just followed Chris home one day, about two weeks ago, like a stray dog. Chris is on the track team and is an avid runner who often runs the roads of Geneseo. He could have very easily picked up some sort of wayward entity somewhere along the way.

It is late now, (2:15!) and I've said all that I can remember, so I'll end this discussion here, although I'm certain that

Above — The relationship of temperature and electricity to the ghost is discussed by Chris and Jeff as they look for ways in which to better detect the ghost, and possibly minimize its actions by controlling the environment. Here we also read the first suggestion that the haunting is now being actively discussed outside of the tight-knit group of Chris, Paul and Jeff. Additionally, Jeff's primary theory on the ghost's presence is shared.

14.

we've not seen the end of it. Right now
Paul is yelling at Chris for teasing the
ghost and Chris is threatening to sleep in
Brian's room. They are trying to convince
me, Ed, and Brian to sleep in their room!
No, way?! Chris even suggested, much to
his own shock, that we all go in turn
off the lights and call to him. This has
all evolved into a pretty morbid or terrifying
joke. We shall see what tonight will
bring. By the way, Paul admitted some
of the stuff so the secrets seems to be
out-of-the-bag. I, however, still won't
say anything. But before I stop,
I will leave you with a coincidence
to think about; Chris says that the
hauntings probably started about two weeks
ago around Feb 1. He was incredibly
shocked when I pointed out that the
Ghost seminar that the Warrens presented
was Jan. 30. (See my notes)

Did some ghost follow Chris
home, despite the Warren's assurance of their
protective "Christ-light"? They did admit
that it had happened before.

As always... Believe what you most!
See you tomorrow, I hope...
John Jeff Unger.

Above — The start of the interpersonal turmoil between Chris and Paul is noted here. With Paul angered at Chris for 'teasing'(?) the ghost, and Chris threatening to leave Paul alone in the room with it. Jeff is able to capture this information listening through the wall that separates his room from theirs. Chris later suggests to Jeff, Ed, and Paul that they try to 'call the ghost', which will be done the following night. A possible connection between the haunting and Ed and Lorraine Warren is brought up as well.

The C2D1 Haunting: Part III

Thurs
1.6, 14
C2D1
10:30 a.m.

This is becoming redundant! Apparently Tommy is here to stay, although he is less active than Tuesday night. I got up early with Chris (after 4 hours sleep) and accompanied him to the Union for breakfast at 8:00 AM. where he told me of the happenings of last night. The main manifestation occurred not more than 10 minutes after Paul turned out the light. Chris, lying on his pillows, observed a milky mist flowing across them. This mist then swirled together forming the distorting image of a face with a huge open mouth. Chris called for Paul to turn on the light, but nothing was revealed.

Nothing more happened last night that Chris and Paul were aware of, then, but this morning they found that Chris' chair had moved (I had watched Chris set it purposely the night before) and that the clock previously set for 7:15 now was set again for 9:16.4!? Good thing Chris had arranged for me to wake him up. Yet, although Tommy was not apparent so much last night, throughout the day today, he certainly made up for it. The closet opened by itself again; Paul's chair was moved; Chris had a deck of index cards taken from his desk and scattered on the couch; the room door has even opened by itself twice now, and the grand finale' is that Chris had Tommy call his name twice, once early

Above — Incidents appear to be occurring with greater frequency, and idiosyncrasies with the alarm clock inside of room C2D1 are being reported; events that Jeff himself is able to corroborate. Jeff is also beginning to note the negative physical effect that the haunting seems to be having upon Chris, along with mention of 'Tommy' now appearing in daylight hours as well. This represents a significant temporal shift in the activity.

(2.)

this afternoon, and once just after dinner. Tommy's "voice" is no longer gravelly and low, rather it is becoming increasingly clearer, with a long 'sss' sound, as though Tommy is practicing his "speech" and getting better each time. The first time he spoke, Chris was writing and was not scared (he is growing accustomed to Tommy, although he's still quite scared at times; he does not want to stay in the room). But this time he told Tommy to leave him alone so he could finish his story. I was impressed! He read me the story and it was quite eerie — I won't try to explicate it here. Anyway, Chris is most relieved about the fact that he has not 'seen' Tommy again. That was always a shock. ~~He does fear~~ He does fear that after imagining all the time that Tommy's in his closet, that one day Tommy will be actually standing there.

Now for the interesting stuff! (as if the other stuff is already too common to be of interest). This afternoon I convinced Chris to take my 35mm camera with Kodak 100 color film sass, to try to get some "ghost" pictures; I figured Chris, the focus, could get Tommy on film, as suggested by the Warrens. The problem is that my

---

Above — Reported here is a fascinating observation that the ghost appears to be improving its speech. We find that Chris believes that 'Tommy' had actually complied with his request on this day, and we can note the first mention of the now-famous Valentine's Day photo shoot that would capture not only the effects of the ghost on Chris and the room, but an actual image of the ghost itself.

(3.)

camera is not a polaroid so we will have to wait for any results.

Anyway at 9:00 or shortly thereafter me and Chris entered the room. Chri took some preliminary shots, but I doubt they will come out. We weren't sure how to go about calling Tommy, but we tried to get Ed to sit on the couch where Tommy often was. Ed refused, but in trying to "find" Tommy we started looking for the peculiar drafts we had noticed before. Chris first felt the draft near his pile of books, but then lost it. Feeling about the room, he found nothing until he opened the closet and within was the cool draft! Tommy was hiding in the closet, apparently one of his favorite spots. Feeling about, Chris, quite excited, felt the draft nucleus shift. (I as of yet felt nothing). I wanted to try a picture, so Chris moved back into the room when suddenly he started saying that it was following him on his hands, he was drawing it out into the room, his impression was quite strong. I struggled with the camera but could not achieve proper focus and Tommy went away. Then both Chris and I felt for him and this time we located him in the center of the room; both our hands and forearms were notabl colder in a sphere-like area the size of the glowing ball Paul had seen Tuesday ni

Above — Recorded here are the moments leading up to the iconic 'Ghost Boy of Geneseo' photo, of Di Cesare with his outstretched arms under the glowing lights of the loft inside room C2D1. It is the first accounting of an actual shared paranormal experience between Chris and Jeff. Captured here is a purported 'walk through' of an encounter with a full-bodied apparition.

(4.)

I felt him especially strong, exactly
between Chris' two opened hands (6"
wishing for a picture, I grabbed the
camera and drew back, but at
that moment, Chris lost him. He had
followed me; I felt Tommy's presence
on my bare forearms and hands. I called
to Chris who came over and confirmed
it. Going back to the center of the room,
I called for Ed who had gone next door
again to come and take a picture while
we both held Tommy between us (Remember,
we could only feel him not see him so I
don't know if the pictures will turn out) but Ed
took a picture. At this point I was
worried, for Tommy had stuck to me; I
wasn't nervous apparently because my hands
weren't shaking, actually throughout the
whole experience, Chris and I, were quite
awestruck, too interested to be nervous,
fascinated
but this was a definite unknown, and I
wanted to see if I could be rid of it.
I succeeded. Chris retained it and I
withdrew and took a picture. Then I
went to feel it again and Brian came
in and felt it, but dragged it away, on
leaving.

(left margin notes:) Brian also felt the presence and even apparently dragged it away with his cup of soup he brought in.

I failed to lift the physical though.

This sequence represents the first time Tommy was pulling Chris' shirt.

Above – J. Jeff Ungar records his first encounter with the ghost called 'Tommy' inside room C2D1 on Valentine's Day of 1985. He shares that not just Di Cesare was there, but that his roommate Ed S. and suitemate Brian H. were also present for the uncanny experience. Ungar's side notes make mention of the ghost's effect on Chris' shirt which is evident in one of the iconic photographs taken.

(s.)

We eventually got it back, but it's apparently skiddish now. Chris chased it around the room. We took some more pix, but it was never as strong as before. Chris followed it behind his dresser, to the chair of his desk, on the desk and then lost it. Failing to find it below, Chris went above to his bed and felt for it but found nothing. Then he had an idea; taking a bookmark from his bible, he held it before him. Sure enough, as if curious, he felt Tommy engulf his arm - it was really strong, but as Chris turned to me to tell me to take the picture, he felt Tommy weaken, I snapped the picture, but the flash apparently scarred Tommy, who shot with great force up Chris' arm and disappeared. After this we gave up - Chris' hands were ice cold. We had been playing hide and seek with Tommy or something. Blind Man's Bluff I hope Tommy doesn't think I was trying to hurt him with the flash.

Anyway, we've made contact and even I have felt it. I'm psyched on one hand, but scared on the other.

* note: "Super Pickle" (a stuffed figure was moved by this)

Above — The description of the Valentine's Day encounter is continued in marked detail. Ungar, camera in hand, follows Di Cesare about the room in the effort to record potential interactions between them. That the ghost will respond to Chris (the basis of the Ghost Boy legend) now seems a given in both of their minds. We also read Jeff's statement that he has 'felt' the ghost, and that he is simultaneously 'psyched' and 'scared'.

Whatever, this encounter has helped
to familiarize us with it to some
extent - I can only wait for the
film to see if our ghost hunt was
successful...

I hear Chris showing Paul
the zone of cold, Tommy. It seems,
however, to evade Paul. Paul hates Tommy
and this no doubt shows. Now Luke's
being shown it, but Luke feels nothing.

I just went over there and
felt it again, it stuck to me for a
long time. Man, is that ever uncomfortable.
Chris says it is getting bolder now, leaving
his room. Also, while typing about 1 hour
ago. He heard it call his name several times - Ear
phones didn't help, says.

Oh, well...

Oh, I just remembered.
Last night after the light was turned
on by Paul - Both Chris and Paul fell
asleep with the light still on. In the morning
it was off, neither of them having touched it...

Stay tuned!   John Jeff Ungar

*Above — Most notable to Di Cesare, years later, was that Jeff makes no mention of the
'skeletal image' in his journal notes. Di Cesare explains: "There was no reason for him
too. He didn't actually see what I did, and had no reason to believe that the picture I
took would amount to anything significant. Jeff was as shocked as I was, maybe more
so, when he saw the image for the first time. The night wasn't planned out, or edited,
for public consumption, we were just two college kids looking for answers."*

14. In Search of ...

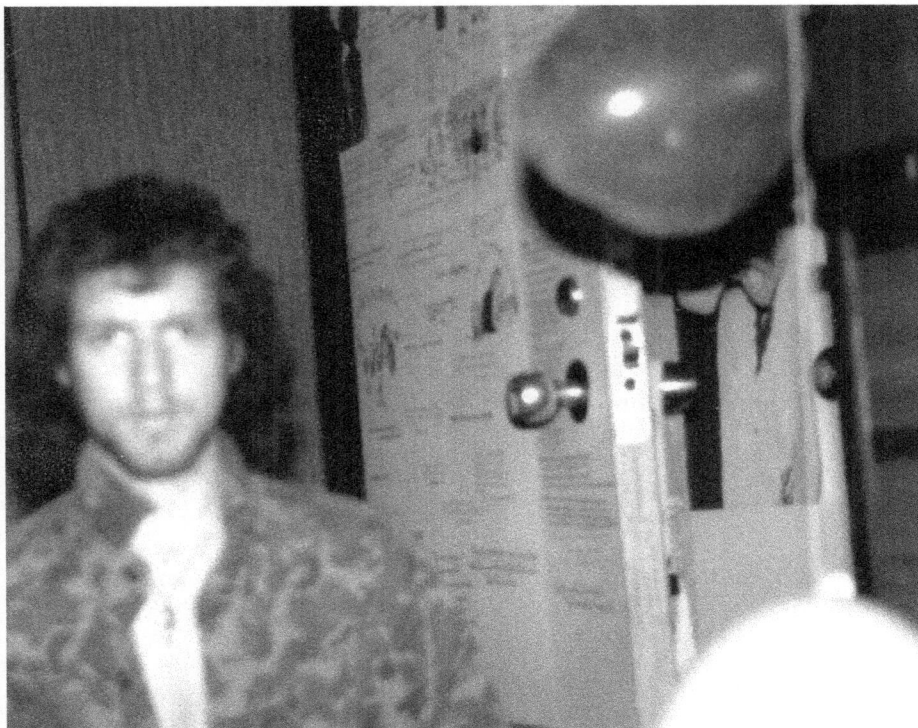

Above - J. Jeff Ungar kneels in the doorway of room C2D1 on February 13th, 1985. Note the two Valentine's Day balloons in the foreground, one red one white.

Jeff wants me to look for a ghost.

He crouches down in the hallway, like a jungle cat stalking its prey, and gazes into C2D1 through the doorway that I had left wide open in my mad dash to safety earlier in the evening.

"I see nothing out of the ordinary," he whispers, "Do you see anything now?"

I have no idea why I am even standing behind him as I nervously wring my hands together in front of me. If I were smart, I would simply retreat back to the safety of his room, and try to forget any of this ever happened.

Hearing no reply, he glances back at me, and asks again "Do you see anything, Chris?"

"No."

I hadn't actually looked into the room yet, preferring instead the boring comfort brought on by examining the light-colored, worn, hallway floor tiles under my feet. I wondered how long they had been there, and if the people who put them down were still alive? It was Ed, who nodded at me to make the effort, and said: "Why don't you go in really quick to see?"

"OK. I'll go in," I whisper over my fear.

Jeff is pleased by this; his reconnoitering will be greatly aided by an advance forward into what has suddenly become a paranormal 'ground zero'. He lifts his 35mm camera up to his face, turns his head quickly to the side to loosen his neck, and then places the view finder to his eye.

[Flash!]

Elevating himself to his full standing height, Jeff glances up into the loft area and then turns his gaze back to me.

"Where did you see it?"

I point to the general area between Paul's desk and stereo, but the vagueness does little to help Jeff pinpoint the exact location that he wants. So, I step gingerly around him, and (with a careful eye on the closet door) I sit down in my desk chair.

I run through the whole encounter, several times, as best as I can. My hope is that I am not speaking too fast to be understood.

Below – A cutout of a photo of Chris (inside of room C2D1) taken during the first few days of the haunting. There are no known existing copies of the original photo. – J. Jeff Ungar.

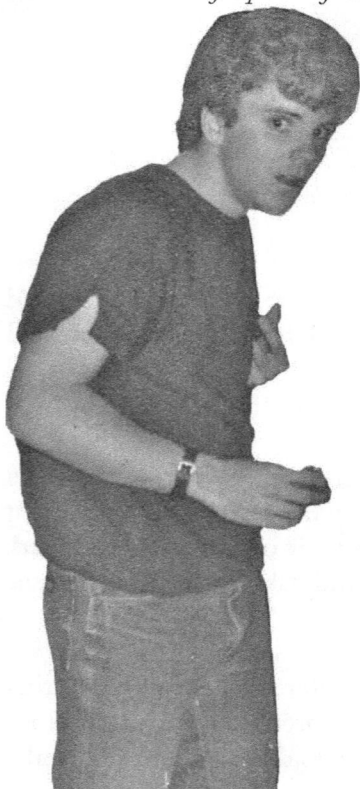

Jeff jots down some words and turns to Ed, who is standing in the doorway, and announces, "The room isn't cold, and that's a good sign."

Ed nods.

"What does that mean?" I ask.

Jeff explains to me that spirits have been alleged to drain the energy from a location, and that people who report having an encounter with a spirit claim that the room the ghost is in becomes uncommonly cold.

This certainly matches my experience, if it *was* a ghost that was actually plaguing me. I noticed the room temperature had been icy cold when the closet door had opened; and when I saw the thing … the wicked thing … appear less than an hour ago, and when I was hiding in the shower stall and Paul came running in, out of breath, claiming he had heard a disembodied voice. In fairness, though, I had been undressed for two of those instances, which may have played a role in my perception of it being colder than usual.

The possibility that Jeff might be bringing some practical information regarding hauntings served to add an element of both structure and stability to the entire situation. Whether the information was accurate or not, I could not say, but I welcomed the conceptual input. The Greek philosopher Socrates was credited with having shared: "I am the *wisest man* alive, for I know one thing, and that is that I know nothing."

So, who was I to pass up an experience to learn?

Jeff asks why there are red candies scattered across the floor, which allows me to explain the horrific encounter in even greater detail. I pick up the now empty fire red candy box in order to scoop the candies up off of the bedroom floor.

Whether or not I am suffering from a flashback, – or the creature has temporarily returned to the room – I see it standing inside the stereo again as I move to collect the candies from the floor. I try to screen my eyes with a hand as I scream: "It's there again! I see it!"

Both Jeff and Ed strain their eyes to see what it is that I am referring to, but nothing is visible to them.

"Chris, I don't see anything," Jeff yells to me.

"What if I'm going crazy? Can we get out of here, Jeff?"

Jeff agrees that exiting the room is the best strategy, perhaps fearing for my mental health.

Ed is already halfway to his room, muttering to himself, and shaking his head in frustration.

Jeff and I take one quick glance back at the room.

"Do you see it now?" Jeff asks.

"No. Thank God," is my reply.

Meanwhile, my mind is still churning, looking for any logical explanation for what I have been experiencing. I recollect that I had not seen the ghost, the first time, until I began eating the *Hot Tamales*, and I saw it again only when I began to pick them up off the floor thirty or forty minutes later. I ask Jeff if he thinks that the candy might be linked to the ghostly appearances. He feels that it is extremely unlikely.

My embarrassment over having asked the question makes me promise myself to screen what I say going forward, *before* I say it.

Adding to the pressure of the situation, it is obvious that Ed wants to turn in for the night, and having a trembling college student, who is claiming to have just seen a ghost, blabbering in the room is not going to help matters any.

I ask Jeff to accompany me back to C2D1, which he agrees to do.

As we stand in the hallway, I ask Jeff if he will continue to write down what has been happening, what I've been going through. If nothing else, it will provide a psychiatrist with a blue print to my illness from the moment that I first noticed it manifesting. To my relief, Jeff is more than happy to oblige, stating that recording the events is something he is very interested in doing. He was already hoping that I would give him my permission to do so.

The C2D(1) journal is born.

I do ask him not to tell Paul about what I am sharing with him, as I don't want to cause him any unnecessary angst; he was clearly already on edge. I am still hopeful that tomorrow morning will bring with it a much-needed clarity on, and space from, events that should not be occurring.

Paul returns shortly after 11PM, looking much more relaxed than when he had left. Opening the door into the suite, he questions why I am standing outside of our room, by myself, in the hallway. The obvious answer is that some freakishly terrifying undead creature might still be in there, but my answer to him is that I am simply 'getting some fresh air.'

A look of comical confusion crosses his face. It was good to see someone smile in the dorm for a change, and he asks, "You are getting fresh air ... across from the *bathroom*? O-kaaaaay!"

Fifteen minutes later we are both lying atop the loft on our respective mattresses having brushed our teeth and changed into our sleeping clothes.

I debate whether or not to tell Paul about what had transpired after he'd left the room. Honest people should not keep such secrets from their friends, especially if it is information that might help them. But I worry that he will think I am crazy. I already know that Ed thinks I am, and for all I know, Jeff might think so as well.

Most importantly, I don't want Paul to leave.

I'll say nothing.

Sleep seems to be a better choice.

15. Tipping Point

Above — Chris Di Cesare, Paul A., and J. Jeff Ungar became the trio around which the C2D1 Haunting seemed to swirl. All were 1983 high school graduates.

For most people, there are few things in the world more comforting, more healing, and more welcoming, than a decent night's sleep. Getting enough sleep is necessary for maintaining one's mental health, physical health and quality of life. Sleep improves the learning process, in preparing the mind and body for the next day, most of the body's growing during adolescence occurs while the person is asleep. Very importantly, the efficacy of one's immune system is to a large degree dependent upon proper levels of sleep.

For me, it is time to sleep.

I am on my raised loft mattress, my bare feet and toes are slowly moving back and forth under my recently washed sheets.

I am warm and comfortable.

The softly-aged pillow that I have faithfully carried with me from my home gently supports my weary face. I hold an edge of the pillowcase in between my middle and index fingers, and then rub my thumb over the point that it makes; something my mother tells me I have done since I was an infant. I choose to lay on my right side, intentionally facing Paul, across the loft, to help make sure I can see if any harm should befall him.

I fall asleep.

Unlike many things in life, where we are aware of the details of what we are doing, it is hard to know — with certainty — the exact moment that we fall asleep. In fact, many people don't even realize that they've actually fallen asleep until an annoying alarm clock, or the intruding sunrise, wakes them up.

At some point in the night, around 1AM, my body craves a shift in position. Stretching my arms up over my head, I yawn, take a quick glimpse over at my still and quiet roommate, and turn onto my left side, facing the cool blue wall. I move my feet slightly, placing the top of my right foot into the soft, padded, underside of the loft, and then doze back off to sleep; or rather, I try to.

A tiny thought, a recollection, perhaps about the size of a grain of sand, is bouncing around my brain. It is knocking into synapses trying to get the neurons moving, it is shouting: *Do not go to sleep!* But I am bordering on exhaustion, and far too comfortable right now to deprive myself of an opportunity for some healing slumber.

I do, however, allow my brain the chance to run through my last few actions to see if there was any credible cause for this microscopic-sized primal internal alarm.

It should be a quick and simple drill.

While still in my closed-eyed half-sleep, I reflect back on the last few things that I had seen: Paul sleeping on his raised mattress several feet from mine; the off-white colored, roughly textured ceiling; the smooth light blue wall ... and the ghost's face.

Something seems wrong.

I am still not fully awake, but I decide to run through the sequence a second time, this time with some rapidity: Paul sleeping; the ceiling; the wall ... and the ghost's face.

Got it!

It was obviously the ghost's face that shouldn't be there. Having solved the apparent cause of my angst, it would be quickly going back to sleep for me.

Wait.

The ghost's face?

I open my eyes, and there, *right* there, mere inches from my own face, I see 'it'!

"Paul! Turn on the light! Turn on the light!"

I am already out of my bed and sitting on the blue carpeted middle (or shared) section of the loft – between our two mattresses - when he flicks on the light near his head.

"What's the matter?" Paul asks as his eyes strain to adjust to the room's sudden change in illumination, "Why are you yelling?"

"I saw something by the wall!"

He scratches the back of his head; his thick and dark hair is now tousled from sleep.

"What are you *talking* about?"

Looking over at the empty space by the wall, I have to wonder myself.

Now that the room was partially-lit, there was clearly nothing visible by the wall near my bed.

"Can you keep the light on for a while, Paul?"

"Dude, it's right in my face. I won't be able to sleep. Why don't you turn on your own desk lamp, under the loft? Maybe that will help."

It is a good idea.

Technically, I could reach down under the loft by my ladder and turn the light on near my desk and I wouldn't even have to leave the comfort and safety of the loft!

As I crawl over to the edge of the loft, gazing down into the large open space below me, Paul switches off the light.

Complete darkness.

Paul laughs.

I yell.

The mad dash back into the shelter of my bed covers and mattress is made without delay. Paul still has no clue as to what might be in this room right now, and I don't know how to tell him, but I am mad that he is making me take unnecessary risks.

"Why did you do that? It's not funny!"

"Go to sleep."

I point a finger, which he likely cannot see in the returned darkness, towards him and warn that if 'something bad happens' I will be blaming him! He smiles and tells me to stop being a 'pussy'.

Moments later, I can hear the deep breaths of sleep once again emanate from his side of the loft.

Wonderful.

Pulling the white and tan comforter up over my head, I curl up into a fetal position; I leave only a barely visible 'air hole' from which to breathe in fresh air from the chilly room.

I am petrified.

My heart is beating hard enough for me to hear it in my ears and to feel its pulse in my neck. The irony of a successful athlete, and 19-year-old college student, hiding under his covers is not lost on me. Sadly, I have no better idea.

If I needed to 'wait out the night' in this fashion, then so be it.

The soft sounds of the song "Glamorous Life" (by Sheila E.) make their way through the closed windows of a car that slowly passes the dorm. I wonder if it is the quiet girl, who lives across the walkway, in that car; I know it is her favorite song, and I bravely push my head out of the bed coverings into the chilled air to look through the window blinds.

Above – The East side of Erie Hall. The C Building is featured to the right. Di Cesare, Ungar, et al. resided on the second floor. The car, as described by Chris was parked next to the visible street lamp. – Screen capture courtesy of EiA Studios.

The street light is reflecting off of the slightly fogged auto windows, leaving me at a complete loss as to whether or not it is her in the car. I sometimes worry about her as she seems to be an unusually quiet person, as though she's still silently coping with some type of trauma that had, against her will, defined most of her early years.

Pulling my tense fingers back from the blinds I am fully aware of the marked chill in the air.

I fall back to sleep.

"Chris, wake up."

"Chris!"

Waking with a start, my mouth which apparently has been open while I was sleeping, is almost totally dry. I moisten it with my tongue as I look over to see Paul's barely visible silhouette sitting up on his mattress.

My eyes do not want to stay open.

"Whaaat?" I ask with a slight rasp to my voice.

Paul is sitting perfectly, and unusually, still. I recognized this reaction. It is the same reaction that I had when I first saw the *thing*.

"There is someone 'downstairs'," he says, referring to the area under the loft.

There is no control of the emotion in his voice.

He is doing an emotional 'survival shuffle' right now; like marathon runners who still strive to finish the race when there is no strength left in their legs. I have been in that place.

"How do you know?" I whisper back.

"I heard someone moving my desk chair across the floor. I'm serious."

Gone now is the Paul who so cavalierly turned off his light leaving me in the creepy darkness. Gone now is the Paul who jokingly questioned my courage and my manhood.

I already missed that Paul.

Listening carefully, I too hear an unusual sound, a 'hissing' sound.

"Do you hear that, too?" Paul asks.

Even though he probably can't see me, I nod my head in affirmation.

The source of the noise could be anything from a drunken student who has mistakenly passed out in the wrong room to a person trying to steal from us. Or, I don't want to consider the 'or'.

"Go check it out," Paul timidly commands.

When I shoot him an angry glance, one that he can probably feel through the blackness, he explains that the sounds are currently coming from my 'side' of the room. I do not argue with him. It was no worse of an excuse than I had given to Luke about not going to the toga party back in January, and was being made under a much more stressful circumstance.

I will check it out.

Inching myself towards the edge of the loft, I peer down into the empty darkness below. The horrific thought that whoever, or *whatever*, is down below is going to grab me by my feet with its sharp nails and yank me down to the ground with it, races through my frightened mind. I am immediately angry at myself for even considering that scenario. If all of this was some type of 'mental creation' I did not want to add any more fuel to the fire.

Better that I play offense.

Crossing myself (the Catholic Sign of the Cross) I decide to jump quickly down to the ground instead of slowly creeping down the ladder. This might allow me the ability to fight whoever is down there; my legs, being as strong as they were, would be able to kick anyone off balance.

I leap away from the relative safety of my bed, forgetting that the loft is less than three feet from the ceiling and smash the top of my head on the roughly textured ceiling.

The pressure of the impact is felt, in my neck, upper back and shoulders. The wind is knocked out of me as I fall to the floor below. The first thing that hits the hard surface is my right elbow; my funny bone. It is not funny. The rest of my body hits, hard, a moment later.

Stunned, I glance desperately about the room, looking for anything and everything at once: a weapon, an intruder, perspective, hope.

Blood is leaking from my tongue, which I had bit at some point. Whether it was from the impact with the ceiling or the floor is inconsequential. The salty flavor in my mouth is unwelcome.

My first scan of the room, while lying in pain on the floor of C2D1, reveals no form, shape or presence. I am relieved.

Standing slowly, a bit wobbly on my feet, I run my fingers through my scalp feeling for any wet spots of blood. There is a growing lump on the top of my head, and some scratched skin, but no laceration. My arm still 'rings' in pain from wrist to shoulder due to my ugly crash landing.

Still, it was time to investigate.

The 'hissing' sound was much louder now, below the loft, and Paul's nervous assertion that it was originating from my side of the room is actually correct: It is my tape recorder.

A power surge must have turned it on.

This problem was simple enough to solve, and I press down on the 'stop' button with my right index finger, my arm still aching.

A welcome silence quickly engulfs the room.

Walking over to the room's only door, I give a quick tug on the door handle: It is locked.

Examining Paul's closet for an intruder reveals nothing; I know better than to check my own. The window is also closed tight and secured. I wonder if perhaps Paul has been sleepwalking, because it is evident that no one has entered our room.

The confirmation that Paul's chair is indeed pulled out from his desk, mine too, is disconcerting. Neither piece of furniture had been in that position when I had climbed up into the loft to go to sleep just an hour, or so, before.

The feeling of dread is amplified when I notice, after I had pushed the chairs back into their customary locations, that the door to my closet is now open.

Open just enough for someone to be watching.

I attempt to put this troubling discovery out of my mind, and I quickly climb back up the ladder trying to project an air of accomplishment to Paul in spite of my new injuries.

"My tape recorder was making the hissing noise," I inform him, as he watches me, carefully, climb back up into the loft. I am wearing a nervous smile that he probably cannot see. "No one is down there; the door is still locked."

"Good," Paul says, "let's try to get back to sleep."

Our peace is short lived.

The moment, I place my head back down onto my pillow, the hissing sound returns to the room.

Paul hears it, too.

"Why don't you check it out this time," I ask Paul.

I did not want to go back down into the area below the loft.

"It's my tape recorder again. Just unplug it, and throw it into one of my desk drawers."

But my roommate refuses his turn to go down to address the situation: "You need to go back down," he says, "you didn't fix it right last time."

I consider crawling across the loft and punching him. But ever since my last conversation with, I purposely don't 'think' her name (*You should have said 'yes'*), I have a hard time saying 'no' to people.

For a second time, in just minutes, I need to go down into the darkness.

This time I nervously inch my way down the wooden ladder, the arches of my exposed feet aching from the hard wood rungs.

Again, my tape recorder is powered 'on' and the tape inside it is spinning slowly around emitting the hissing noise. This time I will allow for no more occurrences. I unplug the device from the wall outlet, wrap the chord around its sturdy rectangular body, and then shove it into the bottom drawer of my desk.

It is done.

I call up to Paul, through the support beams of the loft, informing him that I had properly taken care of the tape recorder and that I wanted to kick his butt for making me go downstairs twice.

Trying to ignore the fact that my closet door is still open (I will close it in the morning) I turn to make yet another ascent up the wooden ladder rungs that by now had the insteps of my feet aching badly.

My concentration, as I prepare to climb the ladder, is broken by the hint of movement in front of me. Gazing through the ladder steps, I see a figure, in silhouette, standing in front of our curtained window. Its head, extended part way up into the loft, is tilted to the side, resting on a neck that must be either damaged or snapped.

It is staring at me.

"Oh, my god, Paul," I scream, "I was just standing where it was!"

As I begin my mad scramble up the ladder, the thought careening around in my head is once again the fear that the *thing* will violently grab me by my feet, its ice-cold nails sinking into my warm flesh, pulling me down to the ground, helpless. I don't have time to be angry at myself for thinking this again; I am more focused on the fact that the thing - the *wicked* thing - is standing exactly where I was when I had spoken to Paul up through the loft.

How long has it been there?

Was it standing beside me at that moment, with its mouth and eyes and face mere inches from mine?

I want to hide like a child; I need to find a safer place.

Stop.

I am not a child; I am an adult.

Steeling myself as best I can, I nervously step back down to the floor. There is a slight tremble in my legs. The thing is still there. I am not sure if I am happy, or made even more afraid, by the fact that it is barely moving. Only its head has moved, slightly, perhaps to better follow me when I move towards the stairs.

A portion of my brain is still not sure that I am actually seeing this; maybe it is some unusual trick of light, a reflection being cast, somehow, across or into our room.

I am taking no chances.

The only semblance of a weapon I can locate is my hard-plastic hair brush; and after snatching it off of the side of my desk, I throw it – just as I would a baseball – at the foul intruder.

For a split-second I am encouraged by the brush's trajectory: the solar plexus. Sadly, my joy is short-lived as it passes through the thing and then caroms in billiard ball fashion off of the back wall, the side of my dresser, and then finally hits the metal base of my standing lamp with a loud 'clank'!

There is silence, until I yell: "Shit!"

Above — Until the 'apparition' arrived, Di Cesare (center) had been able to run his way through, or around, most of life's more difficult challenges. The events in Erie Hall changed all of that. Chris was quick to realize that no matter how fast a person could run, no matter how physically strong they were, and no matter how smart they believed themselves to be, if a person did not understand their environment, they could not effectively survive in it. Photograph by J. Jeff Ungar, 1985.

My muscles flex and strain, harder than they have ever in any race in my life, to get me safely back into the loft. I am already halfway under my protective bed covers by the time Paul has the chance to ask me what is happening.

"Don't talk to me!" I yell from under my covers.

The fact that he had steadfastly refused to go down, and that I had to twice, is not making me any happier right now.

As my mind tries to wrestle with the utter insanity that is swirling all around us, Paul cries out: "Someone is looking at me!"

I say nothing.

I do nothing.

I hide in the darkness like a child who knows that the person who molests them at night has once again entered their room. No one should have to feel as helpless and trapped as I do in this place.

Paul then yells, "I can see someone at the foot of the loft!"

Right then, I recognize how critically important this moment is.

This is my chance to corroborate, or refute, the similarity of our shared experience. This is my opportunity to decide if I am going mad, or if the world around me is.

I ask Paul, from inside my self-imposed prison of blankets and sheets, what the figure looks like. I am very careful not to use any gender-specific pronouns or detailed attributes or characteristics. I decide to use the term 'they'.

"What do *they* look like?"

Up to this point I have not shared with Paul what I have been seeing. He has no detailed knowledge of my earlier encounters other than me repeating that I was seeing something 'freaky'.

I anxiously wait for his response.

Opening up the breathing hole in my comforter, I can make out Paul's form, as he leans slowly forward. Both of his arms are behind him, elbows locked, palms flat on the mattress. His back is straight.

I watch as his mouth opens slowly, in horror, as he discerns what he is seeing inside of room C2D1.

Paul starts to yell.

"It looks like his neck is broken!"

I consider his choice of descriptors: His. Neck. Broken.

I am very frightened.

Paul is staring at me, and I can see that a white mist is now swirling around him.

He asks me: "Oh my God! Are we going to *die*?"

I am guessing the answer to that question will be 'yes.'

16. Haunted

Above – Geneseo Cemetery, 1984. – Photograph by J. Jeff Ungar

The thin layer of frost on the ground is making the sunlit morning seem brighter than usual. I rub my eyes with the back of my two closed hands, removing any particulates that might have formed in them overnight. Not that there was much of a chance for that to happen. It is 9:16 AM. Paul has just made his way to the bathroom to splash some water on his face. My alarm, which was set for 8:10, did not go off, so we will both be missing our morning classes.

For the first time in my life, I am wishing that I was someone else, somewhere else, and anywhere else.

I stare at the sundrenched blue pillow on my mattress, the one with the image of Jesus on it, and I wonder where God is right now. Is He in some great cathedral in Rome? Is He in the eyes of a young couple falling in love? Perhaps He is in the heart of a new born child breathing her first breath? He certainly wasn't in our dorm room last night.

Something was.

I run my waking fingers through my tousled head of hair and then try to lightly massage the tenseness out of my stiff neck. Closing my eyes, I recall the horror that plagued us once darkness fell.

"Oh, my God, are we going to die?" Paul had asked. I didn't answer him as I was still trying to understand the significance of Paul seeing the same form I had, independently. This was no case of mass hysteria, nor was it some grotesque version of suggestion. Some external factor was creating this fear, this terror, and this dread.

Moments later, Paul had yelled out, "It's gone! I don't see it anymore!"

I did. The wispy, human-shaped black shadow – with the tilted head – had found its way over to the area of my closet. In the darkness of night, it was still a shadow. I moved my hands back and forth in the air in front of me. The slivers of light cast from the moon were sliding through the cracks in the blinds, and I was able to create shadows of my own. But the shadows that I made slanted to the left as the moon was in the eastern sky. The human shadow had no 'slant', nor was it of the same uniformity.

There was a dead thing in the room.

Nervously, and perhaps at great risk to myself, I had reached my right arm down into the dark, narrow space between the edge of the loft and the wall in order to pull my blue 'Jesus pillow' up off the couch below. That task safely completed, I pulled my Bible closer to me.

Paul and I then sat still in our beds for a period of roughly thirty minutes, neither of us able to decide what to do, as we tracked the swirling mist that floated throughout the room. All the while, we would catch intermittent glimpses of the dark shape that could be seen swaying slowly and in different sections of the room. I was too emotionally distraught and physically drained to contemplate what was happening. Having the comfort of both my Bible and pillow near me, I was going to try to get some sleep.

Paul nodded and indicated that he would try the same. It was nearing four o'clock in the morning.

The force that tore the pillow out from under my head seemed both impossibly strong and impossible. My head flopped down to the mattress top and the pillow was drawn away from me towards the wall. The abrupt motion sent a quick flash of pain through my neck muscles. I gave a preliminary pull on the pillow only to discover that it was suspended approximately a foot in the frigid air, unmoved by my attempt.

That was my pillow, and I wanted it back!

It wasn't difficult to grasp it, tightly, both fists clenched onto it. Nor was it too much of an effort to wrap my strong runner's feet around the base of the mattress. Pulling my body together (which was much like executing a 'military crunch') in order to take back my pillow turned out to be more difficult. I had strained and strained, gritting my teeth as the force being exerted by whatever that wicked thing was, bent the bottom of my mattress up. My feet were slipping. I needed help.

"Paul, I need your help! You need to see this!"

His reply, from behind his bedding was a simple: "No."

But it couldn't end that way, I wouldn't let it. He had to know, everyone had to know the extent of the physical manifestations. I knew that it would take more than just the word of one lone student.

"Paul! If you value our friendship at all, you will look right now!"

Turning my head for a moment, I see the look on Paul's face. It is a look that says: 'No one should ever have to see this.' His eyes are opened wide, and I fear for his sanity, as I do my own.

"Let go of my pillow, damn it! It's mine! In the name of Jesus Christ, I command you to go back where you came from!"

I used the phraseology that the Warrens had recommended back on January 30th.

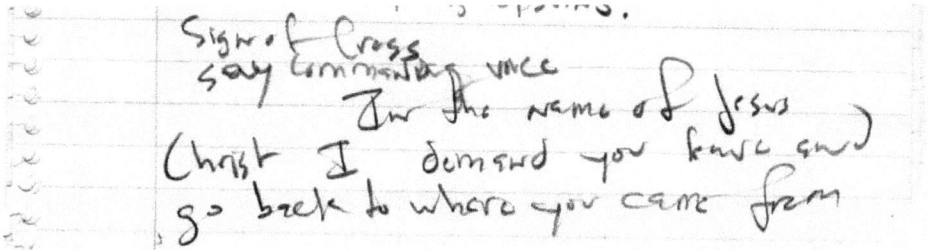

Sign of Cross
say commanding vace
In the name of Jesus
Christ I demand you leave and
go back to where you came from

The sound of Paul sliding open the bathroom door across the hallway pulls me from my uneasy reflection. The mornings always feel safer to me. I stretch out my newly-rested legs and quickly hop down onto the floor. Landing on the spot where I had fallen last night, I notice that   Paul is standing perfectly still in our doorway.

"Are you all right?" I ask.

He doesn't respond at first, then points with intensity and says, "Look. My chair was pulled out again."

There is no doubt in my mind that I had pushed his chair back to his desk area the night prior, although I fail to understand any meaning or purpose behind such a seemingly arbitrary action.

"There was a gold orb floating over your head last night while you were sleeping," Paul adds with the nonchalance one might use while indicating that the morning's toast was ready.

"Oh, really? That's, uh, pretty *strange*. Why didn't you wake me up?"

"You had just fallen asleep."

My thoughts drift back to a discussion I recently had with a student named Dean who was in one of my communications classes. After I had given a required oral presentation that had gone very well, he jogged up to me in front of my dorm and told me that the reason I was such a great speaker was that I apparently had a "golden yellow aura."

Right. Sure. That must be it. It couldn't have been all my hard work and preparation!

Therein lay one of the core challenges of the events that swirled so violently around us. Where was the leverage, the balance, the delineation between objectivity and subjectivity? How long would I need to search in order to know if my interpretations of the events were accurate?

Was it feasible that I actually had some type of golden 'aura'?

Sure.

Was I able to prove that such a thing existed?

No.

So then, was I to put stock in Dean's analysis when it was so easy to dismiss?

To my thinking, the chance that the color of my supposed 'aura' had any impact on the effectiveness of my speech was slim.

But, what if we could prove that auras existed, and that their color (or shape or size) somehow did impact the effectiveness of our abilities? As phenomenal a discovery as that might be, it might imply that we had far less control over our successes, our choices and our lives than we knew. Moreover, it begged the question as to whether or not auras, if they truly existed, were borne of genetics, environmental causes or some divine order.

Jeff, Beth, Ed, me and a few others had, in fact, experimented with auras. It was the night after I had shared with all of them what Dean was suggesting.

We faithfully followed the directions, read from a book on parapsychology that Jeff had obtained from Milne Library, and took turns trying to 'read' each other's auras.

The method called for gazing through a clear glass bottle, which contained in it a colorless liquid. We soaked the label off of a large bottle of white wine. Each person, who was lit from above, had a black or dark background (three sheets of black oak tag paper taped together) behind them in order to create a strong contrast.

Several of my friends claimed that they did, indeed, see my aura, and noted that it was, as Dean had professed, gold in color. It was the largest of those that they could see.

I myself, felt fairly confident that I could see energy patterns around their heads too. But was that what we were actually seeing? Objectively, I had the blondest, and fullest, head of hair of those present, and it seemed just as likely that they were seeing some aspect echoed from that.

Or, then again, maybe we *were* seeing auras.

Above — Sketched image of Di Cesare's purported 'aura' (gold with aspects of green and pink) as described by Beth, Ed, Linda and Jeff during their experiment during the spring semester of 1985. Chris drew the sketch himself while his friends shared their observations with him. It seemed to be a match with what Dean B. had reported.

The continual onslaught of questions that puzzled my brain was exhausting, since the specter of death had arrived. And they usually created even more questions when I took the time to consider them.

The ghost had forced me, angrily and against my will, to accept that life might not be quite so simple or quite as easy as I had wanted it to be; as I thought it should be.

I didn't enjoy what I now had to consider: Can we truly ever prove that we are 'right' about *anything*? Should we ever force ourselves to try?

156

Should I simply accept Dean's unprovable explanation and consider the implications behind it? Or would it be better to simply discard it and hide, safely and comfortably, behind what I felt that I could actually prove?

Turning away from my thoughts, I glance over at my desk.

Oh no.
Oh no.
Oh no!

My eyes begin to well with tears.

"What's the matter?" Paul asks with an unmasked sincerity.

The picture frame that had been on my dresser, the one with the photo of my young cousin in it, has been moved. It has been physically pulled apart. Pieces of it, and what it had (secretly) held, are now scattered across my desk top.

"The damned thing is taking my stuff apart!"

"At least you got your pillow back," Paul offers; and he is right.

But now I have a more frightening problem to deal with.

The ghost has found what I had hidden inside the picture frame, behind the photo: The photograph from Paula, my high school friend who was killed while hitchhiking home.

It is placed on top of the shattered frame.

It knows.

It *knows.*

"You should have said 'yes'."

17. Valentine's Day

Above – Though they have not received much in the way of public attention for their actions during the C2D1 Haunting, (clockwise, left to right) Judy Y., Linda Fox, and Beth Kinsman all played integral roles in both analyzing the haunting and in helping Chris to endure it. In fact, all three would claim to experience some of the haunting's more frightening aspects. – Photograph J. Jeff Ungar, Erie Hall, 1985.

February 14th, 1985 - Valentine's Day: All throughout the campus balloons, decorative hearts, and curled paper streamers of deep red adorn the walls, doorways, windows, and tables. The song, "I Want to Know What Love Is" from Foreigner is, appropriately, echoing out of the many dorm rooms as the anxious young college women fret over their makeup, and the guys search in vain for a pair of nice shoes to wear to a dance.

One rare exception is room C2D1.

The day prior, three of the ladies from the B-building of Erie Hall (Beth Kinsman, Linda Fox, and Judy Y.) had generously offered their assistance and decorated our room in fine style.

In spite of everything that had been going on, they made the room look both festive and beautiful.

The impromptu pre-Valentine's Day party, was quad-wide.

Craig Norris, Jeff's roommate from the year prior, was there. He held court and actively expostulated against unbridled consumerism to anyone willing to listen. Jeff's current roommate, Ed S., quietly whispered his hilarious and pointed observations about people who drew his attention, and Paul had Beth sitting with him.

I sat on the old brown couch, smiling broadly, next to both Linda and Judy, enjoying being around all of the smiles and the laughter. I'm also pretty sure that, at some point, I streaked through portions of the 2nd floor.

Jeff played his synthesizer alongside some members of a popular band called The Rolling Gumbys. I announced that Jeff was a Renaissance Man, to which he nodded and then immersed himself back into the task at hand.

Above — Members of the college band The Rolling Gumbys. — Photo by J. Jeff Ungar.

Everything was glorious inside room C2D1 until first Beth, then Linda pointed out that my mattress, which was situated on top of the loft, had an obvious and unexplained, human-shaped, indent at its center. It appeared as though someone (unseen) was now resting upon it. That sent most everyone nervously fleeing out of the room.

Most of the party-goers carried on for several hours in other locations, but my temporary sense of joy was lost along with the girls' unnerving observation.

I checked my mattress; and it no longer had the indent that we had all seen.

There was no sign of it ever having existed.

The main aesthetic feature in the room's Valentine's Day decorations, along with the many red and white paper streamers, was the dozen or so balloons of red and white.

Less than two hours after the party-goers had left, however, all of the balloons, every single one, popped.

One at a time they popped, almost as though an unseen person was moving from balloon to balloon, and pausing just long enough to gauge our reactions.

Paul had yelled, "Stop it!" to whoever or whatever it was that was doing this, and then turned to me and angrily shouted: "Something is breaking the balloons!"

He didn't have to tell me.

I was watching, fascinated, by the occurrence. This wasn't happening in the darkness; this didn't involve barely discernible shadows or half-asleep impressions. This was empirical. It was provable. Balloons could be weighed and measured, their remnants examined and discussed.

I looked over at Paul, who was sitting at his desk as I was at mine, and wondered aloud, "Why do you think this is happening?"

He leaped from his chair and ran down the hall, returning a few moments later with Brian from C2D3, two doors down. Paul pointed out all of the now burst balloon fragments. Some were lying flat on the floor and some were hanging from pieces of tape or string. I could see that Brian was weighing whether or not Paul, with my help, was playing him like a fool, or if we were actually being serious.

Brian was methodically rubbing the back of his prematurely balding head in consideration, when he asked, "Do you know what's *really* scary?"

"What?" Paul and I asked simultaneously, wondering if perhaps the dread phenomenon had now spread to his room.

"This!"

Brian dropped his pants.

Paul quickly punched him in the arm, then chased him out of our room, angrily cursing at him, all the while poking fun of what he considered to be Brian's oddly curved toes.

I stood up, closed the door, and picked up a deflated rubber balloon fragment off of the floor. There was nothing unusual about it, with the exception of it being ice cold. 'Too cold' for having been in a room that was at a comfortable room temperature, I considered. It was beyond me, however, to figure out exactly what scientific process (ghost or otherwise) could account for this.

Jeff had placed some light pressure on me earlier in the day to provide him with a name for the 'thing'. He preferred not to have to use words like 'ghost' or 'apparition; in public … or in his journal. He was hoping for something more precise, more *personally* descriptive.

Holding a portion of the balloon in my hand, a name had found itself into my thoughts: 'Tommy.'

A slight smirk had crossed my youthful face; Tommy was the name of the blue-feathered parakeet my family had when I was young. It was also the name of my maternal uncle, whose return from overseas military service when I was just four-years-old remains my first cogent memory.

Whatever, it had seemed a safe enough name to use in public, one that wouldn't draw unwanted attention if it was used at a dining hall table or inside a classroom.

After placing the limp section of balloon onto my desktop, I had chosen to approach the room's two closets. I wondered if 'Tommy' was in the room at that moment, proudly reviewing the results of his most recent handiwork.

My eyes studied the doors carefully, looking for signs of anything untoward.

Paul's closet door had been open, his belongings neatly organized and sorted, hangers and clothing carefully systemized, with clean and colorful plastic crates holding any potential loose items on the floor below. By contrast, my closet door was opened just a crack, allowing for a small amount of light (from the room) to slice through the still darkness inside. I had not gone near it after I had seen the shadow lurking there the night before last. Squinting my eyes into two well-focused slits, I was able to discern the ever-growing pile of recently worn running clothes at its base, and a few shirts and jeans hanging scattershot inside above them. After this ordeal was all over, I pledged to myself, I would attempt to become more organized, like Paul.

I had reasoned that if I were able to fully open my closet, the added brightness would assist me in verifying that nothing was inside, and that my irrational fear was mercifully unfounded. It was what I wanted, and it was what I needed.

As I began to step towards the closet, my socked feet making no perceptible sound, I noted a flicker of slight movement near the back.

I instantly froze in place, trying to take as shallow and quiet breaths as I was able to. My abdomen instinctively tightened and an unnatural chill ran from my fingertips up over my exposed arms and settled uncomfortably where the top of my neck met the base of my skull.

For several minutes, I stood motionless and silent, a strikingly similar reaction to the one I had in the bathroom shower just prior to the moment Paul came crashing in, running from some disembodied voice that he claimed had been calling my name.

My mind raced through past actions and scenarios, looking for a moment of prior bravery that might now serve to push me through this staggering fear.

Sadly, there was not much to pull from.

Most all of my successes had been derived largely from combinations of dedication to an arduous routine, natural physical gifts, the intentional limiting of external risks and a certain amount of interpersonal charisma (based largely on my inherited appearance). All of which had been used almost exclusively for the purpose of *avoiding* potential conflicts.

Unable to establish a representative act of bravery on my part, I decided to emulate someone else's: actor Clint Eastwood's.

I had seen him in a few 1970's movies. His characters, like a policeman named 'Dirty Harry', were tough, gritty and often uncompromising in their approach to solving problems. One classic movie line of questioning played itself through my mind with effectiveness: "You have to ask yourself one question: 'Do I feel lucky?' Well, do ya' punk?"

Clint Eastwood, it was.

I smiled quietly to myself in that silent room, as my courage welled up inside of me. I understood well enough that perception can become reality, and if that thing started to believe that I was tough, that I was brave, that perhaps I was a threat to it, I might be able to take better control of the situation that was rapidly spiraling out of it.

Spreading my feet further apart, lifting my shoulders up high, and taking a deep breath as I kept my gaze focused on the closet, I self-assuredly called aloud: "Tommy, come out and play."

Positive that such confidence would serve me well, I took a step forward.

A low-pitched, gurgling, growling sound projected itself outward towards me from the dark interior of the closet.

My jaw dropped.

For a few moments, I stood absolutely frozen in place as the door swayed slightly and inaudibly back and forth. My stomach wanted to vomit.

I sprinted out into the hallway and then through the open door to room C2D2 to nervously share my very questionable actions with Jeff, who shook his head in a rather concerned manner and said, "You have to stop doing things like that, you might provoke it and that would be bad for everyone."

Now, at approximately 7:00PM on Valentine's Day (1985), Jeff enters my room. Paul has decided to accompany some friends uptown for a few hours, and – as Jeff will be leaving the following morning for a week-long family trip to Florida – he feels that this might be the ideal moment to try and collect some concrete evidence of the ghost's existence.

Other than abject fear of the ghost, I have no strong objections. I haven't had a meaningful Valentine's Day since the 4th grade when Wendy Morin gave me a yellow heart-shaped candy with pink lettering that read: "Be mine."

Having given some thought to my recent actions, Jeff's plan is for me to 'lure' the ghost out into the center of the room, where he will then try to capture a photographic image of it; some proof that it is real.

While preparing his camera, and jotting down some quick temperature readings, Jeff asks me if I have been able to determine some type of name for the ghost yet.

I share with him: "Tommy."

He immediately stops what he is doing, casts me an examining glance, and asks me if Paul had told me to say that.

I shrug my shoulders.

"No. Why?"

"I just spoke with Paul a few hours ago, and when I asked him what he would call the ghost if he were to give it a name, he also said: 'Tommy.'"

"Tommy is a common name," I tell Jeff as I try not to consider the true implications of what this might mean "I have an uncle that everyone calls 'Tommy'."

Jeff considers my statement, says nothing in reaction to it, and then carefully instructs me to push my arms out in front of my body. Apparently, I am calling the ghost 'wrong', and he physically adjusts: the height of my arms, the distance of my hands from my body, and the angle at which my hands are held.

I ask him how he knows to do this, unable to hide a slight smile of amusement.

"I saw it on a television show," he responds matter-of-factly.

As I prepare for my attempt at 'calling a ghost', Jeff's roommate, Ed, on his way out for the evening, sticks his head into the room. He looks more than a bit perplexed by what he is seeing. I am embarrassed that he sees me kneeling, motionless, in this odd bodily pose.

To my continued dismay, Jeff asks Ed if he 'would be willing' to take a few pictures in order to help us capture 'the moment'.

It is obvious by the manner in which he reacts that Ed remains largely confused as to what exactly is going on, perhaps even *why* anything is going on, throwing his thick woolen scarf over his right shoulder, but he politely agrees to do so.

I attempt to stand completely motionless as Ed takes a few snapshots with Jeff's camera. All the while I am unable to rid myself of the notion that anyone who sees these images in the future will think of me as a complete fool. Most in society would expect me to mock this endeavor. And even though I understand that this might be a valuable, potentially ground-breaking, even *life-saving*, course of action, I allow myself to mock it, by virtue of a slight smile, in order to not be judged too harshly by some unseen people in the future who I will never know.

In the pictures, I am a coward.

As Ed departs the room, I silently berate myself, hoping that someday I will be given a chance for redemption.

C2D1 is once more secured, and without the perceived threat of societal judgment, I rededicate myself to the task at hand.

Jeff instructs me to "call" the ghost.

"Jeff, how do I do that?"

Above - Valentine's Day, 1985. The insincerity of his expression in this photograph 'haunted' Chris from the moment it was shot. – Photograph by Ed S. using J. Jeff Ungar's 35mm camera.

I jokingly offer to dial the operator on our suite's shared phone, and ask for a 'Mr. Ghost'.

"Get it?" I offer, tongue in cheek, "Call the ghost?"

Jeff does not find that prospect to be an amusing one.

He redirects me, and offers that, while my arms remain outstretched, I should use the ghost's name, in a friendly tone, and formally invite him into the room.

I take one last glance around my room, trying to note every object and detail, wondering if this is when people, looking back, will say that I had lost my mind.

I begin.

"Hello, Tommy. It's me, Chris. My friend wants to see you, and so he has asked me to invite you here."

Jeff is looking around in a fashion that suggests he is worried that he might miss the 'magic' moment. His fingers are poised, set exactly as they need to be, in order to take a photograph with as little movement, or time, expended as possible. He looks how I imagine a *National Geographic* photographer might look. Of course, I am the one standing on the savannah, calling the lion out of its den!

I can discern a growing grayish mist inside the darkened closet, that now seems eternally opened, and my exposed skin is now very aware of the precipitous temperature drop.

Jeff is, too: "If the thermometer is accurate, the room temperature has dropped from 66°F to 61°F in less than eight minutes. That shouldn't be possible in a closed room."

Focusing my sight into the closet, I watch as the mist shifts and grows in what appears to be a vertical fashion. It is happening. The … *thing* … is listening, is understanding, is complying. I wonder if, in Mary Shelley's literary mind, Dr. Frankenstein felt the way I do right now, when his monster's heart beat its first beat: dizzied excitement mixed with a deep-seated fear.

The face is now visible: the pale unblinking eyes, the hint of what should be a nose, the misshapen mouth, once again beginning to open.

Make it stop! Make it stop!

My throat tightens and all of my muscles seem to constrict. I try to tell Jeff that the ghost is here, but I cannot utter as much as a single sound. The horror is too overwhelming.

I've made a terrible mistake.

I try a second time to speak.

Nothing.

I need to problem solve. I recall a particular technique that some runners use to reduce air trapped near the rib cage in order to reduce cramping. The technique involves slightly compressing the solar plexus. Using my back and stomach muscles, I am able to slightly reduce the length of my spine.
This in turn puts added pressure on my lungs.

The third time is a charm, and I am able to emit a slight, raspy, soft breath: "Hhhhhhhhhh … "

Out of the corner of my eye, I can see Jeff scrambling in front of me and to my right. His back is now to the door, he kneels down.

I am frozen with fear.

My thick navy sweatshirt is being blown back at its sleeves and into my torso, the nearby cardboard poster paper by the couch is also affected. These are tangible indications of the spirit's presence, or at the very least, its impact on the environment.

[Flash!]

"Got it," Jeff announces.

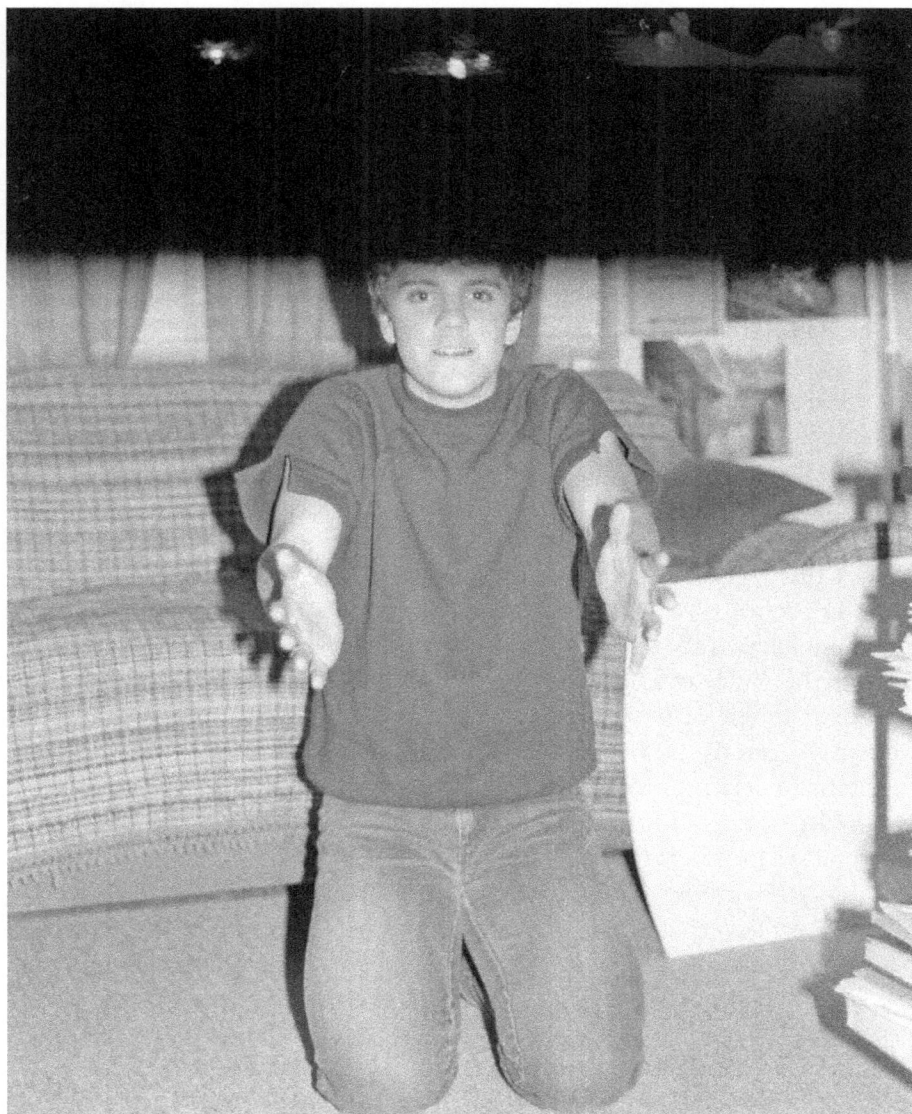

Above - The image taken by J. Jeff Ungar on Valentine's Day 1985, that may forever be associated with identifying Di Cesare as the 'The Ghost Boy of Geneseo'.

This time my faint smile is different: it is a cautious triumph. I understand in that instant, that Jeff might have just captured what my own testimony would have difficulty proving. There will now be 1,000 'words' to describe the event, if a picture is truly worth what 'they' say.

I do not know it at the time, but this photograph will someday grace the cover of a book; it will become the 8x10 glossy image that I will sign for fans at conventions in place of the traditional (and tacky) 'head shot'; it will be how the paranormal field will likely remember me: as 'The Ghost Boy of Geneseo'.

My celebratory mood is short lived.

The flash, or perhaps it is Jeff's quick movement across the room just prior to it, sets the wicked thing into motion and it is coming straight towards me!

1973.

It is my first ever baseball game.

The Saturday morning skies are clear and bright, and I am too nervous to bat. My father, who is the Colden Park Little League coach, asks me what is making me afraid.

"The ball is going to hit me in the head," I tell him, nervously squeezing my seven-year-old hands together until they are sweating.

Putting his hands on my two shoulders, and looking me directly in the eyes, he says in a reassuring tone: "The ball is not going to hit you in the head, Chris. You're making yourself scared. You just need to relax."

He crouches down next to me as we watch Mike, one of the more experienced players approach the plate. The third pitch in the at bat crosses the plate, and he lashes out and connects with it. With the sharp-sounding sound of wood on leather, the ball is lifted up into the air and Mike bolts out of the batter's box towards first base.

The ball falls in for a double, and Mike wipes some of the base path dirt off the legs of his uniform.

My father looks at me.

"All right, Chris, pick a bat and give it a try."

There are several bats to choose from, so I lift each one to see which best fits my hands. The one with the royal blue stripe on its handle seems the best. The number '27' is stamped onto its end. I give it a few awkwardly uneven swings and cautiously walk into the batter's box.

"Remember, only swing at the good ones," my dad counsels.

I nod.

"C'mon, Chris" Mike yells with a sincere look of encouragement on his face.

The pitcher goes into his windup, and releases the ball.

CRACK!

The ball hits me in the head.

There was nothing I could do back then, and there is nothing that I can do right now.

As the creature approaches me, its physical details mercifully begin to blur into an amorphous whitish-gray energy, which spares me seeing its eyes, mouth, and teeth as they approach my face.

Without my permission, the thing passes right through me. An eerie awareness washes over me, and it feels to me as though I can sense every single cell in my body freezing. Just as a cold iced tea or lemonade drink might feel as it pours down your throat in contrast to the hot summer's day, my body seems to feel the full effect of this unwelcome and surprise intrusion.

My physical form then seems to 'unfreeze' just as unexpectedly and rapidly as it had been 'frozen'. This forced encounter leaves me angry, afraid, and physically drained. I fall forward onto the floor of C2D1, with the sense of having in some way been 'spiritually abused', if such a thing were possible.

I want out!

Jeff is yelling to me: "Chris, where is it? I can't see where it went! Do you see it?"

He is darting back and forth around the room, his camera in his hands, at the ready. The colors of the Christmas lights, strung across the loft's underside, reflect in his eyeglass lenses.

I use the side of Paul's desk to help lift myself off of the dorm room floor. It feels as though someone had just punched me in the chest with an invisible fist.

Most of my body aches.

My resentment of room C2D1 is growing by the day; and is growing by the minute.

"I don't care *where* it is," I complain loudly, "I'm getting out of here!"

"Chris! Wait!"

Jeff has not given up on his mission to somehow capture the ghost, 'Tommy', on film.

"I don't see it! If you see it, tell me where it is!"

Understanding how much his friendship has helped me over the last few days, I do my best to collect myself, and I begin to scrutinize the room.

I am looking for something that I do not wish to see.

My eyes scan the unfriendly room for any mists, shadows, or odd distortions of shape. There is nothing by the closet door, or Paul's stereo. It is not crouching by my desk or near the window.

As I open my mouth to share this disappointing news with Jeff, I see *him*, suspended near the ceiling above my bed.

Tommy, with his dead-looking eyes, is looking right at us!

"Jeff, over there!" I scream, pointing with an outstretched arm to the area near my bed, above my pillows, in the upper southwest corner of the room.

I absolutely abhor the fact that he is near my pillows again.

Still holding his 35mm camera in front of him, Jeff runs over next to me in order to better line up the shot, but apparently, he sees nothing.

I am fully confused as I can see the ghost as plainly as I see the poster of marathon runner Bill Rodgers, tying his shoes, on the wall nearest him.

Jeff is frustrated, trying to line up the shot.

"Where, Chris? I don't see anything!"

My mind is boggled. I am able to discern 'Tommy' just as clearly as if I were looking at a living person who had decided to sit in my bed.

"Right *there,* Jeff – the thing staring at you: *that's* the ghost!"

I continue to point at the figure in order to direct Jeff's line of sight, but in spite of his honest efforts, he simply cannot see the ghost.

Fortuitously, an idea strikes him and he urgently commands: "Chris, take my camera. If you can see him, then *you* take the picture!"

I am hesitant.

I have only used a 35mm camera once before (with mixed results at the toga party in January) and I don't want to be the one blamed, years later, for letting the 'big one' get away, if I screw this up. Nor did I want to have to see the thing while taking its photo.

Jeff places the camera into my hands.

I'm so nervous that my first I fear is that I might drop it, thus destroying all hope of getting the evidence that he seeks.

Jeff quietly guides my hands and fingers into the appropriate camera locations with his, and then tells me to do the best that I can.

With a quick, encouraging nod from Jeff, I place the view finder to my eye, hesitantly line up the ghost in its center, and then press the button.

[Flash!]

I hand Jeff his camera, and run out of the room.

J. Jeff Ungar wrote the famed "C2D1 Journal Notes" during the extreme haunting of the same name which took place at SUNY Geneseo's Erie Hall Dormitory, room C2D1 in 1985. In relation to that, he is featured in the award-winning docu-thriller film *Please Talk with Me* and the Syfy channel's *School Spirits*: "Dorm Room Nightmare."

18. Capturing the Moment

I can trace my interest in photography to the small Kodak Brownie Hawkeye camera my mom, Gail, gave me when I was about twelve years old, around 1977. I still have negatives showing my dad with our two black Labrador retrievers up in the branches of an apple tree. Yes, the dogs were climbing the tree.

She gave me her camera. She gave me my life. I've never formally mentioned that my mom attended Geneseo Teachers College. She actually resided in Erie Hall back in the early 1960s when it first opened. I have her to thank for encouraging me to follow what started as a casual interest in photography and has become a consuming pastime. Just ask any of my family and friends who can confirm that I've probably taken tens of thousands of pictures in the last few years alone.

By the time I was a young adult, I'd learned some fundamental skills with photography. In 1981, I bought a Minolta SRT-201 35mm camera that is still in my house to this day. It seems strange to think of now, but it was actually pivotal to my role in the haunting that I took that camera with me on my trip to Germany for my junior year in high school as a foreign exchange student. It challenged me to learn the operation of it and react as much as I could *in the moment*, crystalizing the otherwise effervescent snapshots of memory – holding them sacred in that medium. I wanted to capture moments, to preserve them. That's the sensibility I brought to

Geneseo along with my habit of chronicling events in notebooks. I do not know if I would have been as ready to help (not that I was truly ready) when Chris asked me to record the life changing occurrences that started to transpire in the winter of 1985. As I acclimated to the campus, my mother's alma mater, my camera helped me to become – as I sheepishly refer to myself on the SyFy *School Spirits* program – the "eyes and ears of the campus." I'm actually embarrassed by that epithet, but much like Chris, who became known as the Ghost Boy of Geneseo – a moniker it has taken him decades to accept and embrace – I'll try to wear the title proudly now. With that in mind, let me tell you about one of those moments during the C2D1 Haunting that was captured on film and forever distilled.

On the second night of what turned out to be an extreme haunting that persisted for months, Chris and I conducted an investigation in his room, C2D1, where the ghost had first appeared to him. In my journal notes from that period, I mentioned taking my "35mm camera with Kodak 100 color film [...] to try to get some ghost pictures." Here was an opportunity to react in the moment as I had been practicing since my mom gave me her camera. Maybe getting evidence of what had happened to Chris could help him deal with this paradigm shift. Perhaps taking these pictures could even address broader metaphysical questions about the nature of life and death. There are a half-dozen fascinating exposures from that roll of film we took, and it's that last shot that famously held the key to the true nature of the haunting.

When I got the photos developed, I took them straight to the college library. I did not want to risk summoning the ghost by looking at them in our dorm, Erie Hall, so Milne Library seemed like a more controlled location for in-depth study. The library had an open area with big windows looking out on the valley. I was seated at one of the large tables as I considered with mounting anticipation that in my hands I might be holding an answer to help unravel what it was we faced in room C2D1. I took a breath and positioned the stack of prints on the table, now as portentous as Tarot cards. With Tarot, a reader utilizes a specialized deck of playing cards to divine the future or unveil a certain mystery. Just so, I laid the photographs down, one by one, in a very slow, deliberate way. After each card was placed on the table, I studied our future.

I stated earlier that it was the final, famous shot, what we would start calling the 'ghost photo,' that profoundly changed how I perceived the haunting moving forward. But the two photographs that preceded it, while lesser-known, are also instructive in providing a setting and context that enriches and supports the ghost photo itself.

For your consideration: the first of these photographs was taken below deck, or under the loft in this case. The dorm room was divided into what we considered to be upstairs and downstairs by a wooden loft platform – the beds being upstairs, the desks, couch, and other furnishings downstairs. Chris is depicted in the photo with his arms stretched forward in a searching posture, hands held approximately six inches apart. We were in the middle of our investigation, as my notes describe "looking for the peculiar drafts we had noticed" that had pervaded C2D1 recently.

Using this method: "Chris first felt the draft near his pile of books [...] I wanted to try a picture, so Chris moved back into the room, when suddenly he started saying it was following him on his hands." There are multiple examples of our attempts to feel for the ghost in this way, but in this photo I want to point out something to the left of the poster of the bikini-clad woman with the martini glass, at nearly the center of the photo, just below the bottom rim of the lampshade. There we begin to see the faintest wisp of an anomaly visible against the shaded portion of the far back corner. It is important to note that location as we move on to the next two photographs.

Above – Di Cesare, as directed by Ungar, looking to find 'peculiar drafts' in the room.

"Failing to find it below, Chris went above to his bed and felt for [the ghost]" – here my notes describe what is occurring in the second photograph. I shot this image from the foot of the loft. You can see the flash reflected in the television. Chris by now had already reported to me that he had witnessed the ghost several times in this location. My notes continue: "Then [Chris] had an idea; taking a bookmark from his Bible, he held it before him. Sure enough, as if curious, he felt [the ghost] engulf his arm – it was really strong. But as Chris turned to tell me to take the picture, he felt [the ghost] weaken. I snapped the picture, but the flash apparently scared [the ghost], who shot with *great* force up Chris' arm and disappeared. *Note [in margin]: Super Pickle, a stuffed figure was moved by this." I did indeed observe the plush toy swinging after the flash; I feared for Chris. We had no idea what this thing was capable of. Now let us consider again the far corner of the room. 'As below, so above' – again we find an anomaly, more than a wisp this time.

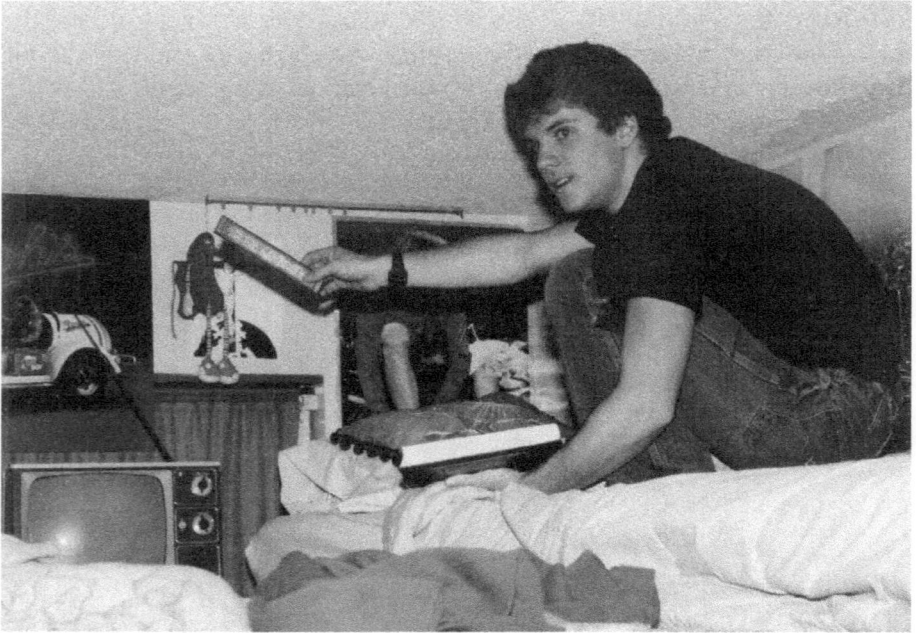

Above – Chris holding out a bookmark that seemed, for a moment, to interest the ghost. Apparently bothered by the flash, it moved away towards the wall on Di Cesare's right. Both he and Ungar observed the Super Pickle toy swing, apparently, as a result of this rapid movement. The plush toy was a recent addition to the room, given to Chris as a gift from the girls in the B-building after discovering he had done some figure modeling.

Now the third and final photograph. It was taken just after Chris descended the loft, his hands had become "ice cold. We had been playing hide and seek with [the ghost]" and were both spooked and eager to retreat from the room. But as Chris looked back, I could see he was startled by something. He pointed at the back corner near where he had just been and said, "There it is! The ghost! Take the picture!" I didn't see it. I quickly thrust my camera into his hands and said, "If you see the ghost, *you* take the picture!" I theorized that, since Chris seemed sensitive to psychic phenomena – and because the ghost appeared to focus on him – our chances of capturing it on film could be increased if the camera were in his hands *while* he was seeing it. Chris pointed the camera at the ghost, took the shot, and we fled the scene.

That was the photo I was most excited to see when I had the film developed and opened the processing envelope at Milne Library. It was the photo I was waiting for as I turned each picture over in sequence, the one I had the most hope for finding something in. However, the first time through I noticed nothing out of the ordinary. When I got to the last print, all I could see was the loft. I wanted to see a full-bodied apparition: something recognizable as a figure, as a person – a human form as described by Chris in the moment. If not that, then maybe some phenomenon like a white haze or distortion, but nothing immediately seemed unusual. I stopped and decided that maybe I'd missed something. I went through the deck again a bit faster this time. When I got to the photo of the loft I was hunched over, really looking at it, focusing on all the recognizable everyday objects in it, how the flash interacted. I focused on the corner where Chris said the ghost would be and suddenly recognized a pattern. And, so, what I had initially dismissed as a reflection at the corner, along the right edge of the Bill Rodgers running poster, I now began to discern what resembled, not so much a human form, but a human *skeleton*. Once you see it, you can't *not* see it! I was almost in disbelief. I hadn't seen a skeletal apparition in any of the ghost photos I'd ever encountered in books or TV. Yet there it was, right where Chris said it would be!

What struck me most was the anatomical detail. I was thrilled, but I wanted to make sure there was not an alternative or mundane explanation for what I was seeing (such as an imperfection in the processing of the film). One of the first things I did was grab an anatomy textbook from the library shelves to compare. I deduced it was a male skeleton. Based on the holes in the pelvis I could see that it was turned away. This was different from the frontal view depicted in the anatomical diagrams; from the back view the pelvic opening is more eclipsed. If you follow the line up, you can almost see individual vertebrae leading up to a ribcage, an opaque gap suggesting scapula or where shoulder blades should be, and then a collar bone above that. And, at the highest point, there is a rounded crescent that resembles the top of a skull, the curve of which suggests that it is tilted to the right. Chris always communicated that the head was tilted to the left. The fact that it is tilted right in the photo relates to the observed physiognomy of the skeleton, underscoring that the ghost is facing away from the camera.

Above – This is the photograph in which Ungar, upon careful re-inspection, noticed what appeared to be a human skeleton. One of the factors that most intrigued Jeff was that it was visible in the exact location that Di Cesare claimed he had seen the ghost.

Once I'd established what I thought it was, I studied it for a long time. I wanted to rule out other explanations like pareidolia or reflections in the room. I analyzed how the flash moved in the picture. I scrutinized the back corners and the levels of the wall. The two halves of the figure were not symmetrical. I could tell this was a structure that was in front of the wall – but behind the pillow (which would have blocked the flash). The brightness of the pelvis was behind the pillow in such a way that it couldn't have been illuminated in that manner if the flash were causing it. These were all arguments in my mind that supported the idea that I was seeing something paranormal. Our experience of the ghost was as a compact ball of energy, a zone of cold, this ghost-light that would float around Chris or hover near him. I theorized the reason we caught the apparition in skeletal form might be because the ghost was just beginning to manifest when

Chris called it out below the loft. I suspected it went through several stages of developing. It passed through Chris and maybe picked up energy as it went (as described in the first photograph that we discussed here – as well as the classic 'hands out' image of Chris that's been featured at numerous paranormal symposia). Perhaps the ghost had retreated to the corner after the flash went off in our second photograph and then defensively turned away. At that juncture it might have been in the process of materializing, and if we'd stayed longer, we'd have captured a fully formed apparition.

This was one of the first tangible signs that what was happening to Chris was external and not internal, and that was crucially significant to our understanding of what was haunting him. By this time, my attention had been so rapt by my study that it was surreal to lift my eyes from the evidence of a strange new reality, now laid out before me, only to find myself still sitting in the quiet library. A new piece of our future had been uncovered. I hoped it would help.

As I write this now, I feel proud of the ghost photo. I'm convinced we captured a skeletal apparition in the process of manifesting. I'm also gratified to see the path of our friendship. Chris and I worked together to take this series of pictures. He trusted in me enough to set aside his justified terror, and I believed in him when I handed him my camera before we exited. I still do. I'm continually amazed when I look back at all the images from that time. I am so glad when I hold them in my hands now – moments captured.

Above – J. Jeff Ungar's *photographic efforts offer to those who view them the opportunity to effectively travel back in time. His landscapes, portraits, and candid photos capture moments that cannot be recreated, but that can now be enjoyed long after the fact.*

19. Drifting Through the Nightmare

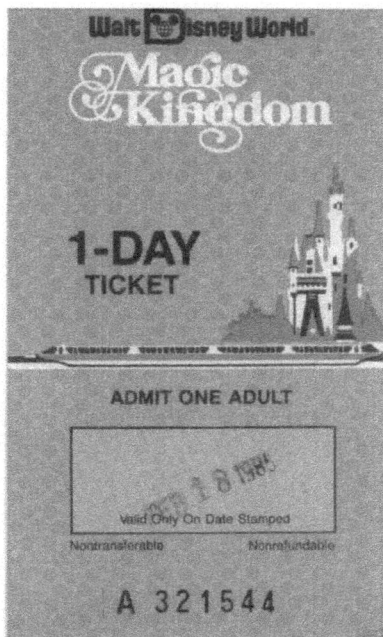

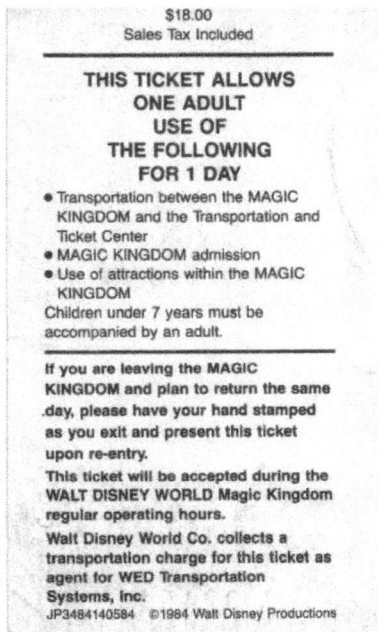

Above – J. Jeff Ungar's Disney World Day pass, dated February 18, 1985

By the time that Jeff had returned from his Florida trip in late February, my friendship with Paul was beginning to fray. Tommy's daily activity had taken a toll on both of us, and Paul, who still desired to keep the haunting a completely private matter, became upset with me when he found out that I had spoken of it to some of the girls in the B-Building.

In the absence of Jeff as my confidant, and considering Paul's reticence to discuss matters, I had turned to my lady friends.

Everyone copes with crisis differently, and Paul and I were certainly in the midst of a crisis of epic proportion!

On the night of February 16th, we were again terrorized. I had fallen asleep relatively early that night, but was plagued by a frightening dream that involved being trapped by a spike that pierced my right foot as I attempted to escape from an enormous glowing sphere that resembled a ball of twine. I awoke with a terrible 'Charley horse' (an intense muscle spasm) in my right calf that had caused my entire foot to stretch, tighten, and then cramp.

The pain was extreme.

My moans of discomfort woke up Paul, who was very relieved to discover that it wasn't another Tommy episode. I laughed aloud, almost uncontrollably, when it had dawned on me that things had gotten so bad that one of us being in immobilizing physical pain was now considered a 'positive' situation.

Laughter tends to be contagious, and soon Paul was chuckling as well.

It was a nice moment.

The laughter slowly subsided, and I turned onto my left side.

Tommy's ghostly face, which was now just inches from my own – and with an impossibly broad smile torn across it – greeted me. The sight was so frightening that, had I not taken care of certain physical matters just prior, I would surely have defecated in the loft. I screamed, and blindly leaped from the five-foot loft; too much adrenalin was flowing through my body to feel the pain of smashing my knees, shoulders, and elbows on the floor.

I found a quiet spot in a nearby lounge and sat myself on a well-cushioned chair, pulling my legs up to my torso; just the way that my childhood friend Joe S. had the day he told me that his mother had been killed by the drunk driver back in 1977. We were both twelve.

Her name was Grace, like my grandmother's.

His mom was working as an overnight nurse at a hospital across the river. I remember she had a towering beehive mound of platinum-bleached hair atop her head and usually wore a smile whenever I happened to see her. I thought that she was glamourous and would sometimes sit on my front lawn in the hopes that she would smile and wave at me. She left behind three boys, my friend Joe being the youngest.

It was my mother who had sat me down and told me the bad news. My first thought was that I was thankful that my Grace was alive, and sad that Joe's Grace was dead.

A few weeks after his mother had passed I saw Joe while I was in my front yard hitting a plastic ball with an oversized plastic bat. We sat down under the protection of the red maple tree that stood in front of my house. I'm not sure why, but I was relieved that Joe looked the same as I had remembered.

With some hesitation, he asked if he could tell me something. I nodded in silence, eyes opened wide. Joe then verified, after pulling his long, skinny legs up against his torso, that his mother was killed by a drunk driver. What confused him he said was that while his mother was killed, the drunk driver – who had caused the accident by veering into her lane – was not. Apparently, he wasn't even seriously injured.

We both made a promise on that day that if we ever saw a drunk driver coming at us that we would relax all of our muscles so that we would live. Just as the man who killed his mother had apparently done. Our reasoning was that stiff things, such as peanut brittle or a tree branch, snapped. While loose and flexible things, like rubber bands, stretched. Arranging our bodies in various positions we attempted to approximate virtually every accident scenario that our children's minds could envision. It was a worthwhile distraction from his terrible loss, but eventually the sadness washed over his face and I could see his soft brown eyes darken. His large lower lip trembled for a moment, and then he stated with as much force as he could muster: "I know one thing for sure; I'm never going to drink and drive."

"Me neither," I vowed.

He was very afraid that day, afraid of what might someday become of him. Joe would die, allegedly in an alcohol-related car crash, at the age of twenty-one.

I understood now.

Before he had left for Florida, Jeff had noted in his journal:

"As I'm writing this, Chris and I are in my room. He is extremely reluctant to be alone in his room, especially at night, the witching hour, 'when fancy stalks outside reason and malignant possibilities stand rock firm as facts'" (Thomas Hardy, *Tess*).

My admiration for Jeff, and his bravery in the face of the unknown, was ever increasing.

He would be back in eight days.

The rhythmic electrical hum of the nearby vending machine was at once relaxing, and annoying. After collecting myself for a few minutes, and putting my thoughts of the death of Joe's mom to rest, I uncurled my legs and loped back to C2D1. The door was still open, as I had left it, and Paul was sitting up on top of his mattress with his light on.

"You OK?" he asked with a tired voice.

"I saw the ghost," I inform him as I climb back up into the loft, "it was right next to my face, smiling a grotesque smile at me."

"I know," he said, "that's why I put the light on.

"You saw it again?" I asked intently, "What did it look like this time?"

I wanted desperately to know what he was seeing, to be able to understand how much of this harsh madness remained external as opposed to internal; to know if I was truly alone or if others were on this crazy journey with me, for the duration.

"It was looking at me, from where my desk chair is. Its head had that weird sideways tilt again. I can't take much more of this, you know."

The way in which he had added "you know" at the end of his statement suggested to me that he was trying to get me to understand something, something important that he was not actually saying.

I wasn't sure exactly what.

"We have to do something or we might die in here," Paul continued in morose fashion. I felt my innards tighten. It was a possibility that I did not want to have to consider. Maybe he was right. All I could do was reply, "I know."

He shifted his legs a bit and added: "Looking at that thing, it might be a very painful death. They may not even find our bodies."

Paul's eyes were a study in seriousness.

"Please, stop," I requested nervously, "saying all of this is only going to make us more afraid, and … (I whispered) … you might give 'it' some bad ideas."

Paul nodded his agreement and, after looking around the room, said, "We need to do something. We need someone to help us get rid of the thing."

The thought was not new to me, but hearing someone else echo it brought me a degree of comfort. On several occasions, I had considered simply packing my bags and heading home, leaving both Geneseo, and the creature, behind forever.

I understood that Paul still had that option.

What had stopped me from leaving, each time, was the never-ending shame that such an action might carry with it. My father was the first Di Cesare to attend college; I did not want the ignominy of being the first Di Cesare to drop out of college. Dropping out amongst the potentially hurtful rumors of a mental breakdown, drug abuse or lack of toughness was not an option I allowed myself. I couldn't bear that family disgrace.

No.

I was here for the duration, whatever that might entail.

"What do you want to do?" I asked Paul, almost afraid to hear his answer.

"Let's get a priest."

February 25th, 1985. Jeff has returned from his trip. He is tanned and relaxed, his hair lightened further by the southern sun, and is speaking of warm weather, theme parks, and the large assortment of foods that he had sampled.

He looks happy and is a very welcome sight.

Apparently, he has also brought the warm Florida weather with him, as the temperatures are reaching up into the mid-fifties, after having been below freezing for most of the month.

His presence meant that my research partner, my sounding bound, and my soon-to-be best friend was back in action. Back to possibly help me make sense of the chaos that had continued to swirl around me, around us, even in his absence.

Gathered in a sun-drenched C2D2, as Sunday's rain clouds cleared away, Paul, Beth, and I begin recalling some of the odd events that Jeff had missed while he was away on vacation. We share about the early morning walk into the village and how Paul and I had resolved to go to St. Mary's Catholic Church with our request for aid. We take turns relaying to Jeff how a priest would not see us, but that a woman who was working there had provided us with a slip of paper, and a name.

Jeff asks to inspect the pencil-written message on the rectangular cut scrap of gold stationary; our veritable Golden Ticket.

On it was the name of a priest (who, we were advised, had mentioned, or perhaps shared, a story about ghosts at some point in the not too distant past) as well as his office number at the college's Interfaith Center.

"Fr. Charlie. Hmmm. Are you actually going to speak with him" Jeff wonders, peering at us from over the top of his wire-frame glasses, "Is that what you want to do?"

Jeff understands full well that both Paul and I desperately desired to contain any talk, or mention, of the haunting, and such a move would certainly run counter to that intent.

Both Paul and I shrug our shoulders in uncertainty, we are both much braver in the daylight.

"Maybe," I say.

Beth relays For Jeff an incident that had occurred on February 18th when she and I were studying in C2D1: a pencil fell from the ceiling near the closets and rolled around on the floor for an odd length of time. And she tells of how we had decided to move our studying out into the C2 common area after that.

Jeff uses the term 'apportation' to describe events such as objects dropping from 'nowhere' into a room. An 'apport', he explains to us, is typically associated with paranormal events such as poltergeist or séances.

I smile, it is good to have him back.

Paul says nothing when Beth speaks. The emotions from their break-up are still strong. The tension is palpable, but it does not dissuade Beth from maintaining her new-found place in this circle of friends.

I share a particularly unnerving experience from February 22nd that began with me sitting at my desk, wearing only a pair of nylon running shorts, while working on a school assignment. I had not done my laundry for a while (due primarily to my fear of unintentionally interacting with the ghost) which I felt might occur if I attempted to retrieve my basket of unwashed clothing.

The abrupt waving motion of the light brown curtains was the first clue that Tommy was making a, then unheard of, daylight appearance!

Above – Cemetery by Daylight, photograph by J. Jeff Ungar, spring 1984. Tommy's 'daytime' appearance now had Di Cesare questioning the parameters of the haunting. During the initial weeks of the haunting the ghost had been visibly 'active' – to those involved - primarily during the evening hours; well after sunset.

What was particularly unusual about this situation was that it was occurring during daylight hours.

Except for the initial audio encounter (the one with Paul's headphones and the voice calling my name) over the course of the first few weeks of the haunting, the ghost had virtually always acted in the evening hours, when the darkness surrounded us.

Being it was mid-afternoon, and feeling comforted both by the sounds of students bustling about the dormitory and the process of reading my baseball book, I chose to ignore the activity.

Yet, as I continued to stare down into my book, that familiarly unnatural and icy cold began to move in towards me, it's faint caress washing over my unguarded skin, especially my bare back.

"Disbelieve, Chris" I counseled myself, "it is daytime."

The night time might very well have belonged to the creature, but the day was mine; mine to go to classes in, and to run in, and to talk with my friends in; and mine to eat in and to function with some semblance of comfort in. It was important to me that I felt safe, and in control of my environment, for at least minor, pre-set, portions of each day. It was better than nothing, which was what this thing was now apparently pushing for.

"Leave me alone," I demanded, my eyes not leaving my desk area, my head not turning to acknowledge its presence.

The concept of sarcasm ran across my mind when I realized that the book I had been holding in my hands, only minutes before, was entitled *Man and His Fictions*.

Oh, how I wished it were that simple.

I noticed that it had drawn closer to me; I could now make out the outline of its head and upper torso in my peripheral vision, not unlike the night that it first appeared to me, by Paul's stereo.

"Not now!" I yelled aloud, still determined to ignore Tommy's intrusion into *my* day. The possibility that another Erie Hall student might hear me yell did not concern me. In fact, I secretly hoped that one might burst through my door and see the damned thing lurking over me.

The icy cold breath on the top portion of my right ear served to move me into a more upright, and rigid, posture.

My rate of breathing had increased, while at the same time the actual depth of my breaths had decreased.

Instinctively, I drew my legs closer together, tightened my muscles, formed my hands into fists, and pulled my head forward away from the ever-nearing frigid breath.

I waited.

I waited … for the sickly whisper of my name … up close, in my ear.

It did not come.

Instead, what felt like frozen finger tips – thin, hard bones of dread and death – began touching the soft, sensitive, skin on my neck!

Screaming in sheer terror, I fell onto the floor, landing at the foot of the old brown couch. I curled up into the fetal position like an oversized shelled shrimp on a plate of Chinese lo mien, only much, much, colder.

I understood in that cruel moment that it didn't matter how fast a person could run, or how smart they were, or how physically strong their body might be that if a person could not control their environment, or worse, not *understand* it, they simply could not survive in it.

How many thousands of noble and capable warriors over the centuries had fallen, fallen due to tragic circumstances that were simply beyond their control?

How many had their lungs burned and poisoned by gas that they could not see, or lost their limbs to disease that they could not detect?

How many were crushed by crumbling, fire-lit, buildings falling above them, or swept away by waves whose approach was unseen in the darkness?

In that moment, the sense of dread inside of room C2D1 had felt like it was taken right out of the epic Gericault painting, *The Raft of Medusa*. Me? I was the young man lying, injured, prostrate, and exposed, on the front of that raft.

The one who would most likely be unable to survive it.

"Get. Away. From. Me." I breathe through my clenched teeth, too afraid to look at the ghost.

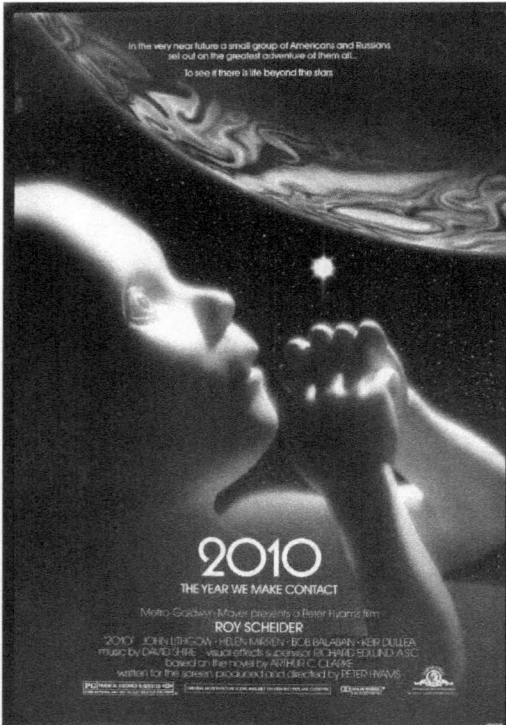

Instead my eyes focus on an 8x10 poster for the Science Fiction film *2010* that I had recently taped to the wall on my side of the room close to the window. That date, 2010, would occur some twenty-five years in the future.

I wondered if I would still be alive then.

Left – Poster from the film 2010.

I lay, for several minutes, until I noticed that the ghost was no longer hovering over me, and that the room had now returned to its normal temperature.

The sharing of these frightening recollections leaves room C2D2 and its current occupants, in a sustained silence. The frightening 'goings on' now have my friends, just as they do me, deeply worried.

I can see it in their eyes.

When the silence becomes nearly unbearable, Jeff reaches for a green and white, thin, cardboard, photo envelope, packed with 4"x6" images.

I know what they are.

They are the pictures that were taken on Valentine's Day.

They are the proof Jeff had sought: proof of the haunting, and proof that a dead thing was actually following me around and whispering into my ear.

They are proof that I did not want.

Jeff hands the envelope over to them, and Paul and Beth fumble their way through the double stacks of photographs, most of which are unremarkable.

Both of them pause, almost at the same time, on one particular photo.

It was the photo that I had taken.

Paul says nothing, but his mouth opens slightly in reaction to what he is seeing: What he should *not* be seeing … again.

"No way," Beth murmurs under her breath, but loud enough for all of us to hear "this can't be real. This *cannot* be real."

But it was.

Jeff had shown the 4x6 photo to me, just an hour earlier, and it had sent chills through my body.

Like the rest of the photographs in the roll it captured the varied contents of room C2D1: the old television set; a PUMA shoes poster of marathoner Bill Rodgers; my mattress and pillow; a section of a poster of the New York City skyline (with the World Trade Center Towers still standing); and the *American Greetings* 'Super Pickle' stuffed doll hanging in a watchful pose on a string from the ceiling.

All of these things I was quite comfortable with, and quite aware of.

There were two distinct differences with this photo however: This was the one picture on the roll of film that I had taken. And in it, in the very place that I had pointed to that night, in the area where I had seen Tommy looking at me, in the place where I had pointed Jeff's camera, was a human skeleton!

Several years later, the photograph would be sent to Dale Kaczmarek, the President of the Ghost Research Society which is located in Oak Lawn, IL, for independent analysis and peer review.

Many who had been involved in the haunting were particularly anxious to hear his analysis might yield.

Among his quotes and findings: "I've had a long time to look at and analyze [the photograph]. First, I made working slides from [it] and later scanned these images into a computer for analysis. While I assume it could be possible for [the image] to be a reflection off the highly [reflective] and glossy poster over the bed, I don't see any indication of what it could have reflected. Surely, there wasn't a skeletal image of something or someone standing in the room when the photograph was taken. I have only seen two other images that come to mind that appear to be skeletal in configuration. I would tend to place this photograph into a 'ghost' category as it shows a recognizable form or shape."

This validation brought smiles to many of the people around me.

The truth of the matter for me, back in 1985, was that even if the photograph would not, one day, receive Mr. Kaczmarek's important stamp of approval, I knew that life for all of us would never be the same.

Above - Hand-written note from Beth Kinsman, to the Chris, inquiring about the results of the 'Valentine's Day' photography attempt to capture the ghost on film.

Dale Kaczmarek is the President of the Ghost Research Society, a clearing house for reports of ghosts, hauntings, poltergeist and life after death encounters, based out of Oak Lawn, Illinois. Mr. Kaczmarek is a frequent public lecturer, paranormal instructor, and the author of six books including *Field Guide to Ghost Hunting Techniques* and *Wind City Ghosts* I and II.

20. The "Skeletal Image"

I was honored to be asked for my expertise regarding a very strange and unusual photograph that was reportedly captured by a college student, Christopher Di Cesare, in 1985. I have long believed that ghost images are the most compelling evidence that we can gather for theories such as the existence of ghosts and the possibility of life after death.

I have been a paranormal researcher for over half a century. I first began serious research back in 1975, and since then have investigated more than 4,000 cases around the globe. I co-founded the Ghost Research Society in 1977 with fellow investigator, Martin V. Riccardo (b. 1952). Since then, I have traveled around the country and even the United Kingdom in search of proof as to the existence of ghosts and life after death. My group has traveled to some of the most recognized haunted locations in the world including: Waverly Hills Sanitarium (Louisville, KY); Rolling Hills Asylum (East Bethany, NY); Bachelor's Grove Cemetery (Cook County, IL); Trans Allegheny Lunatic Asylum (Weston, WV); Gettysburg, PA; the Hannah House (Indianapolis, IN) ; the USS North Carolina (Wilmington, NC); the Joplin Spook Light (Joplin, MO); Lemp Mansion (St. Louis, MO); the

Ohio State Reformatory (Mansfield, OH); and hundreds of other locations.

I have experimented with all types of film as photography is my forte. I have used 35mm film; SX-70 Polaroid film; color and black and white high-speed infrared film; Tri-X black and white film (which is extremely sensitive to the ultraviolet end of the spectrum) and have used various cameras in my work including: the very early 110 and 126 Brownie Instamatic; Polaroid Square Shooter cameras; 35mm's; and have now graduated to the more sophisticated digital cameras of today including full spectrum; 1080p high-definition full spectrum cameras; digital trap cameras; Sony Nightshot camcorders; digital infrared cameras; and the X-Cam Structured Light Sensor camera.

Through the use of these cameras, I have captured a wide variety of anomalous images including strange light formations; unusual mists; dark shadow people; and even full-bodied apparitions. A number of 'orbs' were also captured, however current research indicates that over 99% of orbs are likely to be nothing more than dust particles; bugs or insects; water droplets; obstructions; or digital flaws. The images that have always fascinated me the most were ones that depicted shapes resembling persons. I have accumulated the vast majority of such images via actual investigations of haunted locations across the country.

When I first began ghost research, back in the mid-to-late 1970s, I used either a Polaroid SX-70 or 35mm camera. Contemporary paranormal equipment did not exist back then, and I visited alleged haunted locations as part of investigations and snapped pictures with the hope that something would show up later, after the processing of the film. I never knew if I had acquired a paranormal image until a week or so later, when the film was developed. I was amazed, however, at what appeared to be my early luck in being at the 'right' place at the 'right' time and pointing my camera in the 'right' direction. It was literally hit or miss.

The advent of paranormal equipment, bettered my chances of capturing a ghost image as the devices would alert me to an area that had electromagnetic deviations, cold spots, or electrical disturbances. This greatly increased the chances of producing a plausible image of something that wasn't always visible to the naked eye.

Then digital technology hit the market, which allowed the photographer to actually see what he or she had captured in real-time. The picture would immediately appear on the LED (light-emitting diode) screen. Even when the digital age arrived, I continued to use 35mm Rebel EOS and Canon AE-1 cameras in my work. Since the investigator can see what was just captured using the digital technology, he or she can instantly snap another picture with a 35mm in order to document that digital file.

In 2002 I decided to write a book, *Field Guide to Spirit Photography*, (ISBN: 0-9766072-3-9) as a way for both novice and experienced paranormal researchers to better their chances of capturing an image on film or through a digital camera. This heavily-detailed labor of love offered the reader a wealth of practical information on basic camera operations; the 'ins-and-outs' of film use and developing; various types of equipment; how to analyze spirit and natural photographs; plus a collection of fake, accidental and authentic photographs of ghosts.

The book answered the questions: What types of films and filters to use on 35mm cameras? What types of cameras are best-suited for the conditions of a paranormal investigation? And what are the step-by-step methods of using cameras for ghost research? It not only addressed the 35mm cameras of yesteryear, but explored the history of spirit photography, digital cameras, camcorder operations, as well as how to use cameras in conjunction with paranormal equipment. It continues to be one of the best-selling books from the Ghost Research Society Press collection.

Spirit photography has long been an important part of my life, and it can serve as definitive evidence for survival of the spirit after death. Approximately thirty years ago, I began offering a free service via the Ghost Research Society and my website. I encouraged people to send the pictures that they believed portrayed something 'paranormal'. Without delay, I received thousands of photographs through 'snail mail' (e-mail) that I offered my opinion on. While I do not claim to be an expert on spirit photography, analysis, or even ghost research, I have seen more than enough images over the ensuing decades as to offer a sensible - and often accurate - analysis of what I believe created the image(s) that appeared in the pictures. In truth, nobody is an expert. I have always said that it is simply a case of people who have "more whiskers" then others.

Following the launch of the World Wide Web in August of 1991, I began receiving pictures via the internet and through my website (www.ghostresearch.org). I offered this free service to anyone who wished to have their picture examined. The only criteria that I required for this service was that the submitter provide information regarding: The type of camera and/or film used (images should be in .jpg format); some accompanying text sharing the circumstances behind the picture-taking process (this includes weather conditions or surrounding conditions of the location where the image was shot); why the picture was taken; and that the person(s) always send the original photograph, and not an enlarged image, or one with items 'circled' on them.

I would then load the picture into analysis software that I use, such as JPEGSnoop or other analysis software. I would often attempt to enlarge the suspect area, or play with the brightness and contrast, in order to make the alleged image more 'readable'. I have, without exaggeration, received tens of thousands of pictures over the past 30-plus years. And while most do have natural explanations (some are outright frauds and can be uncovered as that), a small portion of those images cannot easily be identified as real or unreal. I have always classified alleged spirit images into three distinct categories:

1) Natural explanations or unintentional spirit images. These can be caused by reflections; camera straps; orbs; lens glare; double exposure; explainable mists; bugs/insects; cigarette smoke; camera malfunction; 'blurs' caused by camera movement; obstructions; people walking into the frame as the picture was taken or matrixing; pareidolia or simulacra.

2) Paranormal Images that I cannot find a logical explanation for. The word Paranormal simply means 'unknown'.

3) Supernatural Images that are most likely caused by a discarnate (not having a standard physical body) entity and do not fit into the other two categories.

In fairness, you could also add a fourth category which would be 'Frauds and Fakes', where there is a deliberate attempt to pass off an obviously fake image as being real. A good number of picture files that I receive nowadays are created using ghost applications and cell phones. There are clear indications where these come into play as when the supplemental "ghost" image is inserted and the file resaved before sending it to me. The result: The EXIF setting are changed.

As to using JPEGSnoop (a free downloadable program that can be found on the internet) once a picture is inserted for analysis, the program will quickly send you a complete report of the photograph's parameters. The software indicates if the image has been processed or edited because the EXIF settings would show as having been altered from when it was originally taken. Once a picture is taken certain parameters are saved exclusive to that particular picture. If the picture is then altered (in any way) through another commercial program (i.e. Photoshop or alternate paint program) and then re-saved, those EXIF settings will be different, and the software that I use will indicate those changes, that the settings have been altered in some way. This automatically sends up 'red flags' that the image could have altered, manipulated, or edited either at the time of the picture taking process, or sometime afterwards. It should be noted that the simple action of entering a picture into a commercial program for viewing purposes, and then re-saving it can, unbeknownst to the user, also serve to change those critically important original settings.

When one captures a photograph with a digital camera, the camera will not only store the current date and time into the image file, but the camera settings as well. The information that is recorded by the camera into the photograph may include: details about the camera model itself; the lens that was used; shutter speed; aperture; focal length; and so on. Some modern digital cameras and camera phones are GPS (Global Positioning System) enabled. This means that the location coordinates (latitude and longitude) associated with the photographs are captured and preserved as well.

This 'metadata' is then embedded into photographs using the standard EXIF format that can easily be read by most image editing programs, as well as online photo sharing websites such as Flickr and Picasa Web Albums.

But why would anyone want to modify the EXIF data of photographs? Well, there can be several genuine reasons. For instance, the internal date of your camera might have been incorrect and therefore all the pictures were captured with an incorrect timestamp. Or you might want to add your name to the photograph's metadata, so that people immediately know who the owner is. With an EXIF editor, you can also geo-tag your photographs manually, even if your camera doesn't have GPS.

You may be a bit surprised, but Windows Explorer is actually a wonderful EXIF editor. Just 'right click' on any image file, select Properties, and then click the Details tab. You can now edit a wide range of metadata associated with that image from the camera model, to the shooting date, to copyright information and more. Windows Explorer will not let you edit GPS related information of photographs, but Google's innovative Picasa software is a useful choice for doing that.

Finally, if you want to change the EXIF data in multiple photographs, you can edit them all in 'one go' by using dedicated EXIF editors like GeoSetter or Microsoft Pro Photo. GeoSetter can pull EXIF tags from one photograph and then apply them to all your other photos, while Pro Photo is more suited for geo-tagging pictures. Similar modifications can also be done with the help of command utilities such as Jhead and ExifTool. These are very powerful tools, and implementation can certainly be a bit 'geeky'. Change can also occur when someone purposely manipulates or inserts an image into a picture and then resaves it, thereby changing the EXIF signature. This is where many of the fake images come into play.

However, there are a large number of what I believe to be authentic examples of spirit photography. The picture taken by Christopher Di Cesare, inside his college dorm room, is one of those examples.

In 1985 a most incredible picture was taken by a teenager named Christopher Di Cesare while he was a student at Geneseo State University of New York in Western, New York. The picture was taken inside room C2D1 of Erie Hall (a pretty creepy name). Strange drafts were felt by many who lived in, or visited, this room and physical objects were moved around.

One evening, Di Cesare was shocked to see the very life-like apparition of a young male who appeared to be wearing a striped rugby shirt. It's head was unnaturally tilted to one side. The ghost was soon called "Tommy" by those who became involved in the months-long haunting. After many years of research, some have concluded that the apparition was a young boy who had hung himself at the college several years earlier, while others believe it to be the spirit of a long-suffering Revolutionary War soldier (of the same name) who was tortured to death by a local Native American tribe.

The picture in question was taken by Di Cesare, at the insistence of another Geneseo student named J. Jeff Ungar, who owned the camera used and was in search of documented evidence. It is an enlargement of a poster hanging on the dorm's wall and depicts a four-time winner of both the New York City and Boston Marathons, Bill Rodgers. It was taken with a 35mm camera and apparently - with the noted exception of Di Cesare himself - not seen by the naked eye, as most ghost images are not seen by the naked eye but captured with a camera.

Our eyes are like video cameras. They take in and process motion pictures. A camera can capture a moment in time in a fraction of a second, sometimes as fast as $1/1000^{th}$ of a second. Camera's freeze that moment in time and within that very short space of time an apparition can appear, but not be recognized by us. In that fraction of a second, there typically isn't enough time for our eyes to recognize that particular image via our optic nerve, and then send a signal to our brain that would confirm that something was there. The camera, however, because it freezes that fraction of a second, can capture something our eyes did not effectively 'see'.

Above – Kaczmarek analyzed the image captured by Geneseo student Chris Di Cesare inside his dorm room on Valentine's Day 1985 using J. Jeff Ungar's 35mm camera.

On the right-hand side of the poster there appears to be a skeletal figure in white. There is clearly a spinal column - with ribs protruding to the left and the right - and a very well-defined pelvic bone structure. Unless there was a skeleton hanging in the dorm (and all present claimed that there was not) there is no reason for that to appear. I also find it highly unlikely that it is a reflection. And reflection off of what? Throughout all my years as a paranormal researcher, and analyzer of photographs, I have only come across one other similar figure. But that one was not as well-defined as this particular image.

The date was October 17, 2015. I had been invited by Chris Di Cesare (via event Coordinator Bill Edwards) to attend a conference: The C2D1 Haunting 30th Anniversary Symposium, being held at SUNY Geneseo, New York; the location of the now famous haunting and the 'skeletal image' ghost photograph that I had examined some twenty-five years earlier. I gladly accepted as this was an opportunity for me to see Erie Hall, the dorm where all of the paranormal phenomena had taken place in the distant past, and where this highly unusual picture was taken.

It was a great time, and I and others taking a tour of the dorm were more than a little amazed at the reactions from the room's current students occupants when we stopped in to talk about the 1985 ghost encounters.

Many, perhaps, had never heard of this before ... but are very aware of it now!

Above – In 2015, at the C2D1 Haunting 30th Anniversary Symposium in Geneseo, NY, Dale Kaczmarek, President of the Ghost Research Society, met fellow researcher Alan Lewis. It was Lewis, a high school friend of J. Jeff Ungar, who took the initiative to send Di Cesare's 'Skeletal Ghost Image' photograph to Mr. Kaczmarek for study almost a quarter century earlier.

21. Heaven Help Us

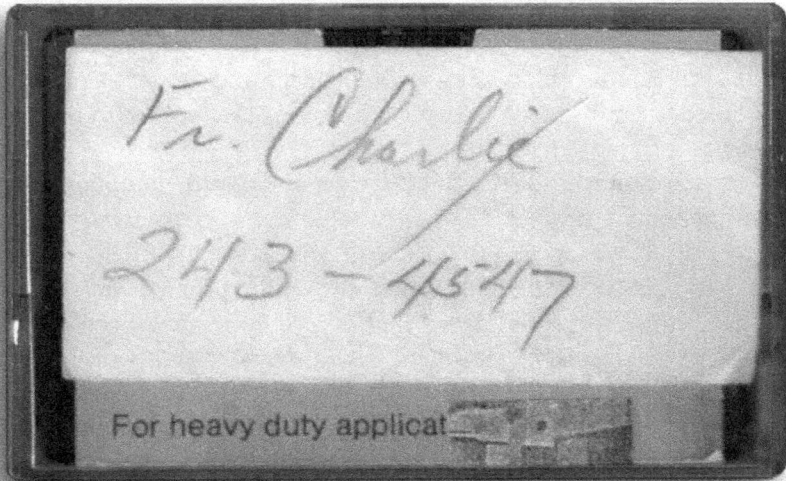

Above - The small section of gold colored stationary with Father Charlie Manning's phone number written across it. The Interfaith Center was just up the hill from Erie.

The photograph weighed heavily upon me. Until its existence, all of this, no matter how many people had become involved, could have been written off as some type of mass hysteria.

I wouldn't have minded.

But not anymore.

Jeff had retrieved an anatomy book from the Milne Library on the SUNY Geneseo campus, and was able to match bone after bone, from the skeletal image in the photograph that I had taken, with the illustrative chart in the thick medical guide. The photo was detailed enough for Jeff to determine that the figure in it was actually facing the wall!

His conclusion: Tommy did not want to be photographed.

This matched my impression, recalling that the ghost had bolted across the room, away from the flash of the camera, when it had passed through me and left me on the ground.

So then, if the ghost did not want to be photographed, and if I did not want to photograph it, then what right did the photo itself have to exist?

What right did we have to show it to anyone?

Word of the eerie photograph, and of the boy who could 'speak with ghosts', began to spread across the campus like a California wildfire. There would be no more cover, no more privacy, no more peace. The events, and the haunting itself, was about to enter into the public consciousness. We would now have to deal with both the living and the dead, and – we did not know it yet - the haunting was only in its beginning stages.

I wondered aloud, on several occasions, if the ghost photo should be destroyed. No one wants to keep a physical reminder of a vicious assault and it seemed to me that it had felt an awful lot like that, at least in a spiritual or emotional sense.

With this new-found proof, would come huge choices, and a potentially huge responsibility. It seemed that, moving forward, things would now depend on how I reacted to a proof that I just did not want.

A man who hires a detective to follow his wife on the suspicion that she is unfaithful ultimately wants proof that his worry was unfounded. He is, in a sense, paying the private eye in the hopes that he finds nothing untoward at all. If the detective returns a week later with an envelope full of pictures, I would posit that there would be some type of initial hesitation in the man before he decides to open it. For while his money was invested wisely, does he truly want to see what the pictures might show?

In that scenario 'failure of proof' brings a sweet relief, and 'success of proof' provides a heart-breaking betrayal. Such it was for me and the photograph of the ghost.

Our scientific success (the same type that current day amateur ghost hunters spend so many hours of their lives in search of) offered me only more suffering, and more dread: Something from beyond the grave was watching me.

With Jeff sitting at his desk, Paul sitting at Ed's desk, and Beth and I sitting on Jeff's bed we begin to discuss our options.

Paul recommends that we all try to spend as much time away from C2D1, and even Erie Hall, as possible. We decide that this plan will work for both Paul and Jeff, whose families live only 40 minutes away, but not for me. I don't have the time, or the resources, to travel five hours each and every Saturday and Sunday. In addition, there is my running to consider.

Coach Kentner had called and expressed his concern that I had been missing too many practices, and if I wanted to stay on the team, there was no escaping the fact that our meets were primarily on the weekends.

Beth mentions that Paul and I could ask the Residence Director for a change of rooms. I put a halt on that one, as explaining to the person in charge that there was a ghost in the room would likely have them thinking we were using drugs. It might also fan further the already rapidly-spreading news of the ghost all across the campus, something that neither Paul nor I wanted.

Besides, I also felt that it would be somewhat immoral to simply stick some unsuspecting people in room C2D1 during an active haunting while we turned tail and fled.

Jeff agrees with this point.

Paul offers that he and I ask our parents to allow us to switch colleges, that the ghost might stay behind in Erie Hall.

That is certainly an idea worth considering, but it is more of a long-term plan, and at the moment we were seeking immediate remedies.

Beth references that she had been taking a psychology class and that her professor, a man named Dr. Lawrence Casler, had apparently taught an entire class on parapsychology. Or was it abnormal psychology? She couldn't remember. But she does offer to get his contact information for us in case we want to reach out to him for help, or some advice.

This possibility immediately rouses Jeff's interest.

With no clear course of action chosen, Beth turns to me, gently puts a hand on my thigh, and asks me what I would prefer to do, since the ghost seems focused solely on me.

I hold up the golden ticket with Fr. Charlie's phone number on it.

After all, the church worker had indicated to Paul and I that the priest had mentioned ghosts in at least one past conversation, and I saw no reason why we shouldn't follow the lead that her generosity had provided us.

Paul shrugs his shoulders as though to say 'Sure, why not?'

It is agreed: Paul and I will pay a visit to Fr. Charles (Manning) the following morning. As part of a functional back-up plan, both Jeff and Beth offer to call Dr. Casler's office in order to facilitate setting up a potential appointment with him as well.

At 9 AM on Monday morning, March 4th, Paul and I march up the short steep hills, beyond the student parking lot just east of Erie Hall, to campus Interfaith Center. It is a quick walk, and the weather has become slightly warmer and a bit breezier, the temperature is expected to rise up into the low-40's by mid-afternoon.

We take with us Jeff's journal notes, reasoning that it will be easier, and much less stressful, to have the priest read Jeff's notes, rather than us attempting to take turns speaking back and forth – possibly leaving out relevant information – or getting our timelines mixed up. Revisiting the emotional trauma was also a key consideration in or choice.

Not to mention that credibility will likely be the key in successfully obtaining help; and for that, Jeff's organized notes are decidedly the best option.

Reaching the fairly modern, nondescript-looking structure, I remind Paul that we had promised Jeff that we will not allow Fr. Charlie to keep the notes. We joke about the likelihood that Jeff is watching us out of his C2D2 window, even now, ruing his decision to ever let us borrow them. I look back but do not see his face in the window, but I'm still not convinced.

The priest who greets us at the door of 11 Franklin Street is much younger, and far more friendly looking, than I had anticipated.

In the horror movies, the priest/exorcist was typically portrayed as aged; his skin wrinkled by experience, his eyes hardened by wisdom, his hair whitened by trial, and his hands trembling with a power that simply could not be measured. His mere appearance, the sound of his voice, was enough to be a threat to any demon or creature that dared to stray from the depths.

Our current situation was certainly as horrific as any scary movie, and unlike them, this was real.

To me the young cleric appears more like the bass player of a local cover band, than what my nineteen-year-old mind had envisioned a distinguished 'man of the cloth' to look like. I am hoping that this fresh-faced gentleman, who is certainly under forty years of age, is a local seminary student sent here to assist the aged priest.

He immediately introduces himself as 'Father Charlie', as he reaches out his right hand to greet us.

The breath is knocked out of me.

I reason to myself: If a dedicated, physically fit, and accomplished athlete such as myself was being outmatched by that thing in my college dorm room, this well-intentioned non-athlete, this casually-dressed man of cloth, would certainly stand no chance against it!

He would be cannon fodder.

If this were an episode of *Star Trek*, I mused; we would throw a red shirt on him, beam him down to the planet's surface, and watch him quickly die at the hands of the Gorn.

Paul and I make eye contact.

Neither of us want to go in.

We go in.

After refusing coffee, and other breakfast amenities, we get down to business. Handing Fr. Charlie Jeff's journal notes, Paul and I sit down into two wooden chairs that face his desk. Manning studies us for a moment, then considers the notes before him.

Ten minutes soon turns to twenty, and twenty to thirty, as the youthful man of God carefully examines the fancifully-written words before him, noting with some humor that Jeff had taken to signing his journal notes every few pages.

I let out a welcome laugh.

Only when he reaches the last sentence of the notebook, haven taken in all the seemingly bizarre events contained inside of it, does he glance up at us, examining us.

"I believe you" he says, adding the statement: "I want to help".

A look of steely resolve is etched across his calm face.

At right - Fr. Charlie Manning circa 1985. Manning's Blessing of the Erie Hall dorm room would provide the students with a temporary sanctuary during the haunting's most violent moments, and have a profoundly positive effect on Chris' wavering faith.

It would appear that I had profoundly misjudged him, just as our suitemates had misjudged Paul and I that weekend night back in September.

A brief wave of shame washes over me, a clear reaction to my immature arrogance. I am hoping that he will not now, in turn, misjudge the two of us.

We need his help.

He places a finger to his pursed lips, glances out of his office window. I follow his gaze over to Erie Hall.

The building stands silent and still.

I study him, as he watches a young woman, adjusting the small maroon wool hat atop her head, come into view, momentarily blocking the front of the dorm. She is struggling with some loose papers in the windy weather.

Then he turns to us; to me.

"Are you using any type of drug?"

I am once again unsettled.

My eyes widen in active protest to his question, one that would obviously not be considered had he known me. But that was just the point: He did not know me … yet.

In obvious response to my non-verbal reaction, Manning carefully explains to Paul and I that he *did* want to help us with what certainly sounded to him like an on-going and highly traumatic experience, if what the notes described was indeed true.

"If I offer to help you, and you are addicted to some type of substance, without my knowledge, then I might not be able to do effectively. I need to rule some things out first" he explained, "to better understand what type of help you actually need."

His thinking was certainly sound, and I realized that I should show at least some measure of gratitude for the simple fact that he was actually taking the time to ask us these questions, rather than assuming, right from the start, that the answers to them would be 'yes'.

It was certainly more fairness than I had initially offered him in my own mind.

Paul's severe facial expressions and continued direct eye contact, combined with how I nervously rubbed my hands together, and sat forward in the chair when pleading for understanding told Fr. Charlie Manning what he needed to know: We were sincere.

So was he, in terms of his offer to assist us with the matter of the 'ghost' living in our dorm room.

He informs us that he is going to attempt to 'bless' the room, and his cover story will be that he is there to 'fix the stereo' (that he read about in Jeff's notes) so as not to attract any undue attention to himself, what he intended to do, or us.

It was a brilliant and creative approach that saw my new-found respect for him grow even stronger.

Fr. Manning is clearly serious about his craft. He understands the importance of studying a situation before acting on it. His desire to help those in need is ingratiating. It, temporarily, infuses me with a dose of some much-needed humility, much in the same way my friendship with Jeff did.

I knew, as Paul and I made our way back to Erie Hall, that we would be in good hands with young Fr. Charlie. I was glad that he had chosen to help us.

Two days later, on March 6th, one day before a full moon, Fr. Charlie stands in the door frame of C2D1. It is 8 PM and the snow that fell earlier in the day remains on the ground as the temperature had never climbed above freezing.

But I am not concerned with events on the outside, I am solely focused on what is about to transpire inside.

"Is this the room?" he asks, now looking quite impressive in the large black overcoat with his priest's collar visible on his neck.

He holds a large, dark briefcase in his left hand.

"Yes," I reply, "this is *the* room."

1974.

The tree, in the woods behind my house, had been knocked down by a violent winter storm. It lay on its side, bereft of leaves and life. I pondered how long it had stood guard over the forest before the end came. Like the great ship, Titanic, there was nothing too large or too prestigious for Mother Nature to send to the grave. Months passed, and by summer I had used an assortment of silverware, mostly butter knives, to carve a makeshift control panel into the side of the tree. In my nine-year-old mind she had become my version of the USS Enterprise. Moving old logs and large stones from a long ago neglected farming wall, I had constructed my own Bridge, Captain's chair and all.

Weeks of solo adventuring had left me a bit bored and so I made a command decision: I invited two of my friends to join me. I now had a first officer and a doctor to assist me as I steered my imaginary space cruiser through the Solar System.

We drew 'rank' insignias on pieces of loose leaf paper and taped them to our t-shirts and 'planet-hopped' until the sun was setting and my mother said that dinner was ready.

Two days later I returned to find that my hard work had been vandalized: the chairs were turned over, the carved-out controls had been destroyed, and the tree was lined with offensive words made with a can of white spray paint.

One of my 'officers' had talked.

Walking back home, across the old wood footbridge that connected the back of my family's property to the woods, I decided that some things in life were just too personal to be shared.

Now, as Fr. Charlie politely explains to Jeff that he cannot be present for what is about to occur, I understand. And as Paul had opted not to be present, in the priest's mind this was now a matter between me, God, and the restless spirit. Had I not experienced that wrecked 'spaceship' incident, I would have argued for Jeff's inclusion.

Jeff hands me one of his spiral notepads and a finely sharpened no. 2 pencil, and asks me to record as much of what the priest says as possible.

I ask him why.

His gaze holds mine, and with a considered intensity, Jeff attempts to ensure that I understand his objective: "We may need to know how to do this in the future, Chris. If a priest is not available, it might be up to us."

I find it a compelling argument, and I carry the chronicling instruments to my desk as Fr. Charlie opens his briefcase to prepare for his ceremony.

Resting carefully inside it, beside his *Holy Bible*, next to the three white candles, close to what I guess is a container of Holy Water or sacred oil, is a small dark green book whose cover reads: *Pastoral Care of the Sick, Rites of Anointing and Viaticum*.

Interesting.

When, a few minutes into the ceremony, Fr. Charlie makes the sign of the cross on my forehead (having some type of ceremonial oil on his thumb), I transition from observer to passive participant. I can't very well be writing down his remarks and actions if I am now an actual part of the ceremony. I figured that, even if Jeff was upset that I had not followed his instructions, providing him with a first-hand account of the Blessing would be just as, if not more, interesting anyway.

Nonetheless, it was fascinating to watch this man move from place to place inside the room, Holy Water being dispersed at certain intervals, prayers being recited with intensity and his hand making the Sign if the Cross with regularity.

The ceremony was nothing like what I had anticipated it would be, it was much better, more solemn and much more inspirational.

Approximately twenty-or-so minutes later the ceremony apparently comes to an end.

I am not sure how I know, except for the fact that the priest's voice falls silent for a short period of time. Nor am I sure that the ghost has been expelled from the room, but there is a great sense of calm echoing off of the four connected walls that I can already sense. A sense of warmth, long since absent, has now returned to the room with the colorful Christmas lights and poster-lined (now minus the half-naked women) walls.

The oil that he had dabbed onto the center of my forehead with his thumb, when he said a prayer over me, was still present. Not many, but some of the words he had quietly uttered (ex. 'The Lord is our shepherd and leads us to streams of living water') were now recorded for Jeff's benefit. A lingering cloud of incense wafted silently in and around the loft's colorful underside lights.

It all felt like a soothing dream.

Still, I remain convinced that I could no longer put full trust in what my senses perceived.

When I ask Fr. Charlie if the 'exorcism' had gone well, he chuckles a bit, then explains that he had performed a 'Blessing'.

A Blessing, apparently, whose dual purpose was to help ease my fears and to ask the spirit to find rest elsewhere.

This sounded like a fair approach to me.

So, I ask Fr. Charlie, point blank, if the ghost can "get back into the room."

"Only if you invite him back," he answers without hesitation, as he repacks his items.

"*That's* not going to happen!" I assure him, for as Fr. Charlie returns his items to his briefcase, I can state with an honest heart that there is no possible scenario in which I can imagine myself ever doing so.

Before he leaves, he cautions me that I might have some type of 'gift', and if that were indeed true, then 'situations' like this one could possibly happen again. He shares a section of *1 Corinthians 12* with me that refers to the rarest of gifts, and infers that I might have one of them.

"Call me if you need anything else, Chris" he offers with a look of sincerity on his broad face, as he begins his walk out the door of C2D1.

"I will," I lie.

For just as I have no intention of inviting the 'dread Thomas' back into my newfound sanctuary, I also have no intention of bothering the priest a second time. It seems to me that to have to call him back (and possibly more than once) would be akin to admitting to a certain amount of failure. It would be a failure that might point to my own lack of faith, or lack of follow through.

A history teacher might spend weeks preparing a lesson on the importance of the Nile River on ancient Egyptian civilization. The lesson might include maps and hieroglyphic samples as well as detailed contemporary analysis. Yet as organized, informative and effective the conceived lesson plan may be, there is simply no guarantee that every student would be inspired by it or fully comprehend it. Some students may still not answer the test questions correctly, and through no fault of the instructor. I do not want to be that student. Nor do I want Father Charlie's efforts to be wasted ones. Trust in him and a belief in the likely success of his Blessing are not items that I choose to question.

I am too overwhelmed with gratitude to even dare.

Jeff, while still moderately disgruntled over having been excluded from the ritual, is quite pleased when I turn over my notes to him. Even happier when I sit and share with him inside C2D2 for a while, no longer afraid of what might be lurking on the other side of the wall.

He quizzes me on the details of the ceremony. I provide him with what I can, although I do feel some pangs of guilt in doing so. 'A gentleman never tells' is an adage that I was brought up on, and much the same, there was a sacred aspect to the evening that made it seem intensely personal and private to me. Father Charlie, after all, could have easily chosen not to have gotten involved, not to invest himself so fully in the events.

The appreciative part of me knew that he was there not just to get rid of the ghost, but to help me as well.

Me.

Chris.

I now consider the large, folded, poster resting inside my garbage bin. It had cost me $20 at a time when I had not much more than that in my bank account. The fit, bronze-skinned, red bikini-clad, woman with the light-reflecting, martini glass in her carefully posed hand, had certainly been a pleasant distraction inside of my college room. One than many of my suite mates had found a shared interest in. But the possibility of losing her was an acceptable one if it means that the ghost might finally be gone.

That night I sleep alone in the room, and for the first time in twenty-eight days, I am not afraid.

Charlie Manning was serving as the Chaplain of the SUNY Geneseo Interfaith Center in 1985 when he was contacted by two frightened college students who claimed to have a ghost in their room. Manning attended Saint Bernard's School of Theology and Ministry (1970-1974), Master of Divinity, Theology, and Pastoral Ministry. Now retired, Manning agreed to sit down with CITA Production's Bill Edwards and converse with Christopher Di Cesare on January 5th, 2019.

22. The Charlie Manning Interview

Di Cesare: Good afternoon, sir. Happy New Year. Thank you agreeing to this interview. I will be making record of your answers on my PC. This is to add your voice to the upcoming book on the 1985 occurrence. I feel that it is important that people are provided with a more developed sense of your contributions. My first question, the most important one, is how are you feeling?

Manning: Good the last few days. The doctor thought I might have had a stroke, but I'm fine. I honestly thought that I was going to meet my maker, but I'm fine now.

Di Cesare: That is great news for everyone! Do you feel up for some questions?

Manning: Absolutely.

Di Cesare: I thought it best to start with some background questions. If you can remember, why did you want to become a priest.

Manning: My Italian grandmother, she felt that I was going to be a priest, it was as simple as that. I was also a 'goody two shoes', and I decided that I wanted to be helpful to people in their spiritual growth and in the receiving of the Seven Sacraments (Baptism, Confirmation, Eucharist, Penance, Anointing of the sick, Holy Orders and Matrimony). As I grew in the priesthood it turned out that I was good with teenagers, and so I was asked to run the youth retreats. I had some great experiences. One particular moment that stands out in my mind is a retreat that we held at St. Mary's in Waterloo (NY). Before the students left, I had the parents write down on a piece of paper why they loved their children. Well, the night before we were to return, I had the staff hand out the letters to the kids. They started to cry when they read them. The moonlit sky was very bright, and as I walked around comforting them my shadow was cast over them. I felt so inspired, as though the spirit of Jesus was walking amongst the people with me. It was such a spiritual moment. Then the staff surprised me, as they had wrote letters to me. It was such a powerful thing. Then I had the kids write a letter to their parents, just like they had received, telling why they loved their parents. The last day of camp, before they could leave, before the processional, while the parents were sitting in the pews, the children gave them the letters that they had written. It was such an incredible feeling for everyone. Because of the positive feedback, I was put in charge of the Youth Ministry Family Camp, as it's spiritual Director. That was in the early 1990's

Di Cesare: Did you ever expect that, one day, you might find yourself involved with matters such as ghosts or spirits. Was that on your mind when you began your priesthood?

Manning: At no point in time. Not until in Geneseo. It wasn't even in my vocabulary!

Di Cesare: When did you discover how to handle a paranormal situation? Did you receive any training?

Manning: No. There was no training. I just said, "Jesus, you put me in this situation, it's your ballgame. Show me what me what to do."

Di Cesare: Looking back, what would you recommend to a minister, priest or pastor who is asked to go to a location that might have some active spiritual activity?

Manning: I would tell them not to go. To run the other way! (Laughs).

Di Cesare: Yet, when you were approached by Paul and I you agreed to help us. Why didn't you run the other way?

Manning: Two young guys went up the hill in Geneseo, to St. Mary's Church, to get the pastor to help them out. They get turned away. The secretary suggested that you go down to the Interfaith Center, that the chaplain there, was more open to these sorts of things. When I heard that, I wanted to help you, not to necessarily go get some ghost. Although I am still surprised that Fr. Bill Gordinier (1932-2016) was not willing to help, it was not his forte, but he was fairly open minded about things.

Di Cesare and Manning then discussed an incident that might have led to that decision. About a month or so earlier, around the Christmas holiday, Chris had been present for an incident that involved two students who were trying to steal the communion wafer, 'the body of Christ', in order to run some experiments on it, in order to prove that it was nothing special. Fr. Gordinier saw this and yelled at the students, "Do not walk away with that! That is the body of Christ! Put that in your mouth or return it!" The peer pressure was so great, and the students were outnumbered by a ratio of about 200:1, so they complied and swallowed the wafers.

Upon hearing of this incident Fr. Manning replied that the students' act was considered a 'desecration of the Holy Eucharist, and that he recalled that around that same time that Gordinier began to complain about some of the students who were attending his church. Fearing that this story of a ghost was yet another way for some students to potentially mock the church, he declined his assistance. Manning mentioned that Fr. Gordinier had recently passed.

Manning shared that he never understood why so many students chose the stained glass windows of St. Mary's over the more open approach of the Interfaith Center. Whereupon Di Cesare remarked that he loved those stained-glass windows at St. Mary's and would watch as the sunlight would bathe the parishioners in different colored rays of light. They both shared a laugh. "That's the way it was," Manning added.

Fr. Manning was then shown some photos by Bill Edwards, and was asked if he could provide any information about any of them.

Manning:

"Well he's one hell of a handsome dude (laughs). That photo taken with my sister, she was in the original picture. That was when I was in the seminary, and I was home for the weekend.

Towards the end of my four years at St. John Fischer College, I became the manager of a rock band without the director of the seminary knowing. Then, the Democrat & Chronicle did an article on the band, and published name with it. All hell broke loose! Across the loudspeaker I heard: "Manning get your butt down to the office right now". As the director was yelling at me, I explained to him that all of those 'rockers' are now going to mass on Sundays! That was another reason that I was put in charge of youth ministry. Another funny memory is when the director announced during mass that there will no more playing of that record from Floyd Pink! Everyone started laughing and he looked at me to find out why, and I replied: "It's Pink Floyd!

I know that right off the bat. That's the Anointing of Sick book that I used in your dorm room. It contains prayers and information for the sacraments and last rites. I adapted it to get the ghost out of the dorm. There was no training that cane with it, you received one when you became a priest intern, The Pastor Supervisor would have taught you how to use that. Fr. Al Shannon at St. Mary's in Waterloo had me study. I still have a copy of it. Even though I am retired, I am obligated by canon law to function as a priest and provide last rites if the church cannot get someone there in time. The book has its origin at the Vatican, they put it together, in Latin. Stateside it is translated into English.

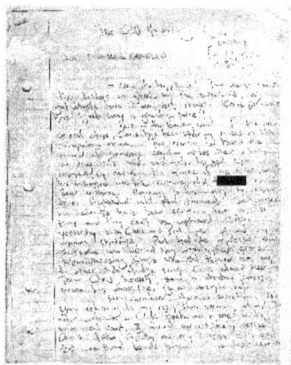

That's the journal. I remembered how you appeared, how you came across, the fear in your eyes.

Manning admitted to Di Cesare that he really can't remember much about the details of the notes anymore, but that it was how Chris appeared, 'so sincere', 'so terrified' that was what ultimately made him decide to act in the first place. Manning said that he thought: 'This kid is for real!'

I barely recognize you (Chris) there, lol. Wow!

Di Cesare: Many, many years have passed (thirty-four) since the event inside Erie Hall. Are you able to recall any sights, sounds, feelings or impressions from that night when you went into that room?

Manning: It was a very powerful experience. I remember going into the room and getting a feeling of, 'Wow!' It's hard to put it all into words. I just knew something was there, it was a very powerful feeling. I knew then that you (Chris) were sincere, and I knew why you were scared out of your mind. I, distinctly remember Blessing you, I anointed you with Holy Oil. Then I blessed everything around me.

Di Cesare: Was there anything tangible that you can remember, anything that you could see or hear? Something to help people understand?

Manning: The physical thing that I experienced, was a coldness in the air! I realized that we had a spirit in there, a spirit that was very unsettled. We also had a frightened kid. The Holy Spirit was directing me to do whatever I did in that room. You know, here is the other thing ... it made me wonder why ... did he pick you (to torment)? But I figured that with the Blessing, if the thing came back, you wouldn't be as cared stiff. You know?

Di Cesare: You have mentioned in the past that it should be clearly noted that you performed a Blessing in the dorm room, not an exorcism. Why is that an important point for people to understand?

Manning: If I understood things correctly, Tommy was asking for help, but he was doing things that were scary. That was the problem, and Tommy didn't want to talk to me, he wanted to talk to you. I would have needed permission to perform an exorcism. That's where I could have gotten in serious trouble. You have to be assigned to do that, and it's not usually a public thing. There is a lot of politics to that. Besides, I didn't want a devil in my face, there to talk to me about my own sins when I am trying to help you. No thank you! That's why I asked, 'Was the ghost inside you?' This was *not* an exorcism.

Di Cesare: That's right. I remember that! And I said 'no'.

Manning: Exactly, it was a ghost, not a demon. It was obvious. If it was, I would have told you: "I cannot do this". That part is still fresh in my mind: It was a haunting. As I've said before that Tommy was not a demon, he was an unsettled spirit. That is why I knew that I could use a Blessing. It was a Blessing between you, God, Tommy and myself.

Di Cesare then shared with Manning the fact that while Tommy respected his Blessing of C2D1, that the ghost began to move to other locations, and bother other students. That he felt it inappropriate to call Manning back to bless room after room, so he never re-contacted him.

Manning: (Thinking) I suppose could have given a Blessing to the whole building, there would have been a lot of people. (Reconsiders) But it would be on state grounds, and performing a religious ceremony out in the open was a concern that I already had at that time. So, maybe not.

Di Cesare: I have a philosophic/faith-based question: Why do you think, in the grand scheme of God and the Universe, that ghosts exist, or are allowed to exist?

Manning: Let me get my seventy-one-year-old brain to work. Let me pause to think. The ghost's spirit was unsettled, it was a person struggling in spirit form. So, I would say that ghosts are designed to help someone make peace with God.

Di Cesare: That's beautiful. Is there anything that you would like people to know about you or your involvement with the C2D1 Haunting?

Manning: To sum it all up - I am an instrument of His peace.

23. Survivor's Guilt

Above – Erie Hall as viewed from the SUNY Geneseo parking Lot R, on the north side of the campus near Court Street. J. Jeff Ungar's many and varied photographs provide C2D1 Haunting researchers with an expansive look at the location, people, and events some thirty years later.

March 10, 1985

Last night, and for the last three nights, there has been no sign of the ghost.

He has not come into the room.

The morning radio deejay had announced that it is a balmy 51°F, and I was not going to pass up the rare opportunity (in Western New York) to wear shorts in March.

At 2:45 PM, I run along the dirt roads that separate the local farming fields. The azure sky is lined with wispy clouds of white who are being hurried along by an unseen wind current.

It is so peaceful out here, so tranquil. I have missed this aspect of my life, the one that used to define me.

Almost a month has passed since I was last able to stretch out my runner's legs like this. But things are different now. The priest, Father

Charlie Manning, had done his Blessing, and the thing, that horrid thing, is gone.

In the three and one-half days since he raised up his cross, whispered his sacred prayers, and cleansed my college dorm room my life has returned to a healthy normalcy.

Still, a number of significant questions remain, the most pressing of which is: why?

Why has all of this occurred?

Jeff's prevailing theory is that the ghost had followed me home (to the dorm) much like a stray dog might, on one of my many long runs through the countryside; just like my run today.

Likewise, there was the possibility that attending the Warren lecture had predisposed, or 'opened', my youthful mind to certain events or possibilities that might have otherwise been overlooked. In spite of my skepticism, I had listened attentively to the presentation, and Lorraine's statement afterwards — that she did not want to know her 'future' — suggested that she had felt that some sort of 'gift' or ability was already a part of who I was.

Both Jeff and Fr. Charlie, in varying fashions, had agreed

Maybe the Warrens had inadvertently brought the whispering spirit to the college themselves, where I then caught its attention?

I can't help but wonder at that possibility now as I pass an old rusting farm structure at the side of the dirt road.

According to some of my college friends, the conventional wisdom that was now circulating around the campus was that some young college student likely had taken his own life, years ago, in what was now my dorm room. The tilted head perhaps being indicative of a snapped neck on the apparition. It was said that colleges 'were known for' covering up events that might possibly generate negative press, and thus limit enrollment and the money that follows.

Of course, if colleges did cover such things up, then how would anyone know that they did this in the first place? It was a circular argument.

There are other persistent questions as well.

Questions that went well beyond my own experiences, the first of which being: What *are* ghosts?

It still seems rather strange to me that we can view star systems millions of miles away, and view microorganisms inside a petri dish, but we have no consistent or effective way by which to see spirits or human souls, that are said to watch over us, guide us, and when things go terribly wrong, haunt us.

Even though most people tend to have a ghost story (or two) to tell, they are just that: stories. Quick, often nonsensical, tales of deranged asylum patients who walk the hallways opening and closing doors, or women in white who appear to drivers on lonely roadways, tales that are designed to send children scurrying away from the campfire and into bed so that the 'adults' finally had a chance to party themselves.

The only saving grace that I can afford myself in this mental exercise is that science can't actually prove what love is either. After all, even though most all of us have professed to have felt 'it' at one point in time, no one has been able to come up with a formula, or a machine, to provide proof of it.

What proves love?

Is it placing a ring on someone's finger?

Buying someone an expensive gift?

Sharing oneself through physical intimacy?

It seemed to me, as I approached the crossroad up ahead, that if you felt loved, that you probably, in some way, were. Likewise, if you felt haunted, then you might very well be.

I am approximately 3.5 miles out, and I turn left onto Rt. 20A and head back east. Over a railed bridge, and up some rolling hills, is the college.

My home away from home.

3:35 PM

"Chris! Chris! Are you all right?"

I am able to blurt out a soft "mmm …" but not any words.

Now there is a flutter of movement, the noise of sneaker bottoms starting and stopping on a wet bathroom floor. There is also the sound of nervous breathing, but it's not *my* breath.

I open my eyes when I sense I am being pulled up by two hands that are clasped together near the middle of my chest. They successfully pull me up onto my knees, but the arms attached to the hands seem to be trembling a bit from the strain.

They cannot do this alone.

There is a quality of friendly determination to them, I trust them. I command my legs to stand. They refuse, but the effort shifts my balance enough that the arms are now able to prop me up against the wooden door which rattles angrily as I lean into it.

"Chris, can you *hear* me? You're bleeding, what happened?"

A dry towel – perhaps my own - is wrapped, very tightly, about my waist. The warmth that it creates around my lower half is welcome.

I mumble out a weak: "Thankssss."

"No problem. Are you OK to walk? Here, just lean on me."

I follow the words to Jeff's face, and I can see that he has worry etched deeply across it. Seeing him now, assisting me in this manner, makes me regret that I was willing to accept the crows only moments beforehand.

I never want that to happen again.

Jeff navigates me across the quiet hallway into the safety of his room, C2D2. His roommate, Ed, is standing as we enter, his expression implies that he is concerned. I am shivering uncontrollably from the cold, or the fear, or the exhaustion; maybe all of these things.

"And …?"

Ed queried, raising both of his eyebrows in expectation.

"He was attacked, in the bathroom."

Jeff had been determined that if increased trouble found its way into our lives, that he would be ready for it. And when it did, he was. It is too frightening a thought to consider what might have occurred if Jeff had not heard me screaming in the bathroom, or had he decided not to help when he heard my screams.

As Jeff carefully sits me down at the foot of his bed, my cold and wet feet leaving imprints on the tiled floor, Ed apparently catches his first glimpse of the cuts.

"Oh, my God … Oh, my *God*!"

There is a pause.

Then he continues: "All of this is *real,* isn't it?"

I am angry, and I reply in a straightforward and aggravated tone: "Do I get my Purple Heart now?"

Neither the pain from the back wounds nor the shock of the attack has lessened.

Ed's incredulous tone, as understandable as it was, bothers me.

He knew that something bad has been going on for over a month now, certainly since the night that I came banging on his door in an emotional frenzy. The understanding that it takes my very blood being spilled for Ed to put any real stock in the situation does not sit well with me; at least, not while I am still bleeding.

Still, I am fairly sure I would have reacted in the same manner if our situations had been reversed, and my temper quickly subsides and is replaced by the fear that I might now lose his friendship for snapping at him; maybe the others as well.

There is a quick movement to my right, but as I am still exhausted and afraid, I do not turn my head to see what causes it.

Her voice gives her away.

"Is he OK?"

Beth asks nervously.

She somewhat out of breath from what must have been a hurried trip to Jeff and Ed's room from wherever she had been.

"Chris was attacked," Jeff repeats.

I hear Beth emit a soft gasp of horror as she gets her first sight of the three bleeding scratches on my back.

The blood-tinged towel does nothing to improve the grim aesthetic.

With no advance notice, Jeff begins using significant force to try and push my hands up into my back. I wince in pain as my shoulders and elbows feel as though they might snap out of their sockets.

"Go easy, Jeffy," Ed cautions, "you don't want to make the poor guy suffer any more than he already is!"

"See," Jeff announces to anyone and all present, "he couldn't have done this himself. There is no way. Something *did* this to him."

"No duh!" I snap back indignantly in lame '80s lingo, "Can you please let go of my arms now?"

"He needs to go to a hospital!" Beth counsels, her tone is severe.

"I am not going to a hospital," I yell, "they'll think I'm crazy! Then they'll medicate me and possibly put me in some kind of strait jacket! No way! If you try to make me go, I'll fight everyone here! I will!"

Over the last four weeks, and up until Fr. Manning's Blessing just three and one-half days prior, I had been sleeping in different locations: C2D1, the C2D Quad common room; C2D2; the C2 main lounge. It had been important, in my mind, to keep moving, to buy myself some potential time before 'it' found me again, before it renewed its focus on me.

To run the risk of medical sedation, of long-term confinement, that a hospital visit might bring with it, only fed into my deep-seated fears. It would have an easier time finding me, attacking me, getting to me.

"Well we have to do *something*," Ed advises, "He's just going to keep on bleeding otherwise."

Beth offers to rush back to her room and get some cotton swabs and some bandages. I have some hydrogen peroxide in the first aid kit that my father had put together for me, one room over, in C2D1.

For the next 43 minutes - 47 if you count the time it took to decide which person will do what - the painful process of pouring peroxide on cotton ball, pressing cotton ball on wound, and covering wound with bandage, repeats itself over and over and over again.

In spite of all of the pain, for me it still remained preferable to being tranquilized, under the influence of some drug, in a psychiatric ward, completely unable to react if Tommy comes back.

Because I know now, with certainty, that he will.

Above - The view from Jeff and Ed's window, room C2D2, where Di Cesare was taken immediately after the shower attack on Sunday, March 10th, 1985. This is the landscape that met Chris' eyes as his friends tended to the bleeding scratches that ran down his back. Photograph by J. Jeff Ungar, 1985.

4:30 PM.

The winter skies outside of Erie Hall are growing ever darker.

Jeff follows my gaze out the window.

"If we are going to get some pictures, we should do it now," Jeff informs the group, seeking tacit approval to do so, "before the natural light fades."

The room is silent for some time, as no one wants to make that particular decision.

So, I make it.

"No pictures!" I shout. "Jeff, if you are my friend, you won't take any pictures.

Jeff opens his mouth slightly, as if to begin explaining the medical, scientific, and journalistic benefits of taking the photos, but then he stops himself. He sees that I am suffering and in pain, and his expression suggests that he doesn't want to add to that.

He lowers his camera, takes a deep breath in through his nose, and nods his acceptance.

"Thank you for not taking any pictures," I say to him, a strong appreciation no doubt controlling my expression.

Jeff's face softens.

"I just thought it would be helpful to have a record of this," he offers softly, "but I can understand why you wouldn't want that."

As I sit there, partially-wrapped in a blood-stained towel, a few remaining icy cold drops of water running down my legs onto my feet, I'm still not sure how to prove either ghosts or love; but this is certainly how you prove friendship.

Afraid that there might be more attacks, I retreat back to the safety of my now-blessed room.

My worried friends will be only one door, one wall, away.

Room C2D1, once the place where for several weeks I had been too frightened to sit alone, thanks to the Fr. Manning's Blessing, is the one place that I now feel safe inside.

Making sure to lock the door behind me, I wad the bloody towel - that had been used to cover me - up into a basketball shape. Dropping it into a black plastic garbage bag, I toss it on the floor right next to my trash can. My mom had sent me back to college this past fall with three newly purchased towels, so 'losing' one shouldn't be a major issue.

Things happen.

I just needed to make sure that I throw the bag in the dorm's dumpster before Paul got back. That is, *if* he comes back. I hadn't seen him since the day before the priest was here. He has no way of knowing that the room is once again safe to be in.

I walk over to the plain, square mirror that hangs on the wall near my dresser.

My eyes look the same, just tired.

They are a light blue, passed on from my grandmother Hubley through my mother.

Yes, my eyes look the same.

It is still me.

One of my high school teachers once told me that the human body is constantly changing, with old cells dying and new cells being created. Eventually, he said, almost every cell in your body is replaced by another so that, in effect, after several years you are a completely different physical person.

While I never completely bought into the application of that particular concept, I *was* impressed by an exercise we did in art class. We were instructed to take a photograph of ourselves and then divide our face down the center. We were to then reconstruct our faces by combining 'same halves' which would accentuate how different each half of our face truly was. This, I suppose, harkened back to many models and actresses who referred to their 'good side' and their 'bad side'.

Above - A magic marker poster that Di Cesare made in high school addressing the theme of duality. He included a 'man descending from the stars' theme as well, after reading "Chariots of the Gods?" by Erich von Däniken as a teenager.

It suggested that we human beings had competing parts, perhaps a duality of sorts, of the same whole. An effective life, one could argue, might be a balancing of these two competing halves of the self:

preparedness, discernment, and strength against pacifism, forgiveness and kindness.

Perhaps it could eventually be boiled down to the conscious and subconscious; or maybe it wasn't all that simple.

In any event, I am relieved that I still look like I am 'supposed to', and for the first time in what feels like weeks, I let my shoulders relax.

The 'Negative Zone', the old brown couch under the loft, that many of the residents of Erie Hall claim is the most comfortable place in the dorm, quietly welcomes me.

I am careful not to place my injured back up against any solid surface. I don't want to pull any of the loosely attached bandages off or get any of my blood on the couch, so I lean forward to a position similar to that of the famous sculpture, *The Thinker at the Gates of Hell*, by Auguste Rodin.

The quiet of the moment is soothing, and the room feels much warmer since it was blessed.

When I wake up, it is remarkably silent.

Sprawled, face down, I notice that my right leg is hanging off the couch; my right foot is on the carpet.

I survey my surroundings.

It is nighttime, and the room is dark now. There is little chance that any student walking through the glass-lined connecting hallway has seen me sleeping in my birthday suit on the couch, or noticed the bandage-covered wounds on my back, from outside my window.

My black running watch, sitting on my desk, was the sole source of light and it reads 2:09 am. I take that as a positive omen as my running hero, Bill Rodgers, had run times of 2:09:55 and 2:09:27 when he set his two American records in the marathon (1975 and 1979 at Boston).

Reaching up, I click on the floor lamp below the loft.

I look for anything positive for my mind to temporarily grasp onto.

My eyes are magnifying the entire room.

I am able to see the fine granules of wood and old scratches in my desk chair as though my face were pressed up against it, even though it is currently several feet away. I recall now, that while I slept, I had dreamed of the green glowing sphere, just like when I thirteen:

Gray. Total gray covers the sky; it is a numbing wall that can never be pierced and it blankets the earth with a stagnant coat. Next there are the wilted trees, branches barren and dying. I find myself alone, wearing only a thin, black bracelet that is weighing me down. I stand on a carefully-sculpted sidewalk that runs through suburbia and on through to a possible escape, a hope in the midst of the drab shuffle, a joyless paradise. A soul-dampening chill runs through me, it is the hand of the grave reaching out for me in order to drain away the dreams of my youth.

Identically shaped box houses line the length of the street in a feigned perfection. Telephone poles, just eight feet in height, run alongside, stark crosses frame my vision, the wires are only head-level off the ground.

On the other sidewalk, I see the men walking in the opposite direction. They appear in suits of drab colors: black, browns, beiges; hats, watches and overcoats completing their outfits. Mandate of the American dream in person, from the perfectly groomed haircuts, to the square cut of their chins, to the immaculate gleam of their shoe polish. But without exception they all wear expressions of the greatest complacency. Everything is all right here. We know who we are and what we want. There is nothing new under the sun. Everything is as it should be. No hint of originality gleams in their eyes.

This is what you have to look forward to.

I walk forward and the men drop away behind me, having taken no notice of the 'child' in their midst. Ahead I notice a hillside set off to the left of the street, on the slope of which is an ominous cavern. The cavern has no place in this suburban vision, but nonetheless I approach as one who has found what was there for anyone else to see, had they only eyes with which to see. In front of the cave is gravel that shifts beneath my bare feet.

Inside is only darkness.

Daggers ran up my spine as I recognized the scene.

Oh, God, I'm here again.

The feeling is accompanied by a compulsion to move forward. The cycle must be completed. I step inside. Crossing the threshold is like stepping into the night sky, the cavern walls open up like the perimeters of the galaxy.

My attention is arrested by a sight at the heart of the cave, like the center of creation itself. A metallic globe glistens with a whitish-green glow. On the surface is a series of lines that show each time the light shifts, as though the gods have left their knitting yarn.

For a moment, I feel a transcendent gladness at the sight, like a lost traveler finding my home. This is always followed by. . .

The answer!

From within comes the awful truth, not yarn but needles radiated from the globe, silver needles whose touch cannot be avoided. Just to gaze upon so many pins hurts my eyes with a stabbing pain that pierces deep into my skull. The globe had sat dormant awaiting my arrival, anticipating this very moment, not striking until I know what it is -- my death.

I take a step back, then another, hoping for some escape from the inescapable. With each step the globe rolls towards me, and as it closes in I pivot back towards the gray world. The first stab pierces my left foot, spearing me into the world of the green rays.

There is no escaping myself.

One needle continues to hold me in place, as a wave of sweet, stabbing energy flows up to my torso, leaving the sensation of pins and needles numbing my senses. With the wave comes a paralyzing power that seems to resonate within the fabric of my soul. Then it hits the eyes, jolting me awake in breathless panic: home ... again.

Now that I am awake, I wonder how this magnified sight might be possible. Just as I had initially thought that my tape recorder had been turned on – twice – by a power surge, I wonder too if maybe some 'super impulse' from my brain (as a result of the intensity of the dream) had somehow overloaded my eyes with energy, and with it an increased my sight capacity.

I sound like Jeff.

I think back to when I was twelve. I had the same dream with the same preternatural result:

I woke up in my bed with cramps in both legs and energy literally shooting through my entire body. My fingers, my toes – all of my extremities – were humming with some vibrating 'pins and needles' that made them completely numb to the touch.

At first all I could see were swirls of color, with occasional flashes of white or gold, and then I swore I could even see the currents of energy flowing in straight lines through the walls until they reached a corner and were redirected to an outlet or a light switch.

Not sure that it was actually happening, I called out to my sister Nicole, who walked sleepily across the hallway and into the doorway of my bedroom.

"Nicole," I stammered, quite happy to see her as she was the proof I needed to verify that I was not still dreaming, "I can see everything like there is a magnifying glass over my eyes! Watch this!"

I instructed her to stand next to the Bobby Murcer baseball poster that was securely taped to my bedroom door. It was the one put out by *Sports Illustrated* in 1976 with Hall of Fame catcher Johnny Bench rising behind him as they both watch the skyward trajectory of a ball that Murcer had just hit.

I closed my eyes tightly.

"Now check and see if there are any tiny words on the bottom somewhere."

"I see a bunch of tiny words on the bottom," she replied.

I opened my eyes.

She was crouched down with her face inches from the poster trying to make out what the words said.

"Watch this, Nicole," I announced, and I proceeded to read each word as it appeared on the poster's bottom edge from a distance of over ten feet away.

"Printed ... in ... the U.S.A ... by ... Colorcrafters ... Trevose ... Pennsylvania ... 190 ..."

Nicole was absolutely dumbfounded as to how I was doing this.

So was I.

This memory is not taking me to a place that I like, where some of the arrows are starting to point directly: at me.

My dresser drawers make commonplace sliding sounds as I open them to retrieve some clean clothing: underwear, a pair of white ankle socks, dark blue running shorts, and a light blue t-shirt with the words "Diet Pepsi 10,000 Meters Series" featured across the chest.

But I find that I can't put the t-shirt on over the bandages running down the length of my back without the risk of pulling many of them off. So instead I walk over to my closet and, opening the door, I pull a large, blue winter sweatshirt off of its hanger. I hadn't worn it before as I normally don't care for baggy, loose-fitting clothes, but this offers a reasonable solution to my current problem.

24. There's No Place Like Home

Above – This photograph, taken by the Di Cesare's mother, shows Chris (left) and his first-year roommate from Genesee Hall, Don Browne (right). They flank two other Geneseo students, Maureen and Celeste. It was taken in March of 1984. Don was Chris' primary ride home for most of their college breaks. A similar trip, one that occurred the following year, in 1985, would leave a lasting imprint on Di Cesare's memory.

The airwaves are filled with talk of the Kremlin choosing Mikhail S. Gorbachev as the new leader of the Soviet Union and of the Boston Celtic's Larry Bird scoring 60 points in a game.

"It should have been 63," yells a student who is telling anyone who will listen to him, that he also played basketball, back home in Bowmansville.

The dorm is unusually busy for being this late on a Tuesday night. My best guess is that it reached almost 60°F during the day, a sign that spring is just around the corner. Our D-Quad common area is jam-packed with students playing foosball, drinking in lounge chairs, and blasting the song *Drive* by the Cars. It is not lost on me that it is 60°F on the day Boston's Larry Bird scores 60 points, that the Cars band hailed from Boston and that the word segment 'hail' is in the new Soviet Premier's first name. Not that any of this represented anything tangible. My brain enjoys connecting things, looking for patterns that are meaningful, or otherwise.

This is probably otherwise.

I am very happy with the commotion; it takes my mind off of the fact that I had been brutally attacked not much more than 48 hours earlier.

The Hawaiian-shirt-wearing dog with the sunglasses on the beer poster in the hallway seems happier today, but it might just be the splatter of guacamole dip that has found its way onto his face. The fact that I'm not sure what guacamole dip is made from, crosses my mind, but does not bother me.

Paul has returned and he does not like the noisy distraction.

As I sit with Jeff on the peripheral of the party, Paul slams the door to C2D1 closed behind him. The sounds of *Tom Sawyer* by Rush waft out from under the door frame:

> Though his mind is not for rent,
> Don't put him down as arrogant
> His reserve, a quiet defense
> Riding out the day's events
> The river

"Paul has been in a dark mood lately," Jeff comments, watching my face for some type of reaction.

"I know. It's true"

Jeff stares, seemingly through the wall, into the distance. He is lost in thought. Seeing people out of sorts made him uncomfortable. I recall his irritation when presented with the image of an elderly Mediterranean woman, dressed in traditional black mourning attire, who had flung herself over her diseased husband's casket. She looked to be wailing in uncontrollable sorrow in the midst of a gathering outdoor street crowd.

"Look at that," he muttered, "what's the sense? All that crying and carrying on isn't going to bring him back."

"Maybe she spent her whole life with him, and she really loved him," I offered cautiously, "Maybe she misses him now."

"Maybe."

Jeff was correct in stating that her emotional outburst would be of no practical help to anyone, but I had seen the look in her eyes – the terror and the fear – before.

I had seen it while staring into the bathroom mirror, the day of the attack.

As midnight approaches the party begins to clear out.

The process is expedited by the Residence Director who offers to write up anyone who is still making noise when she returns in ten minutes.

A few of the scattering party-goers complain about her, but no one takes her up on her offer.

Jeff and I are preparing to return to our rooms as well, when I happen to glance out through the common area window. It looks, at first, as though some – likely drunk – college student has climbed the tree outside the window to get a better view of the party inside.

My guess is he is a good 25 feet up in the tree.

'That would be quite a climb' I think to myself, trying to get a better look to see if I know who it is. The reflection and glare from the lights inside the room make it difficult to see even when I shift my location a few feet. I sit down onto a chair, to lessen the effect, and I can now see the person out in the tree more clearly. He isn't perched on a branch at all; rather he is tied to the tree and drenched in blood. He hangs there, stripped of his clothing and, possibly due to some distortion from room's overhead light on the glass windows, it appears that the tree's branches are actively reaching into his body.

Dear God.

I feel my jaw drop, and as I rise out of the chair, my heart rate quickens.

"What's the matter?" Jeff asks.

"It's him!"

It is Tommy. His mouth hangs open, and it appears as though the skin on both sides of his mouth has been cut. Dark blood oozes out of it and runs down his chin dripping like a slow, leaky faucet onto his battered chest. His hands are stretched out and many of his fingernails have been painted … no wait … ridged sections of flesh are showing where his nails should be.

His genitals have been sliced almost entirely off and are hanging from his body by a very thin strip of skin; blood is leaking out onto his thighs and dripping down his legs. Some of his toes are damaged, and I can't make out one of his eyes. It is either missing or rather damaged so badly that I can only see some red meat in the back of the socket.

It looks as though animals have chewed out sections of his arms.

I want to scream, but I am afraid that the effort will make me spill my stomach contents onto the floor.

"Chris?"

Yet, in spite of all of this gore, it remains the pulsing tree limbs entering his abdomen that are the oddest part of this horrific spectacle. They look almost like thin, malleable, rubber hoses … like …like … his intestines! Those are his *intestines,* emerging from a huge slice in his lower torso, that are wrapped around the tree!

"Why," I scream as loud as I am able to, "why would you want to *do* this to me?!!!"

Jeff, sprinting to my side in an attempt to approximate my view, furrows his brow as he tries to understand who it is, or what it is, that I am reacting so violently to.

"Jeff, it's out there, in the tree!" I am in near hysterics for the second time in a month, "It's trying to scare me by mutilating its appearance! It is so horrible! Why would it be so cruel? Why is it so evil?!"

"Where do you see it?" Jeff asks placing a hand above his eyes trying to block the light from above.

"There, outside the window!"

I point.

Now only the lonely tree remains; no leaves, and no horrific-looking dying man on it.

Just a tree probably patiently hoping, as I was, for the return of spring.

Almost losing my footing as I sprint out of the quad and down the steps that lead to the first floor, I take up refuge in the dorm's Main Lounge, near the ping pong tables.

Out of desperation, I decide to set some new goals for myself.

My first goal will be to get the hell out of Geneseo as soon as I can!

The lengthy ride home, with Don Browne (my roommate at Genesee Hall the year before) and his girlfriend, both of whom lived on Long Island, was quite surreal. While the route we were driving home on was the same as it always was, the conversation proved to be quite telling.

We were discussing our favorite movies (it was a five-hour ride for me, almost eight for them) and Don's girlfriend, who was sitting in the front passenger seat, said that she *loved* horror movies ... all of them.

But she had recently seen *Friday the 13th: The Final Chapter* and said that it was a bit of a disappointment. Don agreed and said that the first movie in any series was typically the best.

"Do you watch any horror movies?" she asked looking back over the seat towards me.

I was in the back seat, leaning forward most of the way. My scratches were just starting to heal, and the friction when leaning back against the chair was making them itch.

"Nope," I replied trying not to get too deeply drawn into this particular conversation, "unless you count *King Kong* or *Godzilla*."

"No," she smirked, "We do *not* count *King Kong* or *Godzilla*; those aren't horror movies, those are ..."

"Monster movies," Don chimed in as he us safely drove down Rt. 17 and towards my parents' home in the Hudson Valley.

"Right, those are *monster* movies," she completed her thought, eying me with suspicion.

"Then, no I haven't," I replied with a sheepish grin, "sorry."

She continued to stare at me in disbelief.

"*What?*" I asked, lifting up my palms.

She tilted her head to one side, which made me very uncomfortable. I wondered if, from now on, every time that I saw a person tilt their head in that manner I would think of the ghost. I hoped that I had not been that badly affected by it.

She held her gaze a while longer.

"You're f**king *hiding* something, aren't you?"

"Hey, he doesn't like cursing," Don interceded on my behalf, knowing my aversion to foul language from the prior year.

"Sorrrry," she sarcastically apologized to *him*, and then returned her attention to me.

"You were *attacked,* weren't you?"

I shot her a nervously quizzical stare, the kind I gave my father back in grade school when he asked if my homework was done, and it wasn't.

"Let me guess, he got you in the back, didn't he?" Her face was 'set in stone' serious. She did not blink. Her mouth was drawn back and straight. Don looked at me via the car's rear view mirror, to gauge my reaction.

They were both watching me.

I heard that faint ringing sound in my ears. My heart rate was already increasing. How could she possibly know? She lived in a different dormitory and I hadn't seen her in almost two full months, since before the haunting began! My mind began to race through the possibilities: She had spoken to either Jeff or Paul. No, not Jeff, certainly not Jeff, he was afraid to talk to girls. Paul? No, she was definitely not his type, plus she already had a boyfriend. Beth! Maybe Beth had told her about … I stopped the guessing game, it was getting me nowhere. Maybe I should just try the truth.

"Yes," I replied calmly and clearly. "I *was* attacked on my back, and I had no clue it was coming."

They both burst out into tremendous laughter.

For a good two minutes, they laughed, and when they happened to make some manner of brief eye contact with each other, they would laugh all over again.

I was at a complete loss. How was me being attacked at all funny?

"No clue it was *coming*," she started to laugh again.

"Good one," the Don added, looking back at me again through the thin horizontal mirror, this time with a smile on his face.

Finally, as she gasped for air between laughter induced coughs, his girlfriend turned to me and said, "I didn't think that you knew what I was talking about at first. So, you *have* seen a horror movie! You look just like him, the guy (Jeff) who got the spear stuck through his body while he was doing his girlfriend (Sandra) on the bed. **SPLOTCH!**"

"That was *Friday the 13th Part 2*," the Don offered for the sake of clarity.

"Doesn't he look just like him though, with the wavy, blond hair and the-always-smiling and everything?"

"Yeah, I can see that," he concurred with little hesitation.

Relief.

I had almost made a critical and, as it turned out, totally unforced error, but my 'cover' was not blown.

My visit home, discounting the unsettling car ride, was pleasant and largely uneventful. It was a much-needed return to normalcy: I visited with my family and relatives; went on a few runs with my dad; took some time to reflect on past fun that I had growing up with my sisters; and ate pretty much every morsel of food in the house. The opportunity to sleep in my own bed, surrounded by the many comforting artifacts of my childhood, helped in to ground my emotions.

Above - "Running is a Family Affair!" A photograph from The Daily Mail, Catskill, N.Y. dated August 9th, 1982. The Chris' father had hopes that all of his children would be athlete-scholars. His mother wanted them to be good people. Sisters Melissa (left) and Nicole (center) are shown above.

My sisters and I watched an animated comedy entitled *Animalympics*, in which various types of animals competed in Olympic events. I most enjoyed the marathon race scene between a French goat, Rene Fromage and an African lioness, Kit Mambo. The two very intense competitors eventually fall in love with each other and run off into the distance holding hands.

Classic.

I also, as briefly and nonchalantly as I could, mentioned that I had stopped running for the college, might be failing one of my classes, and that, oh yeah, there was probably a ghost in my room.

These statements were met with silence.

I always had a fairly odd sense of humor, so I'm not sure if anyone thought that I actually meant what I was saying. When I was seven years old, I watched around fifteen minutes of the "movie of the week" (with actor Scott Glenn) about living gargoyles in which one of the horrifying winged and beaked creatures rises up from the foot of a bed in a motel while the protagonist is sleeping. He wakens and tries to fend it off. The scene was much too scary for me and I turned the channel. My preference back then was for something more suitable such as *The Land of the Lost.*

"Run Chaka, Run!"

That night, as I lay in bed, I wondered if a person really would be able to react that quickly to an unexpected threat. As my dad (who boxed as a youth and was a high school track runner) was likely the ablest to do so, I decided to try that on him. Walking in silence, I made my way into my parents' bed room, whereupon I found both of them asleep. Considering the situation with great care, I opted to take my place next to my father's side of the bed, rather than down at the foot like the gargoyle had done.

There I stood; my face suspended mere inches above my dad's. I was a little, puffy-haired, wide-eyed gargoyle in pajama bottoms.

I am unable to recall how long I stood there, or the precise moment that my father's eyes flicked open, but I do remember the compelling sight of a fast-moving, clenched, fist stopping just a hair's width from shattering my face. And my dad's great relief when he realized he had not mistakenly killed his only son. My mom yelled a lot, and then I went back to bed.

Gargoyles were over rated.

Now, as she brought me some cleaned clothes, my mother pulled me aside at the base of the hallway steps.

"Are you OK?" she asked me with a concerned look in her eyes.

"Sure. Why?"

"You just seem ... different."

Left — A gaunt-looking Di Cesare celebrates his 20th birthday with his family. Chris would lose over fifteen pounds during the first six weeks of the haunting at Geneseo.

My mother had discontinued her higher education to get married and have a family. I was born not long after.

She was as devoted a mother as one could imagine. She would make my lunch for school each day; wash my laundry; buy me clothes; check my homework; and go to every track race and cross country meet that I ran in no matter how far away it was, and whether or not she herself was feeling well. My favorite memory of her was reading the book *Goodnight Moon* to me when I was young. Eventually I knew the words so well that I would correct her, without looking at the book, when she would misread a word, or accidentally skip one. In fact, after the first few readings, I didn't look at the book all the way through because I was looking at her instead. I would watch her read to me. The understanding that somehow I 'lucked out' having her as my mother, was something that I understood from a very young age.

"I don't know, Chris. You look the same on the outside," she continued, watching my face for any brief adjustment in expression, "but you are a completely different person on the inside. Are you *sure* you are okay?"

For the first time in my life, I knowingly lie to her: "I'm fine, mom."

25. The Great Compromise of 1985

Above - C2D1 Journal Notes Scribe J. Jeff Ungar, Fallbrook Park, 1984.

I wasn't quite sure what to make of the fact that a pile of Jeff's books was sitting on Paul's desk as I walked into C2D1 after the long trip back from my parents' house. Nor was I able to surmise what the reason would be for Paul to apparently be washing his bed sheets at 11PM on a Sunday night before classes, as his mattress was stripped bare.

Placing my duffle bag on the ground, I was surprised to see Jeff nonchalantly carrying a large basket of clothing into the room.

"I suppose you are wondering why I am bringing my things in here," Jeff shares, "Paul and I have decided to switch rooms. Ed said he was fine with it."

My lack of a verbal response – or lack of celebration – must have raised some concern in Jeff as he added, "Are you going to be OK with this?"

In truth, my emotions on the switch were mixed. There was no doubt in my mind that Jeff and I had grown closer together as friends. His demeanor was much more positive and his approach to life much more cerebral and artistic than Paul's had been. Moreover, his assistance during this time of crisis seemed essential for me to safely meander through it. In many regards, the move was a decidedly positive one for me.

Still, there was a distinct sadness inside of me. It was the sadness of a valued friendship being lost amongst the floating ashes of the great fire that was the C2D1 Haunting. It was the sadness of not having had an opportunity to speak to Paul before he had opted out of my life. And it was the sadness of the choice being made by those around me, without a single word of warning, because they must have felt that they knew better than me.

My pride was sorely injured.

Before the ghost had intruded, I had been the 'golden boy', a celebrated athlete. Now, just one month later, I was still unique, but had now become some type of dangerous curiosity. Gargoyles sitting atop ancient Parisian structures now seemed more welcoming. As overrated as I knew them to be, at least they seemed to be able to ward off evil spirits.

I seemed only to attract them.

What had once been approving glances of admiration had become cautious scans of derision. Where conversations had once revolved around how fast I could run, they were now almost solely about what I was running *from*.

Worse still, word was now spreading fast about 'The Ghost Boy of Geneseo'.

In spite of all this, I could not deny the objective reality of the situation: Jeff was willing to move *into* C2D1 at a time when virtually everyone else was moving *away* from all of the terror that was swirling around me. I would not have to be alone.

This was enough for me to accept this transition, this great compromise: I would accept being recast as a victim, as long as I would not have to do so alone.

As we settled into the loft, Jeff lamented that the clock was displaying a time well after 1AM.

"So how did all of this happen?" I asked, hoping that I was prepared to hear the answer, "the whole room change thing?"

Jeff explained to me that he and Paul and Ed had discussed the move several times during the weekend. Paul had insisted that he needed to "get out" of the entire Tommy situation and he felt that moving into C2D2 with Ed would be one step closer to his goal. According to Jeff, Paul *was* actually trying to balance his desire to leave with concerns for my safety as the move was discussed. The choice obviously pained him, as Paul never said much more than a quick 'hello' or 'how's it going?' before he left, this time for good, a short time later.

As of this writing, over thirty years later, I have not seen or spoken with Paul since he exited Erie Hall.

In 1994, some nine years later, a high school friend of Jeff's, Alan Lewis, managed to track Paul down. He was living in a suburb of Rochester less than an hour's drive from the college where the horrific events had occurred.

Lewis reported that while Paul was initially reluctant to speak about the events of 1985, that eventually he agreed to do so. He revealed that the ghost warned him, on two separate occasions, and "clear as day", to "leave Chris alone." Paul wasn't about to wait for a third warning, thus the lightning fast departure out of C2D1 that impactful weekend in March.

My mother must have shared her concerns, about my alleged change in personality, with my father.

A few days later a letter came for me in the mail.

This was the first time that my father had written to me, separately from the rest of my family members, so I knew that it must be about something important.

Printed out on old-fashioned lined computer paper, the letter was cautionary in its approach, reminding me of the importance of "stability."

```
                                               A PERSON
ENTERING A FIELD THAT MIGHT DEAL WITH EMOTIONALLY DISTURBED
INDIVIDUALS MUST BE A PARAGON OF STABILITY. YOU SHOULD BE THE
PERSON THAT OTHERS SEEK INFORMATION FROM. WHATEVER YOU MIGHT
BELIEVE OTHERS WILL DEAL WITH YOUR INFORMATION IN A SKEPTICAL
WAY UNLESS THEY ** FEEL  SEE  TOUCH  ** THOSE THINGS YOU DO.
IF THEY DO NOT, YOU AVAIL YOURSELF TO CRITICISM OF STABILTY .
NOW ON THE OTHER HAND A BRIEF NOTE ON PHILOSOPHY--TO SEEK IS
TO FIND. TO DENY IS TO ADMIT THAT THERE MAY BE. THUS : SEEK
AND YE SHALL FIND THOSE THINGS THAT DO NOT EXIST, FOR YOU
SHALL CREATE THEM IN SPIRIT OR FORM, IN REAL OR IN MIND; AND
IF IT IS ALIVE AND EXISTING IN MIND, THEREFORE IT WILL BE REAL
FOR YOU, EVEN IF NOT FOR ANYONE ELSE. BELIEF THEREFORE IS THE
KEY.

I AM ALIVE NOW IN YOUR MIND AS YOU READ THIS. BUT DO YOU KNOW
OTHER THAN FAITH OR BELIEF? AND IF YOU READ THIS 50 YEARS FROM
NOW WHEN I AM DEAD WILL I EXIST ANY MORE OR LESS THAN THE WAY
I EXIST IN YOUR MIND NOW? DO NOT BELIEVE AND I DO NOT
EXIST,BELIEVE AND I DO.
```

Above - A sampling of the letter that the Chris' father sent to him in late March. His initial reaction to the letter was mixed: proud that his father cared for him, but embarrassed that he might have felt that his only son was having some type of mental or emotional breakdown.

I shared the letter with Jeff when I had the chance, and he felt that it was a very positive gesture. In his estimation, most parents simply did not bother themselves with issues as sensitive or complicated as this, and if they did it was usually just to issue a quick condemnation or rebuke.

Fair enough, and it *was* a powerful message being shared.

Doing my best not to irritate the thin, browning, scabs on my back, I continued wearing oversized shirts during this time period. This no doubt fueled the flames of gossip in and around Erie Hall that I had become 'skeleton thin' (no pun intended).

In actuality, I *had* lost between 12 and 15 pounds over the last few weeks, but the irony was that my efforts to lessen the physical discomfort caused directly by the haunting, only served to make it more noticeable to those around me.

Finally, in late March, around the time of my twentieth birthday, I made the frantic call home to my father.

Since the priest's Blessing of room C2D1, Tommy had become alarmingly bold. He was now appearing in broad daylight, and at locations *outside* of Erie Hall.

I saw his head protrude out of a wall of art reference books in the college library where, not surprisingly, a few seconds later a half-filled shelf of books fell to the ground near my feet.

Nervously, I returned the books to approximately location where they had fallen from, and I did not leave the isle for almost fifteen minutes; not until I was confident that anyone who might have seen the incident had left the area.

When the coast was clear, it was time for me to leave.

I next caught a glimpse of him through the shower's mist at the college athletic center, where I went with increased regularity following the attack in the Erie Hall dorm bathroom. It was a quick five-minute walk from the dorm. To my thinking the increased safety of the area was well worth the extra time it took to get there.

This time he was observed by another student athlete as well.

The ghost was watching me as I washed myself down inside the steamy locker room shower area. He was staring in, silently, from the side of the doorframe that connected the locker room proper to the showering area. But he wasn't looking at me like the artists and photographers would when I modeled for some extra spending cash during college, rather the weight of his stare felt oppressive, almost controlling.

As before, I felt as though he was longing to 'be' me; longing to be in control of my legs, my lungs, my youth, and my life.

It all felt 'wrong'.

I shot occasional glances his way, just to let him know that I was aware of his presence, but I refused to adjust my actions because of him.

How did he always find me?

I noted that he looked like a young Caucasian male. Thankfully, this time, without the grotesque wounds and the signs of torture as he had appeared in the tree.

Whether it was me adjusting to his presence or him allowing me to see him with greater accuracy, I could plainly see that he was close to my age. He stood an inch or two taller, but was not as athletically built as I was. The hair on his head was of a medium length, somewhat wavy, and appeared brown in coloration. He was clean-shaven and (without all of the wounds) not unattractive. My guess was that he must have been fairly well-liked by the ladies during his lifetime (whenever that was), and it made me wonder if he had ever fallen in love, if he ever married, and if he had ever produced a child.

Could his life's journey, in some ways, mirrored my own?

The thought of possible similarities between us – between the living and the dead – sent a shiver down my spine. I wanted to be *nothing* like him. There could be no similarities between us that might somehow be used to form an unwanted spiritual bond.

I glared back at him, almost aggressively.

But his eyes were jarring; they stared with a desperation that I had never seen before. And the breathing, the rhythmic pained breathing that I could – faintly – hear, inside my head, over the spraying shower water.

It sounded like a heartbeat.

A few minutes later, I glanced up towards the lockers, and he was gone.

Chillingly, as I was drying myself off (with one of my two remaining bathroom towels) I was approached by a tall, sinewy, acne-ridden student wearing a rather concerned expression on his face. He asked me if I happened to know who had been "standing by the showers, watching" me while I was in there.

I stood motionless, for a moment, considering the many implications of his statement. I shook my head, and told him that I hadn't seen anyone.

"Well, if he comes back, I'm calling the campus police," the student said, judiciously securing his bath towel tightly around his thin waist. Then, with obvious apprehension, he headed off for the showers himself. I watched as he glanced down all of the aisles of lockers as he went; he was clearly spooked. The tops of his ears were reddened, possibly from an increased blood flow caused by nerves, by fear.

A part of me wanted to stop him, right there, and share with him what I had been experiencing since that fateful day in early February. To find out, since he had actually *seen* Tommy, if we had any similarities, any shared experiences, aside from being two young athletes who had somehow found their way to this tormented place; a place that the local Native Americans had called 'Chenussio'.

I chose to say nothing.

It would be safer for him.

The ghost was also making his presence known, in other areas of Erie Hall, and in a most dramatic fashion.

Two days later, when Beth did not show up for a set appointment she had made with Jeff and I, we found her lying on the floor of her dorm room, apparently passed out.

After rousing her, and helping her up off the floor, she claimed that she had heard the ghost calling my name, "Chrissss," and that she had yelled for it to stop.

It had created a state of panic in her.

Before she was able to run for help, she apparently had tried to throw things at it, and hit it. Then she claimed that she collapsed, unconscious, on the floor where we had found her an unknown duration of time later.

Judy, her roommate, told us later that night that she had been feeling abnormally cold breezes in the room and that she felt as though she was being "watched" in the bathroom when no one was there. Also, that in spite of the hot mist created from the warm shower water, that the bathroom now suddenly 'was freezing'.

I knew that feeling.

She mentioned that she planned to talk to her pastor about it when she returned home, which like a safe and logical step.

There were so many options for us to consider, yet few clear choices were presenting themselves.

Early on the in the prior semester, when my life was still as golden as the autumn sugar maple leaves, I read an article in the university newspaper (October 5, 1984) written by a student named Craig Norris.

It detailed the construction of the college's first all-weather running track. As an avid and competitive runner, the piece's subject matter naturally drew my interest. While the cost of $318,000, paid via the State University Construction Fund, seemed a bit steep, Norris pointed out that the new track would benefit both the college's varsity runners (we currently had to train at the local high school's cinder track) in any weather conditions and casual joggers who wished to run on their own, and could use it at any hour of the day. Norris wrote: Many people feel embarrassed or stupid running around the campus by themselves in front of their peers. The new track will give these shy people an alternative to waking at 4 a.m.

When I first read the article, I wondered why anyone would be embarrassed by taking part in the healthy activity of running. What could possibly be so disconcerting about having one's actions known?

The ghost had since taught me otherwise.

Being forced against one's will to face the scrutiny of others, whether it is due to one's physical conditioning, financial status or mental state could become an utterly devastating experience.

Now, five months later, Craig Norris (who had lived in C2D2 of Erie Hall with Jeff the year before my arrival) approaches me as I enter my dorm room, and mentions to me that his roommate was claiming that he too was hearing voices in his head; that he had 'heard' my name in his thoughts.

Craig wonders if I have any opinions, or advice, on the matter.

Not sure as to how to effectively deal with my own situation, I politely decline any unnecessary involvement in his. Why should I risk further failure, the further erosion of my faculties? I have been transformed into that shy student who sneaks off to run at 4 a.m. so as not to be seen by others that Craig had so aptly described in his article.

It can be argued that my inactivity led to disastrous consequence.

I happened to see Craig's roommate, on one occasion, shortly after Craig had interceded on his behalf. I had been gazing out of the window of the room that had become my voluntary prison, enviously watching those who had been blessed by dull normalcy. The dull normalcy that allowed them to smile effortlessly, and not worry about surviving each and every day, to avoid wracking their brains by the necessity of questioning every sound and movement that whirled around them.

Craig's roommate exited Erie Hall.

As he passed beneath my second-floor perch of isolation, his steps looked heavy, his shoulders hunched forward, he wore a look of unmistakable misery. I followed his form as he made his way down the walking path towards the college union. I felt a profound sadness as he exited my line of sight. Perhaps it was born from a feeling of guilt. Or maybe it was that I sensed that I would never be able to help him.

That choice was taken from me, and from all of us, when he chose to end his own life.

The Blessing, while largely effective in its original purpose (to send the ghost from my room) had some unexpectedly negative and unforeseen consequences for almost everyone around me.

Asking for additional Blessings might help, but it would be impractical, and demanding, to ask the priest to perform dozens of such ceremonies.

No.

Father Manning had faithfully done his part. It was time that I initiated some type of plan of action of my own: It was time to call home.

"Dad," I breathed nervously into the lounge's pay phone's receiver, "I'm in trouble."

The phone call was an awkward one.

My father had been a science teacher before he became a building principal, and while possessing a fine sense of humor and being a creative-minded problem solver, he was an empiricist at heart. He had invested lots of time and copious amounts of money in me growing up, and he did not particularly enjoy the possibility that I might be frittering away my vast potential with nonsensical stories about a ghost.

I could hear it in his voice.

After several minutes we found that we were at loggerheads, so my father said: "Fine. I want you and Jeff to go find the biggest, meanest, strong-looking guys you can. You bring them into your room. If they see anything, I'll come up there."

Deal.

Outside the common area window Jeff and I could see a group of about five or six guys, some of whom we recognized from Erie Hall, playing a makeshift game of soccer, or maybe it was rugby, where grass normally grew. It was now a large swampy area of mud from the combination of the melting winter snow and their frenetic activity.

I explained to a slightly incredulous Jeff what my father had requested, and then we set out to collect what were the unknowing subjects of our grand experiment. So positive was I in the existence of the ghost, and in its desire to interact with me - to be near me - there wasn't the slightest hint of doubt in my mind that this test would work.

Four of them, two covered with mud, and all of them six feet in height or taller, agreed to follow us back: Luke and Brian from C2D3, Don from across the hall, and someone who Jeff described as 'a rugby type'.

All we said to them was: "This is going to sound very strange, but we want to show you something absolutely amazing in our room."

Whether they assumed there would be a keg filled with beer, a stolen final exam answer key, or some hot chicks lying topless in our loft, it didn't matter. All I cared about was what their reaction would be when the *real* surprise showed up.

They were immediately annoyed when we reached the doorway of C2D1. Whatever it was that they had expected to see, was not there.

"What's going on?" asked Don, who had a cloth bandana tied around his spikey-haired head.

"Just wait one minute, you'll see."

There was still no doubt in my mind.

Jeff was maintaining the appearance of outward composure as well, save the nervous trembling of one of his legs. I was pretty sure that he was becoming increasingly concerned about what would become of our belongings, and us, if the four unwitting test subjects happened to grow angry.

"Dude, why did you bring us all here?" the rugby player in the light blue tie-died shirt asked, more than a hint of irritation in his voice.

Brian and Luke (who had previously mentioned to Paul that he thought that the haunting was some kind of joke) looked at each other. They had no clue what was going on.

The 'rugby players' decided that it was time for them to go.

As the four stood up to leave, I felt the temperature in the room chill at a rapid a rate. I made strong and direct eye contact with Jeff and mouthed, "It's here."

Jeff nodded that he understood.

Brian, made a strange face, quickly turned to me and screamed: "What's *grabbing* me? Something is on my *leg!*"

The others are now caught between the choice of finding the cause of his sudden delirium, or giving in to their fear that something 'wrong' is definitely occurring.

They chose door number two.

Don, who turned to his left, and Luke who headed to the right, were the first to bolt out of the room.

Brian by then was becoming red-faced and frazzled.

"What *is* this?" he implored.

"The ghost." I answered, deciding that there was no longer any point in concealing the truth with the level of activity as high as it was.

The 'rugby guy', who seemed to be friends with Don, attempted to leave the room. As he did so, Brian seemed to break free of the thing. But as the 'rugby guy' took a few steps towards the door, he stopped and started flailing *his* arms and legs as though he had somehow become caught in a large spider's web.

"F**k! This is too freaky!" He yelled, as he threw his large arms into the air over his head and ran out of the quad.

Brian walked back to C2D3, shot us both a look of extreme displeasure as he rubbed his left thigh, and slammed the door behind him.

None of them would ever asked us another question, or make a snide comment, or speak to either of us about the incident again.

Our mission accomplished, I yelled out into C2D1, "You need to go away now! Do you hear me?"

"How did you know that he would show up," Jeff asked as he jotted down details about the most recent incident.

"He has been following me around," I replied, making sure I didn't see the ghost so that I could finish the next part of my statement, "he is a lot like a controlling or abusive spouse. They are physically and emotionally aggressive to the person that they focus on, who they view as their 'property', but at the same time they remain protective of them.

Jeff nodded his head in approval, and jotted down a few additional sentences in his ever-present spiral notebook journal. He was impressed by the cleverness of my last-minute plan of action, and of my assessment of Tommy's mindset. This further underscored his belief that the ghost could be talked to, could be reasoned with, perhaps eventually made public.

I still wasn't so sure about that.

Also disconcerting was that, in my zeal to win my father's respect and help, I had temporarily permitted Tommy to re-enter C2D1.

There was no formal invitation back into room, but there was a certain tacit acceptance given to his presence. That is why I shouted for the ghost to 'go away', as a reminder that he shouldn't be there in violation of the Blessing.

It was all just some fragile house of cards that I was building on, and I knew it.

With Jeff now standing beside me for moral support, I made the call to my father and shared what had happened.

There was silence on his end for about ten seconds.

"I'm on my way."

He arrived that night, completing the five-hour car ride in almost exactly four hours. He carried with him a baseball bat; a crucifix (from my great-grandmother) with a vial of holy water imbedded in its back; and a handgun.

My dad wasn't there to fool around.

Whoever had been bothering me, whatever kind of intimidation or hoax was transpiring, he was determined to put a stop to it that night.

Jeff was beside himself with anguish as his parents pulled up in their bulky, and to Jeff, "embarrassing" Dodge Caravan to take him home for the evening.

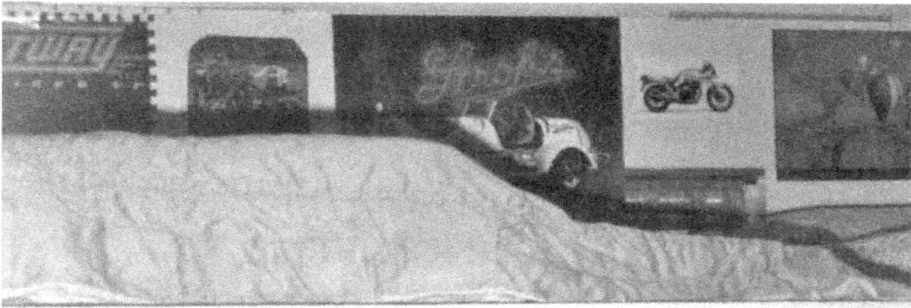

Above – Chris' father, Vito Di Cesare Jr., relaxes on the old brown couch in room C2D1 in the early fall of 1984. Six months later, he would be keeping a tense vigil over his son during the heart of the extreme haunting.

"Sac-re-mént!" he exclaimed, "It *would* have to be now!"

Having been barred from Fr. Manning's Blessing of C2D1 three weeks earlier, Jeff was now angered that he would be missing my father's visit as well. I half-jokingly told him to enjoy the time with his family up at Wolfern. Jeff scowled a bit, for effect, and then trudged out to his parents' vehicle. I watched him from the room's window as he shot one last glance up as he stepping into his parents' vehicle.

I hadn't slept for more than three or four hours at a time since the evening that had I noticed the figure standing over my right shoulder as I ate the *Hot Tamales*. So, after we had some dinner uptown at my favorite eatery on the planet, Aunt Cookie's Sub Shop, my dad told me to 'get some sleep'.

Armed and ready, he placed himself at the foot of the loft.

In the morning, as the sun lit up the room's old curtains, I awoke to find my father sitting in the same location that he was in when I had fallen asleep some eight hours prior. He looked exhausted, but gave me a slight smile when he saw me looking over at him.

"Are you OK?" I asked him.

"I'm fine. Why don't we go for a quick run before I head back?"

There has been much written about the loneliness of the long-distance runner, but that was never the case for me. Running, even during the harshest of practices and in the hardest fought races, was still largely a social event for me. If I wasn't running with my teammates I would run with friends like Gene Piaquadio Jr. while in high school, and Paul and Jeff during my college years.

My favorite runs were the ones with my father.

He had been training me since I was eleven years old, and he was still the primary reason that I ran: I wanted to make him proud of me.

As we ran down the narrow college walkways, up onto the shop-laden Main Street, and then down around a portion of the cross-country course, very little was said. When two athletes are 'in sync' there is not much that *needs* to be said. We had trained together well over three thousand times, in the driving rain, under the scorching sun, and through the frost of winter.

This was something sacred.

Many people are born without a father in their life, and some lose them at an early age.

Experiencing this moment was precious to me.

After we had cleaned up, my dad slipped me a few dollars (in case of an emergency) and then, as he was packing his duffle bag and retrieving his car keys, he composed himself, looked at me, and said: "You know that you can always turn to me; and you can turn to your mother. If you need our help, just call."

Then came the coup de grâce: "And, Chris, move out of this room!"

Alan Lewis, a graduate of SUNY Buffalo and veteran social services caseworker in the state of New York, would be the first to actively investigate the C2D1 Haunting. His journey began only days after the tumultuous spring semester for the students at Geneseo had come to a close. Over the years, Alan has been successful in tracking down and interviewing key witnesses, preserving important haunting-related artifacts and documents, and in helping to shed additional light on the events of 1985.

26. The Ghost Story

From the standpoint of the present, we can always look back and see the pivotal moments when things change for us, when choices we make in the roads we take determine so much of where we are now. And yet sometimes it seems that there was no choice at all, that being who we already were at that moment, we cannot have done differently.

Such a time came for myself in the spring of 1985, in the simple listening to the story of a friend. That friend was Jeff Ungar, whom I had known since the 8th grade, and who had briefly lived with his family across the street from mine. We had remained friends through High School, and in the period after that, when many friends one no longer sees begin to drop off the social radar, we had continued our friendship through a common group of people, and even exchanged letters, when that kind of thing was still done.

As long as I had known Jeff, he had been a person of exacting standards, piercing intelligence, and a lively conversationalist on topics that interested him. A love for the comedy of Monty Python was a given in our group. He enjoyed contributing his quirky noises or witty sound-bites to conversations, but rarely put himself at center stage, seeming to prefer to hover on the social fringes. All that was to be different on this evening.

The occasion was an evening shortly after all of our group had now individually completed our second year of college. We had gathered at a favorite local restaurant called Perkins, when Jeff began his tale. He came prepared for the task, as became clear at the end. And the story he had to tell was, of course, the same one that is told in this book. Jeff imparted these events with a passion and intensity I had never seen in him before.

I do not recall anything else being discussed that evening, the enormity of what our friend had been through dwarfed all other possible topics. This was only a few weeks after the haunting had concluded, and all the details were fresh in Jeff's mind. Though he himself had not precisely witnessed the ghost, he had experienced the side effects, and been first hand witness to the effect the ghost had on Chris Di Cesare who lived in room C2D1 of Erie Hall, and had no doubt that it was really happening. And at the end of the narrative he played his trump card, laying down the ghost photograph, which we all continually stared at, as the image yields more details to concerted study.

Each person has their own standards for what it takes to persuade them. In my case I had enjoyed ghost stories as a youth, and took their reality seriously, but came to regard them as childish, and silly to believe in. That is an attitude wide-spread in our society, and any person expressing such a belief is certain to be dismissed by some people. Few wish to be a potential object of ridicule, and Jeff was certainly not a person to put himself in that situation lightly. No, it could only be because he fervently believed that he had lived through a haunting, but that the reality of such a thing was important. A gamer changer. And so it surely is.

There was no conscious struggle to decide whether I believed the story of this haunting or not. At some point while looking at the ghost photo I felt myself fully convinced. The struggle came later as I attempted to come to terms with what it meant about the world that a haunting could really happen. That evening while standing in the bathroom at my home, my imagination could not help but flirt with the idea that there could be a ghost behind the shower curtain at this moment. Come to think of it, ghosts might be around all the time. If one ghost had authentically existed in the world, there were surely more. If one ghost story was true, many more of them must also be true. Though the initial effect of this belief was a fear that could manifest at any moment, there was a longer lasting effect, the implication that reality must be deeper and more full of a sense of marvelous mystery, and contemplating that mystery was a worthwhile and enriching path to pursue.

I had many other occasions to discuss further details of the haunting with Jeff. This was made easier by the fact that he had assembled all his notes from the haunting and presented them as a package to his creative writing teacher. All his efforts to document the haunting made for a fine writing project it turned out. The fact he had attempted to chronicle events as they took place would do much to ensure that the details of this haunting did not fade away, but would become well known to so many others.

Above – Alan Lewis with friend J. Jeff Ungar inside Wayne Hall on the SUNY Geneseo campus. The date is December 4th, 1986, the day that he would finally meet the person that he had heard so much about. – Photograph by Di Cesare.

The story of the haunting and what it meant to me had therefore been with me for some time before I actually met Chris in person on December 4h, 1986, another event that would have a tremendous impact on the course of my path. I would hear him tell the story of the haunting on many subsequent occasions, and therefore continued to learn more details all the time, but my core belief had already been set, so it could only be sharpened by later revelation. Eyes once opened more fully cannot be long constricted ever again.

That central understanding of the deeper nature of the world and the value of pursuing it remained with me, and several of our friends. We knew that this insight had been valuable to us, and felt perhaps there was some responsibility to share it, that others might also gain. It was in this spirit that in the spring of 1994 my friends and I sought out some of the witnesses to these events.

The individual referred to as 'Paul A.' had always been a prominent figure in any story of the haunting. The original roommate, he was there for the start of the haunting, and had been a witness to some of the most dramatic aspects. The irony of this was sometimes harsh to Jeff, who wanted to experience more, whereas Paul did not seem to welcome any of what he had witnessed. Paul, after all, was the one who left, and Jeff was the one who moved in. But Jeff himself had perceived the cause for why Paul had seen more than himself, as in separate discussions Paul had revealed to Jeff his prior history with such paranormal occurrences such as mind reading, and instances of knowing the future. Like Chris, Paul was more naturally sensitive than the average person.

What Chris knew was that Paul's family had lived in the general area, so the search for Paul started with the local phone book. It was in a suburb outside the Rochester area that the correct 'Paul A.' was located. He agreed to speak to me one evening.

I had a class I was taking at a local college named Brockport, and met Paul at his home after class. This was a step of a different magnitude then all the previous efforts I had made. That had consisted of listening to the recollections of two of my best friends, and making a record of what they stated. Chris has a unique memory, as he has a tendency to forget events that most others can easily bring to mind. However, when he is reminded of what has occurred, some key detail will often spark his recollection, and then once prompted he is able to narrate what occurred with a level of detail that can be astounding. So as I approached the door, I did not come with any particular training as an investigator or journalist, and discussing a potentially sensitive topic with someone I had never met before was far from my comfort zone, but I did bring my sense of mission with me, and a thoroughly detailed chronicle of Chris' recollection of the haunting.

Paul was far from comfortable with the situation also. I recognized him from the old photos, though obviously older. He invited me in politely, but maintained a sense of cool detachment. There was a minimum of small talk. Paul knew I had come to discuss the haunting. He had agreed to this discussion, and at no point did I get any sense he was holding back, but it was clear his cooperation came with reluctance.

Above – Alan Lewis tracked down Di Cesare's first C2D1 roommate, Paul A., nine years after the haunting had occurred. – Photograph, 1984 by Chris Di Cesare.

"I am married," Paul told me, "But I knew my wife would not be here this evening, and will not hear what we are talking about."
"Okay," I said. "Do you own this home?"
"I do," he replied. "And in fact when I was looking for a house, one of the requirements was that the house could not be too old."
He looked at me significantly to see if I understood. I nodded. He did not want there to be any chance that his home was haunted.

As I have pondered this conversation in later times, it has been my strong feeling that Paul did not often make any reference to what had happened in his Geneseo dorm room in his second year of college. I should hardly be surprised to learn that our conversation could have been the first and last time he discussed what he'd seen and heard in any detail. Everything about his demeanor suggested that the haunting might have profoundly affected him, but that he did not ever wish to have any such experience again.

I proceeded to read to Paul the narrative that had been constructed from Chris' recollections of the times when he had been present, and asked for his reaction. I read the account that he had seen a figure in the room with himself and Chris, and that when Chris had asked him what it looked like, he had said it looked like a kid with his head tilted to the side.

"That is what I saw alright," Paul admitted grimly.

I read to him the account of a night of terror, capped by a moment when Chris struggled to keep hold of his pillow, while some force unseen attempted to yank it away from his grasp. Few pieces of evidence could be so unmistakable as the sight of what should be impossible: a man having a tug of war with no one.

Paul looked uneasy to be reminded of this sight, but confirmed it was accurate. After I had real all the narrative to him, Paul said, "That's amazing. I'm so impressed that Chris is able to remember all that. That is exactly how it all was."

If I had not received anything else from this conversation, this much would already have been significant, but it turned out that Paul had more to say.

"You know," he said, "I saw that ghost all the time when no one else was around. I never told anyone what I was seeing."

This news was enough to make me catch my breath. I asked for whatever details he could recall.

"It happened a lot," he said. "But one time when I was in the room by myself, I saw a thin pair of white legs stretched out underneath my desk." He looked at me to gauge my reaction, but I could only nod. I was worried that the wrong word could cause the end of the revelations.

"Another time, again with no one else in the room, I was sitting at my desk, and several of my books began floating in the air right in front of me."

Writing this now, I can think of a hundred follow up questions, but that is all I can recall from that time. It seemed like enough however, more than I had hoped to obtain when I had come. From here we discussed what he thought about the ghost, whose existence he clearly had not come to doubt.

"The thing about Tommy," he said, "I don't think he was evil." (I was aware that there had been multiple events in which Paul had seemed to have been targeted by the ghost, and at the time Jeff had noted, "Tommy hates Paul.") "Rather," Paul said, "I think he was focused on one goal, and that goal was Chris' attention, and he tried to get rid of everything standing in the way of his goal."

It was clear to me that though he might not be in the habit of discussing the haunting, Paul had spent some time contemplating what had happened and why, so perhaps it was a relief to him to be able to relay his conclusions.

Paul followed this up with the observation that the ghost had thus been responsible for breaking up a friendship that he had hoped would last, and that he still had regret about this. It seemed as though he was acknowledging that his choice not to remain in the haunted room had caused him to owe a debt to Chris, and giving these revelations was his means of discharging that debt, knowing his words might someday be revealed to others. Since he has rebuffed all subsequent attempts at contact, it may be that he considered this one instance sufficient.

In legal proceedings, there is a high value placed on the testimony of what is called a reluctant or disinterested witness. Someone who is not directly involved in a situation and is not anxious to discuss what they know is not likely to dissemble. There could be few witnesses more reluctant than Paul, who gave every impression of being a person who had been scarred by his experience, unable to forget what he perhaps wished he could.

Having established the best supporting witness I could imagine, my friends and I discussed other means we might follow up on to support the haunting. At my local library, I read through a reference book on the paranormal and learned about an organization called The Ghost Research Society, whose director would examine potential ghost photos for authenticity in exchange for permission to use the photos. I sent the skeletal ghost photo, and received back a very positive response. That analysis appears in this book.

Looking about for other witnesses, our friend David Flass took the lead in making contact with the priest who had blessed the room, Father Charles Manning. Dave and I travelled down to small community called Cohocton, where he was serving as a clergyman. We found Father Charlie to be an enthusiastic and lively man, who as a result of keeping an open mind throughout his career, reported encountering a lot of strange things along the way. It took him some prompting for him to remember the details of his involvement in the haunting.

He did give us a couple pieces of insight into his actions. He stated that the distinction between him performing a blessing and an exorcism was important, as he would have had to obtain permission for an exorcism. He had gone to the room under the guise of an appliance repair person not just to avoid causing attention, but also to avoid any dispute about performing a sacred ceremony on the secular ground of a dormitory. Lastly, he stated that once he had been convinced there was likely a ghost in this dorm room, the ceremony was intended to not only provide relief to the living inhabitants, but hopefully help the spirit to find rest. All in all the conversation provided interesting insights into events we had so often discussed.

It is a tempting game for people to speculate about the what-ifs of their lives, what if we did not make the choices we made along the way, what if we did not meet the people who are close to us, what if we had different things happen to us. The C2D1 haunting in one sense did not happen to me, but in another it might as well have, since how I thought about the world was never the same after hearing about it, and the people who have been likewise attached to it remain an integral part of my life, as though it could not have been otherwise. Trying to convince another person about such a thing as the existence of ghosts is a fool's errand when that other person does not wish to be convinced, but for those who are open to the possibility, I can only say that my experience has been made richer and more meaningful by such knowledge. May yours be also.

27. The Doctor Is In

Above – The note left for the author by Beth Kinsman, as they prepared to meet the parapsychologist.

It is 10:45 PM, Erie Hall, we are inside of room B2B2. Linda Fox is lying across her bed near her window, which is closed. She is having great difficulty moving her legs, claiming that the ghost is "holding" her down and "sitting" on her. Moments earlier she sent for Jeff and me to assist her in getting Tommy out of her room.

I glance about the room which is swirling with a disconcertingly recognizable light gray mist that appears its densest near Linda.

Approaching her with my arms outstretched in the manner that had worked before, I ask her - as she is now close to tears - if I can move my hands near her. I offer to 'feel' for the ghost, in order to see if I could communicate with it.

She nods her head in the affirmative.

Jeff raises his 35mm camera and takes a photograph as I approach her.

I am conflicted by his decision to snap the photo. While I recognize its definitive scientific, psychological and paranormal research value, I am concerned that it was taken without her consent.

This is a very personal moment.

I peer over my left shoulder, "Jeff … did you want to …?"

Jeff lifts his head up from behind his camera, a look of temporary confusion etched across his intelligent face.

Then he understands.

"Oh. Right. Linda, you wouldn't mind if I take a few pictures, would you?"

"No," she offers with a nervous laugh, "if you guys can get *rid* of this thing, you can do whatever you want!"

In spite of the recent memory of the shower attack, I attempt to talk to Tommy.

I ask him to leave, in my head (and I am still unsure as to exactly how I can hear him).

I 'understand' that he refuses to do so.
It is 10:52PM.

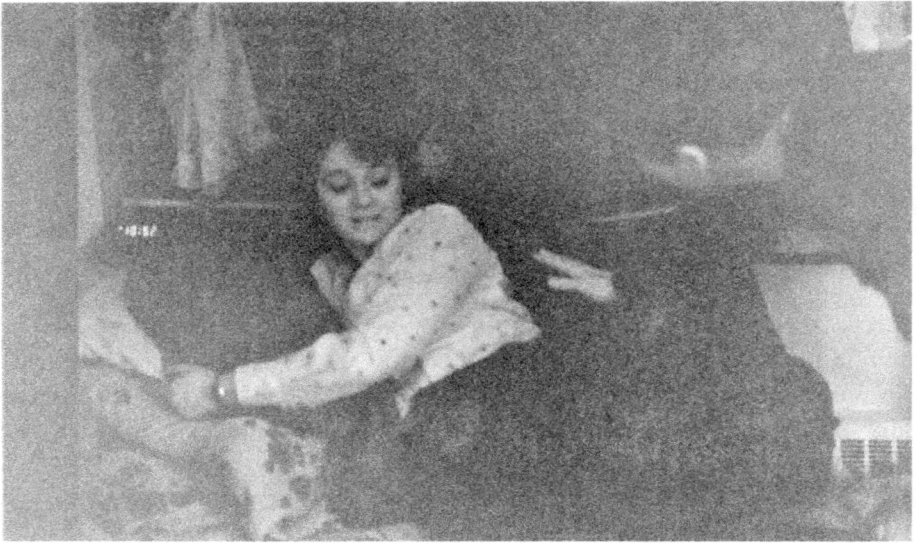

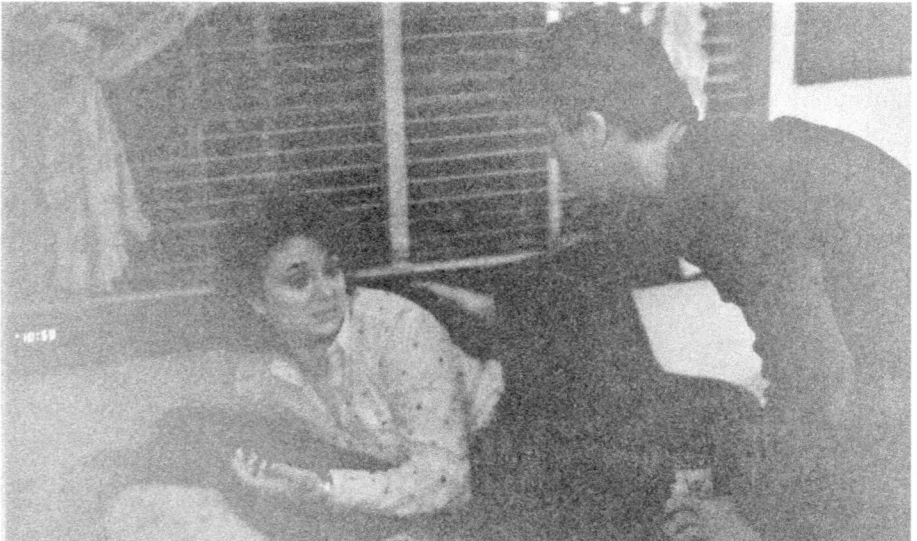

Above - These incredible mist-laden photographs, taken six minutes apart, by John Jeff Ungar, capture the raw emotion that an extreme haunting can have on its victims and offer a real-time glimpse into the C2D1 haunting as it was occurring.

Six minutes later, at 10:58, the misty energy is finally departing. Why?

Likely because I had made a promise to the ghost that soon – not now, but soon – I would try to help him. I offer this repeatedly. I think it inside my brain and say it aloud with my mouth.

His actions suggest that he seems to have accepted my offer.

I make this offer even though I suspect that helping him might mean additional harm to me. However, I think that I have convinced him that it's me that he wants, not Linda. That was my primary goal.

I had decided that he wasn't going to hurt my friends; I wasn't going to *let* him.

After all, I was the 'Ghost Boy of Geneseo'.

I wanted to help Linda.

I wanted to help all of my friends.

Still, an exact plan eluded me, and I did not know where to find one.

Sitting up in the loft later that night, Jeff (with spiral notebook in hand) revisits the idea of meeting with the parapsychologist, Dr. Casler. While he cautions me that the result might simply be a theoretical discussion, and not an actual resolution to the haunting, he feels that it might be worth our time.

I don't want to bother the priest again; he has already done his part.

Breathing out a pronounced 'sigh' of resignation, I consent.

The meeting was set up the next day by Beth, who was pleased by the reality that we were finally acting on what had, initially, been her idea. We purposely missed the first meeting that she had attempted to set up, several weeks prior, as I didn't want Fr. Charlie to think that we were hedging our bets with him.

Now there is nothing to lose, and no other option that we can think of.

Two days later, we have our sit-down meeting with Dr. Lawrence Casler in his office on the Geneseo college campus. I was both embarrassed and honored that he remembered we had missed our first appointment with him. He admitted that he wasn't sure if the initial phone call (made by Beth) had been a hoax, or if maybe we were in some kind of trouble when we did not show up, and he appeared quite pleased to finally see us in the flesh.

Dr. Casler impressed me as a man of great intelligence. His mannerisms, his eye contact, his rate of speech, his verbiage, all bespoke a man who took his work, his studies, and his theories very seriously.

He, in turn, was quite fascinated by us.

A slight smile crossed his thin lips, as he marveled about traveling all over the country for years in search of cases such as ours, and there we were, right at his very doorstep!

I shot a quick glance back at Beth, who was sitting behind us in a chair by the wall. Her hands were folded and she was wearing a proud smile.

She had done it; she had brought together teacher and students, helped her friends, and (hopefully) done everybody some good in setting this meeting up.

I was happy for her.

As Dr. Casler, captivated by the level of detail in the journal notes, turned page after page, I noticed that Jeff was quite enthused by this informal summit. Ever a creature of ideas, this is what *he* needed, this was *his* validation. That a learned man of science, a published author, a noted scholar was finding value in his efforts was gratifying for him beyond measure. The level of satisfaction that I took from winning a 10K road race was mirrored now in him, in this moment.

I was happy for Jeff too.

I was happy for both of them.

Looking down at my white and blue, *Asics* running sneakers, I lifted them to make sure that I had tracked no mud into the professor's office. A soft chuckle, which I disguised by clearing my throat, inadvertently left my mouth as I thought to myself: Wow, you are *literally* trying to cover up your tracks already, aren't you Chris?

I didn't feel like I belonged here.

Dr. Casler asked Jeff what he wished to be 'called'.

Jeff was unsure of what he was referring to, and repeated back, "What do I wish to be *called*? Do you mean, what is my name?"

I could see that Jeff was startled over the prospect that he had made such a minimal personal impression on the psychology professor, especially in light of the fact that he had just pored over the detailed pages of more than two months' worth of his efforts.

For the first time during the meeting, I smile.

"For my papers, my archives, how would you like me to record you? What name would you like me to use?"

"Jeff … Jeff Ungar is … fine, yes … that's good." Jeff stated in an absolutely uncertain tone. I had never seen him this nervous before, not even when an undead creature was assaulting his friends or when he was working through a 10-page paper the night before it was due. I tried not to smile too much.

As Dr. Casler began to jot down some notes of his own, Jeff abruptly leaned forward in his chair, and offered: "You know what? I've reconsidered. I would prefer to be called 'John Jeff Ungar'. Is it too late to revise that for the record?"

"It is absolutely *not* too late," Casler replied, now wearing a smile like my own.

Jeff sat back into the chair and emitted a genuine sigh of relief. He felt good about his choice. Every photographer worth their salt was careful to list the camera that they had used, the location the image was captured, and the film type when preserving or displaying their work. If Jeff was now to become the official 'chronicler' of this haunting, it was important to him that he be listed correctly, and from the start as John Jeff Ungar.

It was going to take me a long time to get used to that.

It turned out that Jeff had called it correctly, the night before, when he cautioned me not to expect any concrete answers in regards to ending the haunting. In fact, much like Jeff himself, Dr. Casler was now advocating that we acquire additional forms of evidence; perhaps a tape recording of the ghost's voice.

Jeff smiled, nodded his head and allowed himself a quick, "Yes!"

I could feel my hands start to tremble from a combination of anger and fear. To prevent my reaction from being noticed, I position my hands under my thighs, and sit on them, holding them still and in place. It was damp enough outside that I could pretend that they were cold, if anyone happened to ask.

Understanding, going in, that Dr. Casler would not be able to directly assist us in bringing the haunting to a close was acceptable to me. Nevertheless, my assumption was that we would at least ascertain ways in which to lessen the haunting's effect. It seemed to me that redirecting our approach to 'evidence gathering' only risked further perpetuating the whole horrid ordeal.

When he noticed my unnerved body posture, Jeff visibly tempered his enthusiasm.

Good.

Beth dutifully reminded Dr. Casler that his next class was scheduled to start, so we began to close the meeting. He instructed Jeff and me that I should be the one to take the lead in these evidence collection efforts.

"Chris, you appear to be the focus of the entity's attention."

"Let's go," I whisper to Jeff angrily, "I want to leave this place, *now!*"

Jeff finds himself in the unkind position of having to decide between inquiring about what was currently bothering his good friend, and bidding a proper adieu to Dr. Lawrence Casler, Ph. D. He chose the latter of the options.

I was quite thankful, as it should make my escape a faster one.

That still didn't stop Dr. Casler, his bright eyes scanning me from behind his shining glasses, "Oh, and Chris, I'd like you to come back and talk with me. Just you; when you get the chance."

I *knew* it.

Less than ten minutes into the meeting with Dr. Casler, I knew that his primary interest wasn't necessarily in the ghost at all.

It was in me.

When Jeff presented the photograph of the ghost to him, he barely considered it. Inspecting it for no more than five seconds, he placed it to the side of his desk in front of him. I am not even sure if he saw the skeletal image in the background. Instead, he asked: "What made you two decide to take this photograph when you did?"

He wasn't looking for static moments, or photographs for that matter, he was looking for causality, and for *meaning*.

What did it mean that this young boy was seeing a ghost? Under what conditions did it manifest? How had the event affected their belief systems? What did it mean that many other college students were now experiencing this purported phenomenon? What was going on in the minds of these young students, who were clearly horrified by, and completely invested in, the ordeal?

Perhaps most importantly, how was it that this ordinary boy – with no outward inclination towards it – was able to manifest all of this?

Had he been successful in unlocking some portion of the human mind; perhaps he had been able to pierce, to see beyond, some long taboo veil?

The following evening Jeff, Beth, Linda, and I gathered in room B2B2 for the experiment.

My concerns over the psychologist's true intent aside, I had made a promise to the ghost – who by now everyone was calling Tommy – and I was intent on trying to keep it. What might occur if I broke my word was not something that I cared to consider.

Since Tommy had most recently manifested in Linda's room, all involved felt it was the most logical place to start.

Jeff had procured the Sears Roebuck SR2100 tape recorder, the one that Tommy had turned on twice, from my desk drawer a month earlier.

A new fear ran through me: Had the ghost planned this all along? Is this, what had taken us almost two months to decide, what he had wanted from the start? Had we played ourselves into his hands? If so, then we would be no match for him when the 'end' of all this occurred. I was truly fearful for all of us.

But the 'Ghost Boy of Geneseo' couldn't afford to be.

Looking back, the significance of what we young college students were about to do cannot be understated. Just twenty-five years removed from the work of Sir Friedrich Jorgensen, regarded by some as the 'father' of the EVP (Electronic Voice Phenomena) we were going to try to speak with the dead. We had no hand held active recording devices, no infrared motion sensors, and no EMF meters. There was nothing for us to depend upon but our own instincts, a 35mm camera, a tape recorder and a shared desire for understanding and survival.

I glanced about the room hoping beyond all hope that I wouldn't see him smiling down at me as if to say, "I win."

Mercifully, there was no sign of him.

Jeff, in what to this day may very well be the most focused intellectual effort I have ever witnessed, moved from location to location locking windows, securing drawers, measuring distances, gauging temperatures.

There was an understanding that he was now working under: he had seen enough to know that Tommy would come when I called him; now it was up to *him* to ensure that it was recorded properly. The more controlled the environment, the more valid the results would be.

Dr. Casler had lent his academic and professional credibility to Jeff's preference to gather more data, and he was now an inspired man on a mission. Additionally, our social support network had grown with the help that we were now receiving from Beth and Linda (and on the peripheral from Ed).

I was very well aware that Jeff had both logic and reason on his side. Additional data, photographs, eye witness accounts, and voice recordings were all viable means on the road to understanding what exactly we were dealing with at Geneseo.

Moreover, it could potentially lead to breakthroughs in society's understanding of the paranormal as a whole. Imagine being able to talk to the spirit of a dead relative; being able to ask them questions about what the 'Other Side' was like; or even globally-transforming topics such as: what value could be placed in the world's great religions? What about self-determination?

Jeff, Dr. Casler, and Beth ... all of them ... they were absolutely right.

But I had the most powerful motivating force ever to grace mankind with its presence driving my thoughts: Fear.

I didn't want to risk having my eyes gouged out, my genitals sliced half off, my fingernails pulled out, and my abdomen sliced open; because that is exactly what I thought might happen if I failed in what they wanted me to do: To deal with a demon who seemed much smarter than I was.

I had felt his wrath (my back was still not close to healed) and his intentional transformation on that tree just one week prior was ample warning to me that this haunting might be a lot larger than we teenagers understood it to be.

We all cheer when tyrants fall, but rarely are we the ones who are tasked with the responsibility of making it occur. The brave men and women of the armed services are honorable enough to perform the risky – potentially deadly – work that the public lauds from their recliners as they watch their sports, soap operas, and music concerts, all the while asking what else can the government do to make life better for them.

Don't get me wrong, I didn't mind taking another hit for so noble a cause, it's just that in this case, I wasn't even sure I knew how to fight the battle.

The tape recorder is ready.

I gather my thoughts.

I begin.

"Hello Tommy. I kept my promise. I'm here. I'm trying to help you. If you'd like to say anything, I'm leaving this box on, right here, for approximately 15 minutes. All you have to do is speak; it will pick up your voice. At a later time, I can hear you on the tape, and hear what you said. In this way, I can speak to you. I'll come back tomorrow, around the same time. If you have left any questions for me, I'll answer them. As I said [deep breath] I'm trying to help. In order to help, I must know what your purpose is and why you are here. The remaining time is yours, Tommy. Go to it."

I take care to be respectful.

With the tape recorder still recording, we all leave the room. Jeff turns out the lights, and locks the lone door to B2B2 behind us.

He pulls up a chair collected from one of the common room's tables, wedges it under the door knob, and then sits down in front of it. He hands me the key. No human being is getting in, and no human being is getting out.

That shouldn't pose a problem for Tommy.

Beth and Linda accompany me back to C2D1. I am not enjoying the direction that things are heading, and they see that I am suffering. I understand that leaving with them poses a certain 'risk'. Both women were highly intelligent, humorous, attractive, and stacked with positive qualities. Most of the guys in the Erie Hall, on the campus in fact, would have jumped at the chance to date *either* one of them.

Under more normal circumstances, even with my extreme dedication to my running, I might have asked to date them. But the cold, hard truth was that I just wasn't ready for a relationship at that time. My faith was being sorely challenged, my academics were suffering to the point where I had gone from the dean's list to failing, and my body was still trying to recover from the month-old marks that now ran down my back. Adding the risk of a failed relationship on top of everything else was potentially too destructive. Though I was well known for gallivanting around the dorm in my birthday suit (perhaps to the point of obnoxiousness) I had yet to be with a woman.

No one knew that.

When I eventually confessed that truth to Paul, late in the fall semester, he seemed in near shock. To him my situation was analogous to purchasing an expensive sports car and then storing it in the garage, and never actually driving it. What was the point of being involved in a clothing-optional shower party with a bunch of hot college girls, if you simply dried off and walked away from it, empty handed? And while he ultimately respected my decision (or at the very least my willpower) it seemed counterintuitive to him.

The girls and I sit around inside C2D1 for about five minutes.

I am lying on top of my loft, enjoying the fact that I am with living, breathing company. Beth is sitting almost directly below me on the old brown couch underneath. Every once in a while, we shoot each other quick glances through the space that separates the loft and the wall. The space that I had reached down through a month earlier to get my pillow, the one the ghost wanted to take from me.

Linda is sitting, and smiling, at Jeff's desk as she inspects his many books, drawing utensils, and wall art. She expresses her regret at not being able to draw quite as well as she would like, but shares that she was proficient in many other areas of arts and crafts design.

Eventually, probably just to lighten the mood, one of the ladies suggests that we play a quick game of 'Truth or Dare'. I had heard of it, and knew it was often associated with things that got a person into trouble.

The idea has little appeal to me. Being coerced to share my most intimate thoughts and experiences is not my idea of an effective way to relax under the current conditions, nor do I want to risk getting arrested by doing something stupid.

As it turns out, the 'dare' part of the game was actually fun. At one of the ladies' request I re-create my infamous 'Ice Skate' Dance; the one that had gotten me written up by the Residence Director just a few months prior.

It was December 10th; I was blasting Adam Ant's song "Strip" from Paul's stereo, while jumping up on and off of the loft, and racing through the tile-floored hallways (between the C and B Buildings) chasing a pair of happily screaming girls while wearing a pair of ice skates around my neck.

And, eventually, just ice skates.

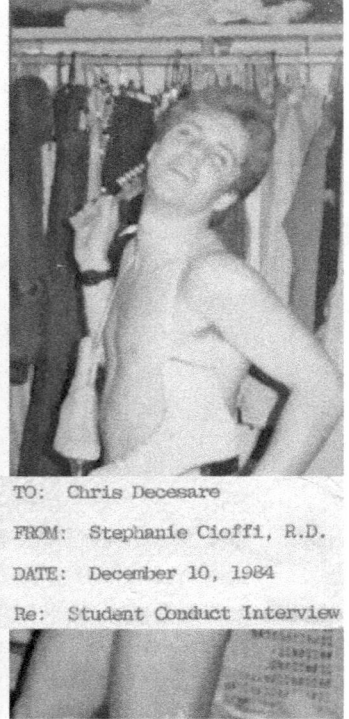

TO: Chris Decesare

FROM: Stephanie Cioffi, R.D.

DATE: December 10, 1984

Re: Student Conduct Interview

Above – Chris Di Cesare doing his initial 'Ice Skate' Dance for the girls in the B-Quad. The commotion that it caused would run him afoul of Erie Hall dorm authorities. Photographs – Linda Fox.

After some nervous and sincere pleading with the Residence Director, I was able to have the write up reduced to a 'noise violation' (akin to playing music too loudly or yelling too loudly at a party) so long as I promised not to do it again.

In 2011, Jeff would share: "My second year in the suite, Chris moved into C2D1 with Paul. I'm not the first guy to run out there and say "hey, how ya' doin'?" He was very friendly very outgoing. Not much in common at first blush. He was into running, he was seldom dressed. Almost spastic in an interesting way. His energy level was fun to watch, and it pulled me into his orbit."

Jeff, who just so happened to be studying at that time in the same area, was mistakenly called down as well, and he sat in the chair next to me, one leg nervously shaking up and down the entire meeting.

He was absolutely mortified.

We hastily fled the RD's office, with Jeff warning me that I'd better not get him caught up in any of my antics again.

As we turned the corner, I gave him an impish smile.

"Chris!"

I raced up the stairs, mooning him the whole way.

Accordingly, *this* time the Ice Skate Dance is done in the relative safety of my own dorm room, and Adam Ant's song "Strip", accompanies me at a very modest volume.

I keep my shorts on.

Our fifteen-minute diversion soon becomes a thirty-minute delay for Jeff, and when we realize that we had completely lost track of time I comment, "Jeff is gonna' *kill* us!"

As we hurry through the glass enclosed foyer that connects the B and C buildings collaborating on the creation of an effective alibi, I realize that I hadn't laughed this much in weeks.

There is talk of adding a third girl to our next 'Truth or Dare' session.

The following day this typed slip of paper was taped to my door:

-Chris: Shall we make it four?

We never did.

Jeff is standing in front of B2B2, an anxious look on his face, when we finally return to him. Since Jeff could not leave the doorway (potentially invalidating the experiment) in order to come get us, he had no choice but to wait it out.

"You *do* realize what time it is, right?" he remarks as I placed the room key into his eager palm.

Beth, Linda, and I make fleeting eye contact with each other, but none of us are able to utter a sensible reason as to why we are late. Beth is unable to contain a short burst of laughter as Jeff shoots her a look, and then anxiously unlocks the door.

The cold draft that blows out of the room immediately washes away the feelings of happiness and joy that I had been experiencing. I can't wait for all of this to be over.

Jeff begins to list, out loud for all of us to hear, the many changes in the room from the way we had left it: the desk chair is pulled out (like it had been in C2D1 when Paul noticed it); the tape recorder's position on the desk has been moved a few inches from where it had been placed; the room's temperature has dropped 6°F; and the closet door in the room is open.

We gather around the desk and listen as Jeff first stops the recording, then rewinds the tape, and finally hits 'play'.

The tape, from the first instance that we all hear it, has a rhythmic throbbing to it. This is no doubt due to the recorder itself. Dale Kaczmarek in his publication *Field Guide to Ghost Hunting Techniques* points out that: Many cassettes and digital units have built-in condenser microphones and while they are good for normal use, thy should probably not be used for EVP experiments as the sound of the motor and pulleys can often be recorded on the tape and can be impossible to separate from the ghost voices.

As sound as that advice is, we are oddly 'fortunate' in that the ghost's wailing voice – once it had begun to speak – was so clear and so distinct, that when it breathed into the recorder there was no mistake as to what it was, even with the internal sounds of the recorder: a voice.

It is odd hearing my voice on the tape as I was leaving Tommy the instructions. I can't help but wonder which was more accurate: the way my voice sounded in my head when I spoke, or the way it now sounds on the cassette tape?

For the first few minutes the tape recorder had only captured varying levels of static, the soft beat of the tape spinning in the old device and the occasional and recognizable squeak of the large door opening and closing in the common area of the building, about fifty feet away. In retrospect, given the mind-numbing boredom that might have resulted had we left the recorder on for hours, I was thankful that Jeff had decided to limit the taping to approximately fifteen minutes.

But then, more distinct sounds could be heard. Sounds made very close to the device's imbedded microphone. Having brought no papers, or surfaces to write on, I scoop up the cover of the cassette case and begin to record what I am hearing and what the 'count meter' reads as I hear it.

At '099' I hear what sounds like a draw(er) or window opening. I watch as Jeff moves around to the front of the desk, only to point out that the desk drawer had indeed been opened a few inches.

Markers '202' and '225' bring with them sounds that I associate with guttural noises.

I begin to lament where it is that I find myself: kneeling on the floor, in a dimly lit room, listening to static (and barely audible grunts). Why couldn't I be like the majority of the Geneseo college students and be doing virtually *anything* else?!

'247' yanks me right back into the moment. I can make out the sounds of a person talking. A lump in my throat forms because I recognize the voice! It is the voice that I had heard coming from the C2D1 closet. The voice that was pushing through Paul's headphones. It was the same voice that had called, "Chrissss" when I was working on my paper.

It is Tommy.

'253' occurs right after, and it is *far* worse.

"Hellllp ... meeee ..."

Dear God.

I drop to the floor, shaking my head back and forth, trying to cover my ears.

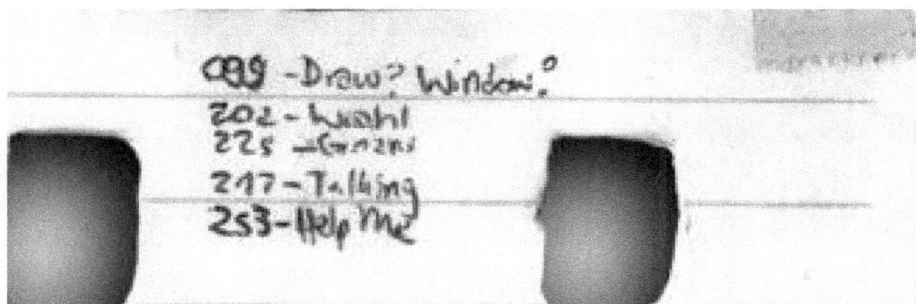

Above - The April 1985 tape recording session may represent one of the earliest recorded 'post-spiritualist' EVP – electronic voice phenomena - recordings in New York state. In 2010, the cassette's audio data was transferred to CD format by members of EiA Studios with an eye towards its long-term preservation.

Jeff is, with good reason, triumphantly pumping his fist in the air celebrating the impressive accomplishment. We had captured what today might be considered a 'Class A' EVP. Back then I simply called it 'horrible'.

"Turn it off!" I yell, "Turn it off!"

Jeff immediately stops the cassette tape playback. He looks thoroughly perplexed by my reaction.

"Don't you get it, Jeff? Don't you get it?", I plead.

I leave him no time to respond.

"The thing wants my help! I offered to help him, and now he actually *wants* my help!"

The room is completely silent for several seconds. The weight of the moment is finally catching up to the events themselves. A moment of choosing is inching its way towards all of us.

"That was the goal, wasn't it?" Jeff eventually interjects, correctly.

"Jeff … I don't know *how* to help it!"

The room falls silent again.

Beth and Linda now sit cross-armed, next to each other on the bed nearest the door. They look very afraid, and are clearly 'spooked' by the voice that they – that we *all* – had just heard on the tape.

I wish that we hadn't gotten them involved in all of this.

Only the sound of Jeff rhythmically tapping his pencil on his pant leg can now be heard. It reminds me of a metronome, keeping a steady beat that the rest of the instruments could then follow; a point of focus for each band member.

Here we sit, four young people who have just crossed into a place that none of us had expected, or could have imagined, we would.

We are communicating with a spirit.

Tommy has called my bluff.

The following Thursday I find myself back at the door of Dr. Casler. Alone.

I have no choice as I see it.

My hand was being forced by everyone around me. If I could no longer control my own destiny, then I felt that I should learn more about the one now being foisted upon me.

Dr. Casler had written a book in 1974 entitled, *Is Marriage Necessary?* in which he argued that many people got married because they wanted to avoid the social stigma of not being married, not necessarily because they benefitted from, or were satisfied with, monogamy.

In fact, he wrote an article in the December 1969 edition of *Psychology Today* in which he proffered that love was actually a 'disease' as it propagated an unhealthy dependency on someone else rather than on one's own individual maturity.

In addition, Casler had gained a measure of notoriety for his studies regarding nudist camps in the late 1960s as well. Among his findings, as recorded in the June 1969 issue of *Psychology Today,* were that male nudists typically did not get erections when viewing unclad bodies around them, and that this was largely due to the likelihood that the naked body can become deconditioned as a sexual stimulus if enough exposure was offered over time.

As much as I loved to run around au natural, Dr. Casler's ideas were still socially extreme to my way of thinking. Nor did I view marriage as a weakness or a 'disease'. To me, it was actually an ideal.

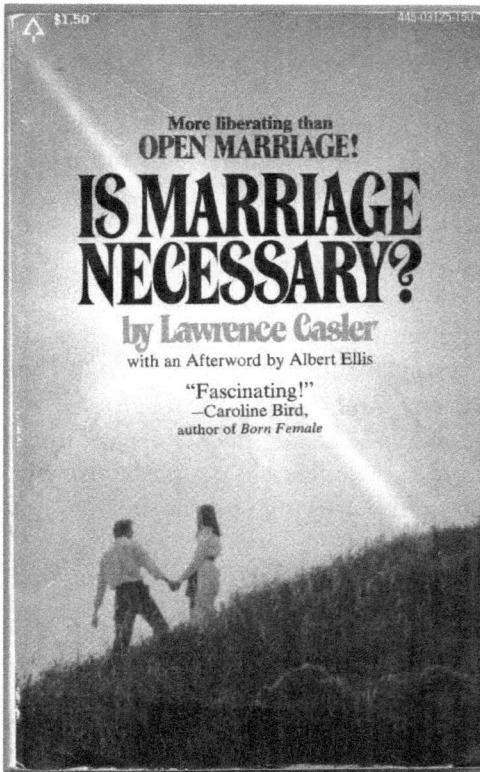

Left – The cover of one of Dr. Casler's books, Is Marriage Necessary? *Chris had no idea at that time how well known, or prolific a writer, Casler was.*

Had I been aware of any of this information that overcast April morning in 1985, I likely would not have been found knocking on his office door ten minutes before his office hours began. Which (looking back) would have been a shame, because I was about to learn a lot from him.

As I had imagined, Dr. Casler was pleasantly surprised to see me. He recalled my name immediately and promptly asked me to take a seat across from him in his office.

The subject had arrived.

In the mold of any decent clinician, he did not ask me how the experiments with the ghost were going, or about any of the evidence that had been presented to him the week prior by my friends and I.

He asked me, instead, if I had any questions for *him*.

I wasn't about to waste this opportunity, nor was I going to pull any punches. I wanted answers, and if he wanted something from me, I would get my answers first.

"Why," I asked him, waving my arms all about, "is all of this happening to me?"

"If what you are claiming is true, regarding seeing and hearing a ghost, then I would suggest that you are quite sensitive; sensitive to your environment in ways that most people are not."

'Sensitive' was the term that Lorraine Warren had used back in January, and the term that Jeff had used shortly thereafter. Now Dr. Casler is wielding it just as matter-of-factly as they did.

But wasn't everyone somewhat sensitive then? Just like the ability to draw, everyone has some level of talent, just some seem to have more than others. In a perfect (and fair) world everyone would be able to draw well, right?

"So, what you are saying is that, in a perfect world, everyone would be able to use their latent sensitivity to see ghosts?"

Dr. Casler pauses for a moment, perhaps my question catches him off guard. Or perhaps it is so far off of his prior statement that he needs time to figure out how to correctly redirect my thinking, my approach.

"I don't know if I would consider everyone seeing ghosts around them *perfect*, but it certainly would be fairer. There are certain people, those with severe emotional instabilities, that I would prefer not see ghosts."

A brilliant mind.

I sat quietly for a moment, reflecting on his words. He was implying that all of this … the ghost, the sensitivity … somehow fell inside the natural order of things, or perhaps at its very edge.

"Then tell me, if you can, how things like ESP or ghosts or precognition are able to be explained through the laws of nature. Science can't explain them, right?"

He was studying me, I could actually feel it.

He liked exercising minds, his own included.

Leaning back slightly in his chair he issued me a challenge: "How can you prove a boat, that you cannot see, is in the water?"

I recalled sitting in the back seat of my parent's car, looking out of the windows, as they drove over the Newburgh-Beacon Bridge (on Rt. 84) and watching the activity on the surface of the Hudson River far below us.

A wave of satisfaction rolled over me.

"The wake; a moving boat leaves a 'v-shaped' trail of waves behind it! Even if the boat had already passed from your line of sight, you could logically still account for its existence, and know that it is still there in the water because of its effect on the environment around it!"

Dr. Casler smiled for the first time.

Leaning forward onto his desk, as though he were about to reveal a trade secret, he said, "That same boat also displaces the water in front of it as it moves forward."

I continued listening.

"A person who is very sensitive can see the water level rise before the boat actually gets to them."

"Precognition!" I respond, in order to demonstrate my understanding.

He relaxed back into his chair, and began rifling through his desk drawers. He collected a neatly stacked deck of cards, then stated, "I want to try an experiment."

Above – Dr. Lawrence Casler, as he appears in this 1984 SUNY Geneseo Yearbook photo: back row, second from the right.

"No, I'm good," I countered placing my two hands, palm out, in front of me as a social shield.

The professor removed his black-rimmed glasses in order to clean them, and looking at me out of the corner of his eye he asked me what I was afraid of.

That was an easy question to answer.

"I've already failed at enough things this semester, and I don't want to embarrass myself in front of you, too."

"Let's just do a few," he replied in a soothing tone, "if nothing happens we'll just stop. What do you say?"

Each (Zener) card was blank on one side and had a shape on the other.

The object was for me to determine what card he was holding up to his forehead, as he concentrated on it. Once I had offered up a guess, he would then proceed to draw the next card off the top of the pile, which sat face down in front of him on the desk.

Fortunately, the experiment moved with greater rapidity than I had expected, because by the tail end of it, I was simply calling out 'circle' and 'wavy lines' and 'square' … whatever … at random.

When we finished Dr. Casler did not speak for some time. This delay was unnerving.

"Did I get them all wrong?" I finally asked.

He looked up, adjusted his glasses, and replied: "Actually, yes *and* no. Your answers were incorrect for almost every single card."

Failure. I knew it.

I had warned him not to do the experiment. Well *this* was a grand waste of time.

Without looking up again, he began to make a series of straight-lined pencils strokes on his paper and said: "But what I *am* seeing here is a very strong case of positive step (or positive one-step) progression."

"Is that good?"

"Well, it is neither good nor bad inherently; those are labels that I try to avoid using. What it *is*, however, is extremely rare."

He then held up his sheet of paper to show me his marks.

"You managed to predict the next card, the card on *top* of the deck, accurately in five of the first seven cases. That is a remarkable result."

I paused.

Son of a gun, I thought to myself, apparently, I *was* somewhat sensitive.

Lorraine Warrens' statement from the presentation, almost two months ago, once again runs through my mind like an echo: "There is a Law of Attraction; ghosts are attracted to compassionate or sympathetic people."

People like me.

Perhaps she and Jeff, and now Dr. Casler, were right: Maybe I did have one of those flashing (psychic) neon signs, the ones that read 'Room Available', shining brightly above my head.

The question now was: How the heck do I turn it 'off'?

28. Resolution

Above – Negative strip, Geneseo in 1984. The tree image was one of Ungar's favorites.

April 12th, 1985. I sit alone inside of C2D1 watching the misty rain that has washed away the final remnants of the snow that had fallen earlier in the week.

I watch as the other students pause, in order to open their umbrellas, and then begin walking towards some destination that I know *has* to be better than where I am. The soft tapping of clear, shimmering, rain drops creates a moving and melodic tapestry on the outside of my dorm room window. I am reminded of the droplet of water that had fallen from my outstretched wrist and onto the bathroom floor just over a month ago.

Rain.

Water.

Life.

The air temperature has climbed in the mid-fifties; the exact type of weather that I used to love running in.

New Zealand's Rod Dixon won the 1983 New York Marathon in this type of weather. Dixon had overtaken (future two-time Boston marathon winner) Geoff Smith in the last few yards of the race by running the tangents, zig-zagging across the roadway in straight lines, cleverly chopping off distance from the course.

Smith, who had bravely led the race for over ten miles, dutifully stared down at the long blue line that ran down the middle of the road, unaware that Dixon was closing in behind him. Unaware that Dixon was about to snatch victory from him, with the finish line in sight, because he, Smith, had 'mistakenly' run the entire distance.

I wonder who I would have been in that scenario, the cleverly strategic Dixon who had won, or the bravely honorable Smith who had lost. I wonder how many times those people who took the short cuts in life 'won', and how many times those people who dedicated themselves to what was actually correct, 'lost'.

Wiping away the fog that my warm breath has created on the window, I can see the bones inside my fingers illuminated by the light streaming into the chilly dorm room.

Then a second thought consumed me. People spend so much time on their appearance (hairstyles, makeup, tanning, working out, plastic surgery) literally countless hours of their lives, and all the while – hidden inside – is the skeleton that no one sees. Ironically, when their physical bodies are eventually consumed by the earth, only that, now invisible, skeleton will be left visible.

Until time eats that away too.

Almost two months later, I'm still not sure why Tommy appeared as a skeleton in that photograph. He didn't look like that when I had taken the shot. Dr. Casler suggested that the ghost might have been in the process of forming (from orb, to shadow, to skeleton, to full appearance) and that had I waited a bit longer to take the picture, he might have appeared as though having flesh, full-bodied.

Still, I worry that there might be more to it than that. The skull and crossbones has been a symbol of death for many centuries; I want to avoid death.

The song, *Nightshift*, by the Commodores is playing when I turn on Jeff's boom box. There is something healing about the song, the sounds of it make me feel better. I had even remarked to Jeff – a week or so earlier – that whatever sound was used in the song (maybe an open 'E' chord), it seemed to have a calming effect on Tommy, who I could sense around the edges of the room, as well. The song is now climbing up the charts, so I have the opportunity to listen to it often.

Above - A cassette tape cover made by Di Cesare in 1989 that featured his favorite songs during his time as a student at SUNY Geneseo. Note that the song Nightshift appears on the Side B listings. Images of Di Cesare and of Haley's Comet and President Ronald Reagan round out the cassette cover.

At the time, I had no idea who 'Marvin' and 'Jackie' were, and I thought that the term 'nightshift' was being made in reference either to people working the midnight shift, or to a comedic movie that I had once heard reference to.

Looking back all these years later, an ode to the departed Marvin Gaye and Jackie Wilson, and reference to the 'nightshift' (being Heaven or the concept of a connected and positive afterlife), I understand now how the song might have been both appealing and healing to anyone, especially during an extreme haunting.

The sound of passing laughter from a group of female students, outside my window, jolts me back from my peaceful moment. Glancing about my room, I see Tommy's face, pushing through the wall, approximately three feet from what is now Jeff's closet. Blood leaks from his mouth as he silently moves it.

I close my eyes.

I am being reminded that I am still a prisoner in my own room.

According to Albert Camus, nothing was more despicable than respect based on fear. Apparently, he never had to face what I am now facing.

My dream, eight days later, is a horrific one. Resembling, in many ways, Michelangelo's fresco, *Last Judgment*. In it, I watched as people that I knew were falling, one by one, into the burning fires of hell below them.

They called out to me, asking for my help, begging for assistance, as their skin began to melt away. All the while, I sat strapped to the darkness, unable to grasp their hands or allay their fear of the pain that we knew surely awaited them.

I woke up with a start, breathing heavily, and sweating to the extent that my forehead, neck and torso are soaked with moisture. My fingers and toes are ringing with an energetic numbness, even when I move them, and my throat is parched to a sting.

At the moment, I squint over, the clock switches to 3:33; Make a wish!

I look for Jeff, and then remember that his parents had called him back home for some family event. The type that he loathed.

"Typical" had been his initial response to this change in his plans.

Not knowing what it was, I wipe some recently-crusted blood from the right corner of my mouth. A high-pitched noise gnaws at my brain.

Damn.

This *has* to end.

The room echoes with a nauseating silence, and I cannot fall back asleep. In fact, I don't want to fall back asleep, afraid that the nightmare will begin again if I do.

The thought of still more of my friends suffering under the weight of the haunting is agonizing, and I begin to wonder if Tommy was warning me that he was about to set his sights on them next.

Shortly before 4 AM, with my body still drenched in a sickly sweat and feeling drained, I decide to climb up out of the loft and start my day a few hours earlier than I had planned.

When my two feet land firmly on the dorm room floor, I reach over for the towel that I had placed on the back of my desk chair the night before, wrap it loosely around my neck and shoulders. I want to conceal the still visible marks on my back. I head for the shower.

The hallway light had been turned off, so that when I push open the heavy wooden door, my sleepy eyes are immediately blinded by the bright light that comes pouring out of the bathroom.

As they begin to adjust, I can see that the room has an occupant.

Standing by the sink to the right, wearing a pair of dark sunglasses and a towel of his own, Craig Norris is shaving his face ... at four in the morning.

This was typical 'atypical' Craig.

My first thought is that he has come back from a long night out on the town, and after drinking too much, had simply found himself in the wrong bathroom at this most unfriendly of hours.

But then, that would make too much sense. This was Craig Norris that we were dealing with.

Craig was the possibly most intense person that I had ever met. He always seemed to be on the move, shifting from one arduous activity to the next. His light blue eyes felt like they cut into you when he turned his attention to you. Craig was so intense that he, at times, actually scared some people away. Not that he ever seemed to mind, it was all too easy to get bored talking with the same person for too long anyway.

I recall that during the prior fall semester I had seen him sitting in one of the cushioned chairs in the large common area. As three of the ladies from the 'A' building walked past – yammering on about which name brand jeans were currently the 'ones to wear' – Craig hopped right into their conversation and lambasted them from paying extra for a pair of jeans in order to advertise for someone else.

"They should be paying *you* to wear them! You're doing *them* a favor!" he smiled as they scurried off to the safety of anywhere else.

Craig Norris grew up in a commune during the 1970's, with the music of the Grateful Dead as a constant background sound. It was an upbringing so unlike my own, an approach to life so foreign to mine, that I typically worked to (politely) avoid him whenever I could.

He could talk about the arts, society, capitalism, sports, the environment, politics, citizenship and teamwork as much as Jeff could. But it was usually in a way that was designed to challenge his listener(s) very concept of the world around them; to force growth in them wherever and whenever possible.

Above - Craig Norris was the most intense, and fascinating, person that Di Cesare claimed to have met while in college. Craig was known for approaching strangers in the hallways and commenting on their conversations. - Photograph by J. Jeff Ungar, 1984.

I hadn't seen much of Craig since the first few weeks of the fall semester when he and Ed and Jeff had been temporarily 'tripled up' in room C2D2, one room beyond my own in the quad layout.

Craig had found a new location to live by early October: across the second floor. Appearances became a rare occurrence after that move.

Why he is now in the D-Quad bathroom, and why he is wearing a pair of dark sunglasses while shaving in the mirror at four in the morning, I cannot say.

I would find out, a few days later, from Jeff that Craig and a friend were heading out for a sunrise hike not long after I saw him.

Stepping around him, I hung up my towel on the metal rack inside the stall, pulled off my pair of red jogging shorts, and then let the warm shower water soothe me. I breathe out as the nervous sweat is washed off of my heated skin.

Craig must notice this because, to my vexation, moments later he sticks his half-shaven face past the new (and still useless) replacement shower curtain, and asks me if I am OK.

"Yup, I'm good."

"You don't seem good."

Why is this happening? Why am I being questioned here in the shower at four o'clock in the morning by a guy who doesn't even live here? And why is he wearing a pair of sunglasses?

"I'm sorry if I don't seem good," I grunt, attempting unsuccessfully to pull the skimpy shower curtain back in between us.

"Everybody is talking about your ghost," he says, "You need to do something about it."

My ghost? *I* need to do something about it?

"What!? Are you saying all this is my fault? That it's some kind of ... poltergeist?"

My reactionary question to his statement is actually borne of my own fears from early on in the haunting. The movie *Firestarter*, starring Drew Barrymore and David Keith, had hit the theaters less than a year prior, and had brought the concept of poltergeist activity to water coolers and mall food courts across America.

Poltergeists were suggested to be a form of psychokinetic energy, often manifesting in teenagers who are going through puberty (which I recently had), or who are unable to deal with the frustrations or pressure of life as they move towards adulthood (which I thought I had been doing, until the ghost happened). It was also purported that the young person displaying this psychic feat might actually be unaware of being its source.

The now-scabbing vertical lines that run down my back from neck to waist seem proof enough to me that the source remains external.

I hope that Craig does not notice them.

Craig sticks his head back into the shower stall.

"Honestly, Chris, I don't know *what* it is. Jeff thinks it's a spirit that followed you home from one of your long runs in the country side. Paul thinks it's definitely a lost soul who has its sights trained on you. But it doesn't matter who is right or wrong if the people around you – if you – are constantly suffering. Does it?"

"No."

"You need to stop running from this and deal with it. If you don't, you're going to continue to run from everything in your life. This is a chance to become the person that you are supposed to be. You can't rely on others to do it for you. Your dad isn't going to be able to see you through this, the priest either."

He places a hand upon my shoulder.

"You have been hiding your whole life; hiding behind your looks, your running exploits, your sense of humor. You have to stop hiding, Chris. *You* are going to have to take care of this, my friend."

Looking at his face, now covered with droplets from the shower spray, I examine his eyes.

At some point in time he must have removed the glasses. They are not eyes filled with anger, or judgment, or any tinge of disappointment. Rather, his eyes are filled with concern. Concern for me.

While still facing him, I reach back, turn the water off, and ask him: "What should I do?"

"What do you want to do. Chris?"

I want to run, to leave Geneseo.

I want to pretend that none of this had ever happened. I want to once again be the golden-haired boy next door that every girl's mother wants them to marry. I want to be the athlete that makes the sports headlines in their local newspaper. I want to be the son who makes his parents proud by doing well in college. I want to be the person that I used to be; the person that I no longer was. I want this thing gone!

"I want to face it."

"Then *do* it."

. . .

I am going to face whatever it is. I am going to face Tommy.

. . .

As I reach down for my clothing, Craig instructs me to leave it behind. He feels that this should be an opportunity for honest communication, and that wearing clothing is not honest. He posits that putting my shorts back on would be like wearing a mask, and masks stifle communication.

"You go in the way God made you. Chris. Bare both your body and your soul to that thing. Talk to it, and get this done!"

Left – This fascinating photograph, taken by J. Jeff Ungar, in the spring of 1985 shows Di Cesare and Craig Norris (often polar opposites in their viewpoints) running in opposite directions. Ironically, the traffic sign in the photo is pointing in Craig's 'direction', which is what Chris eventually ended up taking early on April 14th, 1985.

Although I am uneasy with his suggestion, I trust Craig. I trust his ideas. I trust the concern in his eyes.

After silently nodding to Craig, and wearing only a worried look upon my face, I cautiously walk across the hall.

The cynical portion of my mind (that initially wanted to view this haunting as some type of practical joke) figures that Craig is probably getting a kick out of watching my bare ass walk across the hallway.

By any reasonable standard, my current action certainly creates an unusual site.

Before I enter, I nervously turn back to Craig, who has by now picked my red running shorts off of the bathroom floor, and say: "If something happens to me, just let my family know that I *wanted* to do this."

He nods. His intense eyes urge me forward.

I enter the dark room.

Closing the door to C2D1 behind me serves to shut out the light from the bathroom, and along with it my only obvious physical connection with the living.

The date is April 14th, 1985. It is 4:30AM and I am standing, seemingly alone, in the middle of my own room.

I understand very well that the night, and the darkness, belong to him.

The residual droplets of water from the preparatory shower, that had only recently warmed me to my core, are now instead stealing away my body heat. Silent beads of chilled liquid are running down the nape of my neck, my still-wounded back, and the back of my tightening legs from my still-soaked head of hair.

I cannot help but to shiver.

I also cannot help but think to back to the day I thought I would die, on that bathroom floor, forty days ago.

Amazingly, forty days and forty nights had gone by since March 10th, when I had studied that one mind-restoring droplet of water, the one that clung to my wrist in hopes of hanging onto me forever. Now, with more drops of water running down my shivering body, I had to hope that I could convince this dead thing it too could not hold on forever, that it too would need to 'let go' of me, and 'let go' of all of us.

There is but one candle in the room, and it isn't even mine. Beth or Linda or Judy must have brought it over on one of their visits to make the room smell nice for some last-minute party, probably the one for Valentine's Day. The kind of parties we often had before things became terrible.

My still wet fingers are slippery and cold and make it difficult to light the candle; the drops of water from the bangs on my forehead nearly put the flame out once it is lit. Carefully placing the candle on the floor in the center of the open area, and as close to the center of the room as I can discern, I kneel down beside it.

The hard floor hurts my knees.

Additionally, the slight upward curl of my toes against the floor has me recalling, the only too recent shower attack and its gruesome aftermath.

I do not want to die here.

The 'Our Father' (Lord's Prayer) rolls off my tongue with such a practiced ease that I am left wondering if I had rendered it completely ineffective by not having concentrated on its delivery. I decide to say it a second time, carefully pronouncing and emphasizing each word, with obvious intention this time.

That's much better; it was time.

I cleared my throat: "I know you can hear me."

My soft voice eases through the still room: "I can sense you all around. You are being invited back in this room, against the priest's Blessing."

As my ears listen for the slightest hint of movement, my eyes scan attentively around the dimly lit room. I want to avoid the panic that can be induced through surprise. Too many times had I awoken in my bed only to see that dead face hovering above my own.

Running had taught me that preparation can reduce the chances, and the effects, of such surprise.

I want to be prepared.

The squealing of the heavy wooden bathroom door outside of my room tells me that Craig is leaving the area. I wonder if he was the last person that I will ever see, and if he will remember this insane day.

God, protect me … please.

The waiting continues.

I am fighting against the continued impulse to run. It would be so very easy to grab some clothing from my dresser (or not to) and take a well-needed rest in the common area. I can always cover myself with one of the couch cushions, I reason, should I opt not to take the time needed to dig through my drawers.

Don't be a coward.

The fire atop the wick of the candle is snuffed out as liquid wax engulfs it. I smell the wisps of smoke in the air as the room darkens. Only a scant amount of bluish light, an extension of the moon's gaze creeping through the window's blinds, remains to help me see into the shadows.

The base of my neck and the top of my ears are the first areas to notice the plunging temperature. The chill breeze that advances closer from the area of the closets would have blown the candle out had it still been lit.

Not wanting to be seen in a weak and submissive kneeling pose, I stand up as I prepare for his imminent arrival; for his first and hopefully only 'formal' visit.

Standing, the stinging cold air washes over the front half of my body, causing the muscles in my torso and abdomen to tighten beyond comfort.

The water in the corners of my eyes is ice cold against the warmer lids when I blink.

I can see him!

The dark gray soft-edged shadow – which is distorted and elongated – precedes a darker, more defined human shape. It slides across the wall to my right, disappearing behind the loft's front edge.

After taking a quick, tense step in that direction I am stopped in my tracks by the sight of a face, eye level with my own, and mere inches to my left.

My solar plexus heaves, as I draw in a nervous breath and steal back several feet.

It is not moving. It just stands there, wet blood on its face, neck, chest; arms glistening in the faint light, like dim blue stars in the heavens.

To Craig Norris' eternal credit, the ghost is standing just as naked as I am, and looking a lot like I had seen him on that tree outside the suite window. Maybe he had not been tormenting me back then, maybe this is how he actually looked.

It begins to open its damaged mouth.

Stomach acid races up into my closed mouth, but I swallow the reflux back down into my unhappily stinging throat.

"Help me ... Chrissss."

The words, and the voice that speak them, are very familiar to me by now. However, with a visible form now attached to them they are slightly less haunting and infinitely more powerful! Things have now moved from the realm of the potential to the world of reality.

It is time to speak my piece, while I still have the chance to.

"I have no idea why you had to choose me. You had to know that I didn't want any part of this. I was happy before you stole my happiness and my sanity, before you damaged my faith."

I try to invoke some level of measured anger in my voice, but can only share a palpable sadness.

"Pain ... soooooooo much pain," he rasps out of this mouth, "made ... a missstake ..."

His suffering looks real; both the terrible wounds to his body and the anguish in his voice are strong testimony to it. I can now discern what I think are tears running down his cheeks, and down past where a part of his nose should be.

Remembering advice from Jeff that questions which provided detailed answers were far better than those that invited an open-ended response, I ask: "Who are you, where are you from?"

I am careful not to invoke the name of 'Tommy' as I face him, as it occurs to me that it might not be correct, and I do not want to offend it, or to make any kind of mistake, with it so close to me.

Its head moves forward unnaturally on its neck, as though on invisible rollers, or its movements are faster than my sight can perceive.

The face contorts wildly.

It is gasping for precious air that is clearly not traveling easily between its mouth and lungs. With a wail that sounds like it comes from a parent who had just lost their child, he cries out.

"Dannnnnvilllle ..."

My young hands clench into nervous fists, and I turn my narrow runner's hips (ever so slightly) towards the room's door.

I am ready to run, but he does not attack.

His face and shoulders are marginally wider than mine, but he doesn't look as intimidating as I had worried he might in spite of the many open wounds. His hair, though matted down with what appears to be blood, is minimally darker than my own.

This matches. This the same thing, the same person, that had been watching me in the gymnasium showers just days before. The one that the skinny kid with the acne had also seen. Everything matched: the voice, the appearance, the actions.

This is Tommy!

I consider my final question, as he sways slightly in front of me. I need to understand why all of this is happening, it's not enough to just know that it is. This is too important.

"Why are you here?"

His head tilts further to the side than I have ever seen before. It reminds me of the ghost photograph and of the dark shadow that had haunted Paul and I back in February.

He shares:

"Misssstake ... made ... misssstake. Was wrong ... sssssooooo wrong."

A guttural coughing sound is accompanied by a sudden convulsion that spews more blood down his face.

As I cover my own mouth, I am thanking God that there is no foul, rotting, stench in the air; the kind of stench that likely enveloped Gettysburg, PA after that horrendous and decisive Civil War battle.

Rather, the air around him smells crisply clean and fresh like an ice chest or cooler might. The dark blood that I anticipate will have spattered the floor, possibly freezing my already cold and wet feet in place, is nowhere to be seen.

The ghastly site of his intestines slowly spilling out of his body, and his half-severed other parts, are also not fully visible in this moment. It is as though everything below his rib cage is currently moving between here and someplace else, represented now only by what seems to be an electrically-charged swirling mist.

I am encouraged to stay.

"You asked for my help, and I am going to give it to you: You need to leave. You can't stay here. You're hurting my friends. You're hurting me. You have to let go and believe that you can find forgiveness."

The figure remains still, save for some labored breathing.

With ears that I cannot see, I 'know' that it hears me; that it understands me.

I feel sad.

I feel sad for *him.*

I continue: "You have to believe that there is someone out there who loves you, who forgives you."

He extends a gnarled but still youthful-looking hand out towards me.

Above – Outside the C Building of Erie Hall where the tree, that Chris saw Tommy hanging from, used to stand. Screen capture provided by EiA Studios.

It almost looks like my hand, but mine has never fired a musket or a rifle.

I do not receive it.

Instead, I pull both arms behind my body and clasp my hands together near the base of my chilled back. I can feel the microscopic blond hairs located there standing on end.

I don't want to become attached to him in any way.

No.

His way will not work.

I decide: "You have to go; you just can't stay here anymore. I am sorry. I really am."

At that moment, Tommy groans an ever more pitiful sound. The candle by my left foot suddenly erupts with a high flame. Fearing the well-worn section of the rug it rests upon will catch fire, I crouch down to blow it out.

But there is no fire, and no flame.

The candle is dark and cold.

In that lowered position, I begin my count. The count that goes from one to ten. The count that I am so familiar with, and the count that did not work when the ghost first appeared. This time it *has* to work, or I will be without answers, and without a plan.

If that happens then this dead thing will once again be living in my room with me.

Finishing my count, I keep my eyes closed tightly shut.

There is silence.

Then warmth.

Then a calming sensation.

It is then that a wave of grief sweeps over me, and I burst out into tears because I instinctively know that his soul has gone, and I don't know if it will be in a better place.

When Jeff returned the following day (tax-filing day), with the temperatures soaring to a record-setting 75°F, he immediately inquired about the changes in the room.

They were the same changes that I too had noticed, several hours earlier, when I had opened my eyes after a much-needed long and restful sleep. The first such sleep since my father had visited several weeks earlier.

In what would have certainly constituted an unacceptable safety risk, I had been sleeping on my back, my hands clasped behind my head, with one of my feet protruding out from the bed sheets.

On this morning, though, there was no fear of the ghost breathing in the warm breath from my mouth into his, or of his ice-cold fingers running along the relaxed flesh on the side of my foot.

The ghost was gone!

(Again).

I cast off the smooth, body-warmed, wrinkled, cotton bed sheets and hopped down the loft's ladder. The dark sense of foreboding, some of which had survived even the priest's Blessing, was no longer present.

Maybe it had worked, I thought to myself, maybe I had truly sent the ghost away!

Kneeling on the old, worn couch, I opened up the blinds and curtains. The bright, glowing, late-morning light streamed into the room. I smiled the smile of a victory won, even if it might prove to be a temporary one.

My over-anxious fingers unfastened the 'eternally locked' window, and the warm spring air that rushed in to caress my eager body, smelled of life and hope and possibility.

I remain there, breathing it all into my starved lungs for several long minutes; kneeling winter-pale inside the glorious golden rays. Practically daring someone to see me in this unclad moment of supreme triumph.

I had earned this.

Minutes later, with order now restored, the thought that all of this had been some type of unreal nightmare wandered itself across the landscape of my mind; like it always did and probably always will.

To appease my never-ending sense of curiosity, I unlocked and opened the door of C2D1, crept quietly across the empty hallway, and slowly slid open the heavy bathroom door.

I turned my body to the left; there they were, the remnants of those one, two, three long scratches.

It had happened.

It had happened.

It had happened.

Returning to the comfort of my room, I sat down onto my solid wood desk chair and ran through the most recent events, trying to recall how on Earth the horrid ordeal had finally come to an end.

Then I remembered: Craig Norris!

Craig had butted his nose into my shower, and his sage advice into my subsequent actions.

I had to smile.

It figured that the man who was known for thinking outside of the box would help me find the key to opening mine.

I also had to smile because he had apparently made off with my favorite pair of running shorts, the red ones that I had left on the floor of the bathroom the eventful night before.

But even if, in the worst-case scenario, Craig had simply wanted to score a quick laugh at the sight of me walking butt-ass naked across the hallway, or if he needed an extra pair of running shorts for his hike, his plan had worked beyond my wildest expectations.

"What happened," Jeff asked as he dropped some items he had brought with him from his home on his desk, "why does everything feel so different in here?"

I watched as he summoned forth the talents of all five senses in an attempt to determine the multitude of possibilities. It was an aspect of his personality, the desire to understand, that I hoped he would never lose.

It had helped to save my life, and I was thankful to him for it.

He squinted his light blue eyes, switched his mouth from side-to-side, and then announced, "The room feels like it's back to normal!"

Working on a new art project at my desk, and wanting to get a rise out of the normally unflappable Jeff Ungar, I did not answer.

"All right," he continued, "if you are not going to tell me, then I guess that I just won't know."

He unpacked the rest of his belongings, adjusted his collared shirt, and sat himself at his desk thumbing impatiently through book after book after book.

I could feel his polite level of tension rising.

He opened up his spiral notebook, and began twirling his pencil between his fingers.

Still, I said nothing.

Wait for it.

"Oh, come on! This isn't fair!" he kindly protested, "You're *really* not going to tell me?"

I then unleashed my widest, toothiest, grin and he understood that I had just been teasing him.

Holding up a few pages of a comic book that I had just begun, I offered, "What do you think of this?"

Jeff studied the hastily drawn panels, lightly stroking his goatee with his fingers.

"Hmmm. These two lads look familiar. They look like *us*," Jeff remarked seemingly pleased with the quality of the artwork, "what is it about?"

He nodded his head in approval.

"Cool! It's good that you could tell it was *us* so quickly," I replied, "We have just been transported through a dimensional vortex, and into a dark abyss."

"Does my character, at least, have some inkling as to what is happening," Jeff asked, immediately invested in the potential of the piece.

"You get to observe as I get tossed around by the energies inside the vortex," I replied, hoping to get another rise out of him.

"How typical," he grumbled with a purposeful smile on his face, "Once again I can only *watch* the exciting stuff."

"Exactly," I continued, trying to up the ante, "Notice how most of my clothes get ripped off?"

Jeff considers this.

"You *do* realize that the scenario in your comic plays out in similar fashion to the whole ghost situation, right?"

"I do."

Above — Section of page two of the comic strip drawn by Di Cesare on April 15th, 1985; the morning after he had spoken with 'Tommy', the ghost of Erie Hall.

In fact, the comic (which, looking back, has the worst lettering job ever) was my first attempt at dealing with, trying to explain both to myself and others, what had happened during those terrifying ten weeks. It was just a start, but it was a safe and very important first step in what would become a lifetime journey for understanding.

"Have you seen the ghost, lately?" Jeff astutely asked, watching my reaction, "You seem noticeably more relaxed now."

I placed the comic, which I knew I would never finish, down onto my desk.

"I will tell you what happened soon. I promise. I just need some more time to verify things first."

Three days later, on the evening of April 18th, I began sharing with my roommate, the person who would be the Best Man at my wedding four years later, what had occurred several days prior.

Jeff sat, and listened intently for several hours, all the while recording my latest encounter; writing of the time when the Ghost Boy of Geneseo had set a spirit to rest.

It was a tale that, soon enough, would begin to tell itself.

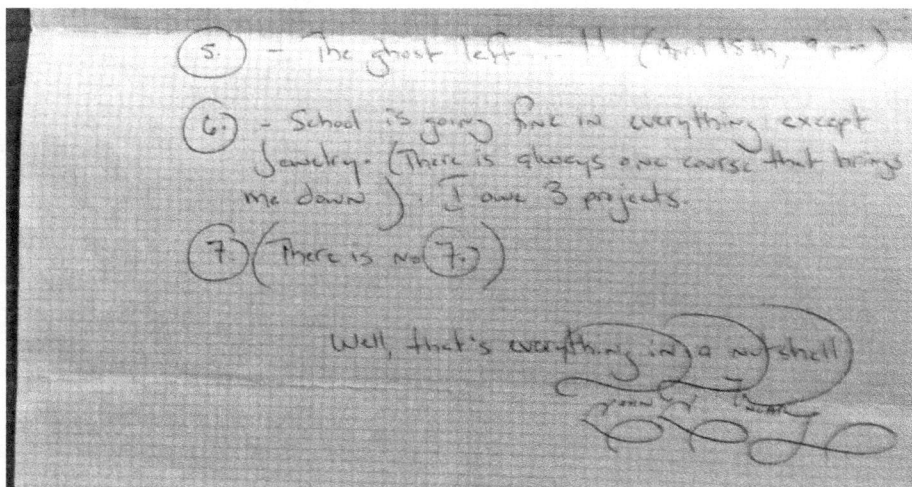

Above — The second page of a letter J. Jeff Ungar wrote to his mother on April 29th. In it he mentions Di Cesare's confirmation, on April 18th, that the ghost had left.

Over the next few weeks — my last at Erie Hall — I rededicated myself to my academics, and was able to obtain a passing grade in all of my classes.

But the haunting had left indelible footprints. Footprints that I, even standing at the center of the haunting, would not begin to understand — or follow — for several decades.

Several newspaper reporters arrived on campus around this time, investigating stories of a 'boy who could talk with ghosts'. With the haunting now finally over (as far as I could tell) I didn't want to take the risk of talking about it publicly. My fears were that it might prevent me from moving on with my life or potentially lead to a rash of 'copycat' incidents in which someone else might actually get hurt.

I chose to make myself 'invisible' to the newsmen.

Whenever a reporter found his way to my vicinity I would hide behind trees, crouch behind mailboxes, and sneak around the corners of buildings.

As I mentioned, I almost talked with one reporter, he seemed sincerely interested in the actual people behind the dark rumors. I wasn't ready yet.

Jeff would be with me, on several occasions, when people pointed and announced to their curious friends: "Look! There's the ghost boy, that's *him!*" Or when a random person would come up to our door and either accuse me of worshipping the devil or to ask me, "If you are Jesus, then who am I?"

Much of my spare time in the days following the haunting I spent reading about Geoff Smith's recent victory at the 1985 Boston Marathon, where he had hung on to win (for the second consecutive year) in the intense heat while battling severe leg cramps.

It inspired me to try and return to competitive running shape.

Losing the fifteen or so pounds that I did during the haunting (while completely unintentional) made running easier than I had originally anticipated. Without the physical and emotional drain of the ghost dragging me down, I found that I was just as fast as I had been the prior autumn. It was a relief knowing that the haunting had not stolen that from me as well.

The weather had been nice all week as the semester was inching its way towards a welcome close, and Jeff, perhaps sensing that I needed the emotional lift, asked me to put on my red, white-lettered, NCAA shirt (that he knew I was extremely proud of) and a pair of running shorts so that he could test out his newest camera lens.

He wanted to take some shots of me running on campus.

I was more than happy to oblige.

Other than the fact that the impromptu photo shoot aggravated the cuts on my back (for which Jeff later apologized profusely) I found the exercise refreshing.

Still, there was a part of me that feared I would never be 'normal' again.

I had been alone in a crowd for far too long, and was no closer, in spite of months of hardship and suffering, to understanding why it had all happened.

Above – Negatives of photographs taken by J. Jeff Ungar of Chris Di Cesare running down the steep-hilled road on the east side of Erie Hall. The Milne Library, where Ungar first examined the ghost photos, can be seen in the background at right.

I continued to ask myself, "Why me?"

As mentioned previously, Jeff had developed quite a few interesting theories as the haunting progressed. We also discussed topics such as the potential intertwining of history and numerology, and Jeff even pointed out early on that the Spiritualist Movement was said to have begun (at the Fox Household in nearby Hydesville, NY) on Friday, March 31, 1848. March 31 just happened to be my birthday.

In any event, I decided that it might be healthier to put the whole ordeal aside now and then, rather than allowing it to consume my every waking thought.

In what was an apparent celebration of Arbor Day (the precursor to Earth Day) Jeff, Don Hunt, and a few of the Erie Hall girls and I made a trip down to Letchworth State Park, 'The Grand Canyon of the East'.

The laughter, the joking, the running water, the fresh air made it feel as though - for the first time in a very long while - my body was healing.

I watched as my friends climbed the tree-lined slopes, hopped across some large stones that made it possible to cross the running waters on tributary streams, and helped each other around protruding bushes.

"This is how life is supposed to be." I thought to myself.

The notable contrast between the months spent in a cold, dimly lit, whispering, haunted room and the sound of my friends' laughter amongst the smell of sprouted grass in the mild spring air was tangible.

For my part, I immediately sprinted into the nearest wooded area, doffed my garments, and flitted about like a carefree, golden-hued, dragonfly.

Moving from location to location with apparent abandon, moving only when the prodded on by the nearest sign of unsuspecting people.

Above – Cavorting carefree inside of Letchworth State Park. The photo was taken just twelve days after the close of the C2D1 Haunting. Photograph by Don Hunt

Eventually Jeff tracked me to an expansive field of leafy greenery, where I had been sitting on my bottom, using a portion of a discarded tree branch as a flute in my Sylvan utopia.

When I was, inevitably, asked by someone about the scratches that still appeared on my shirtless back, I responded with a cocky and pre-meditated: "You know how wild those college girls are!"

Cue the wink.

Jeff preferred to offer the hysterical response that one of our suitemates had concocted that – somehow – I had been attacked by a mother wolverine, while in the act of protecting her 'wolvelets'.

Classic.

May 15th, 1985 was the last day that Jeff and I lived in Erie Hall.

Underneath the broad smiles and sincere hugs there was a palpable sadness in saying goodbye to Beth, Judy and Linda, 'the girls', as Paul and I – and eventually Jeff – had called them.

The truth of the matter was that I had grown closer to them than I had to any other non-related females to that point in my life. Traumatic situations can do that. And there was a shared sense (in spite of that) this was likely going to be a long-term, perhaps permanent, farewell.

I suppose it came down to the fact that we all needed time to decompress, to reflect, and to heal before we could think about furthering friendships that were forged in such a widespread and all-encompassing flame.

Above – Di Cesare, pictured with Judy Y., Linda Fox, and Beth Kinsman during the winter and spring of 1985 at SUNY Geneseo. – Photographs courtesy of Linda Fox.

It remains my belief, all these years later, that the decision to move along, on our own separate paths, was mutual. One that was made out of intense respect for one another's emotional recovery.

Still, I knew even then that I was going to miss them.

Before Jeff and I left Erie Hall that May, we decided to sell the loft that Paul had so willingly left behind weeks earlier.

Two male students, sophomores I think, were very excited to have it, and we watched as they quickly and eagerly dismantled it, and then industriously carried it out of our lives - piece by piece - like worker ants.

While a part of me was saddened to lose it, there would now be one less reminder of the haunting for us to have to address and tolerate each day and night.

Packing up our belongings, Jeff and I agreed to stay in touch over the summer.

He had become my best friend and my battle buddy.

It was a choice that I had made: to trust.

As human beings, we are afforded choices. Some choices are as clear as the pane of glass that separates you and your college dorm from the world on the other side. Others, they are as confusing as the darkness of a hurricane's wind, scattering tree limbs, debris – and all hope of safety – across the scarred landscape. Yet, in spite of all the tools at our disposal, the distinctions of outcome between the two cannot always be predicted.

The distinction between two people, between their philosophies, between their politics, between their backgrounds, can cause separation. A separation that can become permanent. But when it mattered most, there were no separating distinctions in John Jeff Ungar's mind, only his desire to help a friend. It was John Jeff Ungar, who risked it all in those dark days to ensure that proof would exist, and that I would survive.

It was a choice that he had made: to help.

We shook hands, bid goodbye to Erie Hall, to suite C2D and, most importantly, to our room, *the* room: C2D1. As we closed the door behind us, the room was dark and - hopefully – empty.

Sitting in the comfort of my family's black Chrysler New Yorker, I stared blankly out the window. With Robbie Dupree's song *Steal Away* playing on a cassette tape, the long-anticipated ride home with my family reminded me that I had been present for the arrival of the former Iranian Hostages, when they had landed at Stewart International Airport four years earlier.

That was January 20th, 1981, the same day that Ronald Reagan was being sworn in as the nation's 40th President. I was a sophomore in high school.

Left – The buses carrying the recently freed Iranian hostages from Stewart International Airport after over four hundred days of captivity. Photograph by the Chris Di Cesare, New Windsor, NY, January 20th, 1981.

I was there.

I waved to them, as they took the escorted bus ride from the airport's runway to the Army headquarters at West Point, following a lengthy, almost incomprehensible 444 days of captivity.

They were, no doubt, thankful to finally be going home. They were also completely exhausted. Only a few of them had enough energy to wave back at the large cheering crowds that lined the route.

That was precisely how I felt, as the car headed southbound, down Route 390 towards the Southern Tier of New York, leaving behind almost three solid months of unexpected terror. The blossoming spring trees kept silent watch along the roadside, as I made my own way . . . back home.

These were the events that – over both time and distance – would eventually lead to the rise of the urban legend of "The Ghost Boy of Geneseo". It is a story that seemed to want to tell itself from the very beginning, and then did so.

C2D1 Haunting Timeline

09/03/84 - Chris Di Cesare and Paul A. move into Room C2D1, Erie Hall at SUNY Geneseo. They set up a loft.

09/08/84 – Chris and J. Jeff (Jeff) Ungar meet in C2D Quad area.

11/14/84 – Paul has a series of dreams and Déjà vu experiences, warns something catastrophic is about to occur.

01/26/85 – Erie Hall Toga Party.

01/30/85 – Ed and Lorraine Warren presentation at Wadsworth Auditorium, attended by Jeff and Chris.

02/08/85 – Chris receives care package from his family.

02/11/85 – Chris experiences strange creaking noises from loft, hears his name called inside the room, experiences drafts, cold spots, and closet doors opening without obvious cause. Chris' sweat suit unsnaps on its own volition. Chris too frightened to take shower. Later, Paul hears ghost call Chris' name in C2D1.

02/12/85 – Paul is plagued by moving shadows. Chris sees moving shadows wash over his desk top. First sighting of what might be a ghost – with a titled head - is made by Chris as he sits at desk in his room. Chris flees C2D1 in a panic to seek assistance, and runs to C2D2. Jeff agrees to 'journal' the events.

02/13/85 – Chris is heard shouting at Paul to turn the lights on, Paul refuses. Paul wakes Chris when he hears a 'hissing' sound in the room. Chris investigates, throws objects at wall where he sees a human figure, retreats to bed. Paul observes as Chris, who is screaming, engages in a tug of war (that lasts several minutes) for his pillows which remain suspended in the air. Later, Paul witnesses a gold orb floating above Chris' head as he sleeps, and sees a 'shadowy figure' standing on a chair looking at him.

02/14/85 – Upon waking it is noticed that Chris' chair has been moved, a picture frame taken apart, an alarm clock reset. Jeff conducts experiments for proof of ghost. Chris attempts to summon ghost (Tommy'). Gurgling noises are heard. Ghost passes through Chris. Chris panics. Chris' mattress can be seen with a human-shaped indent. Jeff continues takes numerous photographs of events, one photo is taken by Chris before he exits the room.

02/15/85 - Jeff leaves for family vacation in Florida. Chris wakes during night to find ghost near him and 'smiling' at him. Chris' ear, cheek and neck are cold and numb to the touch; he flees the room for several minutes to compose himself. Several hours later, as Chris sleeps, Paul sees a shadow figure – with a titled head - looking at him from the foot of the loft. He wakes Chris and with the information. Paul fears they will die. They decide to seek assistance.

02/15/85 – Chris and Paul walk to St. Mary's Catholic Church at 7 a.m. They are unsuccessful in their attempts to speak with a priest, but are given the phone number of Fr. Charles Manning of the College Interfaith Center.

02/17/85 – Chris and Beth Kinsman (from B-building Erie Hall) flee his room while studying for an exam when they observe a pencil fall through the ceiling above them.

02/18/85 – Beth volunteers to assist Chris and Paul. Beth obtains the contact information of Dr. Lawrence Casler, a psychology professor.

02/21/85 – Chris' track coach calls to express his concern over lack of attendance. Paul reminds Chris of his earlier predictions, and says that his life is falling apart because of the ghost.

02/22/85 – While reading at his desk, Chris (shirtless) feels something 'freezing cold and firm' touch his right shoulder near his neck. He sprints to a corner of the room, and curls into a fetal position praying that God will 'take this ghost away'.

02/25/85 – Jeff, back from Florida, has the roll of film from the Feb. 14th session developed at a 'one hour' photo booth. Notices the photo taken by Chris reveals a 'skeletal apparition'. Chris does not want to see it, but is persuaded by Beth - who also sees the form – to do so.

03/02/85 – After a series of meetings between Jeff, Paul, Beth and Chris, it was agreed that Chris and Paul should bring Jeff's journal notes and meet with Fr. Charles Manning, while either Beth or Jeff would reach out to Dr. Casler.

03/04/85 – Chris and Paul speak with Fr. Manning at the College Interfaith Center. After over an hour of journal reading and discussion, Fr. Manning agrees to assist. He will visit room C2D1 under the guise of a stereo repairman (making note of the events of Feb 12th) so as not to attract attention to the situation.

03/06/85 – The priest arrives at 8 p.m. to 'bless' the room. Paul is not present. Jeff asks to be a part of the proceedings but is rebuffed by Fr. Charlie. Chris agrees to take notes in Jeff's absence. At the conclusion of the ceremony, Chris asks if the ghost can back in the room, and is advised by the priest, "Only if you invite him back in." Following the Blessing, there is no activity reported for several days.

03/10/85 – Following a long run outside of Geneseo, Chris is physically attacked, and wounded, in the dorm shower. Jeff, hearing 'some type of commotion', pulls Chris – who was found on the bathroom floor lying face down and bleeding from his back – out of the bathroom. Ed S. (Jeff's roommate in C2D2) and Beth confirm the wounds which are described as "Three long scratches" that traveled from his neck area to his lower torso. Chris refuses to go to the hospital. Upon seeing the wounds later that evening, Paul begins to withdraw from the friendships.

03/12/85 – Chris (while talking with Jeff) sees the ghost outside the C2D Common Area, its body intertwined with a tree. He claims that the ghost looks 'mutilated and twisted' with an eye hanging out, nose missing and the stomach sliced open. Chris flees the room, with Jeff in pursuit, anguished over why the haunting had not stopped.

03/14/85 – Chris is told by Craig Norris (Jeff and Ed's C2D2 roommate the year prior) that one of his friends is experiencing voices and paranormal activity in a nearby Erie Hall quad.

03/15/85 – Chris travels home (Newburgh, NY) for the weekend to visit his family. He shares with his family a few minor details about the haunting to gauge their reactions.

03/16/85 – Paul speaks with Ed and Jeff about changing rooms. Paul later reveals that the ghost threatened him to "Leave Chris alone." Jeff agrees to move into C2D1.

03/17/85 – His first night sleeping in C2D1 (in what had been Chris' bed) Jeff claims to experience a phantasmal paralysis, wrestling with a shadow figure that kneels on his chest. Jeff purposefully does not inform Chris of the incident who returns and questions the new roommate arrangement.

03/24/85 – Chris' father, Vito Di Cesare, concerned over his son's mental health, writes to him. He counsels for mental stability.

03/31/85 – Shortly after returning to college from a 20th birthday party at home with family at home, Chris calls his father to tell him that he was 'in trouble' and that the ghost was 'real'. Vito quickly drives to Geneseo, and spends the night in room C2D1, sitting at the edge of the bed. While revealing no details the following morning, Chris' father tells him that he loves him, and advises him to change his room as soon as he can.

04/01/85 – Students in the B2 area of Erie Hall, begin reporting 'ghost problems'. Jeff and Chris discover Beth, who was late for a preset appointment, unresponsive and dazed on the floor of her bedroom. She claims that she heard the ghost continuously calling Chris' name inside her room and that she 'lost consciousness'.

04/02/85 – Chris, Jeff and Beth respond to the pleas of Linda F., who claims that there is a ghost in her room and that it is holding her down and angrily grabbing her legs. Jeff takes a series of photographs showing Chris as he attempts to assist by calming Linda down and attempting to communicate with the ghost. "You want me, not her." He yells. The activity stops.

04/03/85 – Judy Y. reports that she felt an abnormal chill in the suite bathroom as she showered, as well as the strong feeling that she was being watched by someone that she could not see. She states that when she returns home, she is going to speak with her pastor.

04/04/85 – Chris, who showered regularly at the gym following the attack at Erie Hall, sees 'Tommy' peering at him through the shower stall doorway that leads to the men's locker room. Convinced that he was simply reacting to Judy's impressions, he attempts to shrug off the situation until the form eventually departs. As he is getting dressed, a flustered student warns that he saw 'some really strange-looking guy' watching Chris as he showered. He tells Chris that 'The guy stood there for quite a while', and that if he comes back while he is in the shower, he would call the police.

04/09/85 – Chris, Jeff and Beth visit with Dr. Casler. He marvels at both the amount, and the quality of evidence that the students have gathered. He encourages them to obtain audio evidence to go along with the photograph.

04/11/85 – Ghost voice 'EVP' collected in B2B2 of Erie Hall. The gathered students (Chris, Jeff, Linda and Beth) hear the ghost on the cassette tape asking Chris for 'help'. While most are enthused by the growing amount of evidence, Chris is anguished, stating that he didn't know how to help the ghost, even if he wanted to.

04/12/85 – Chris begins to withdraw from his friends, spending large amounts of time alone, on the couch in C2D1, watching people pass by his window.

04/14/85 – 4 AM. Chris, after talking with Craig Norris about all of the people who were suffering due to the ghost, decides to enter C2D1 with a singular purpose: to get rid of the spirit. He goes into the room sometime between three and four a.m., under Craig's suggestion that it be done 'as God made him' (without clothing), with the intent of breaking the priest's Blessing. Chris reportedly speaks with the ghost.

04/18/85 – Jeff, not made aware of Chris' efforts over the weekend, notices a positive change in both Chris and the 'feel' of the room. Chris is initially hesitant to share any details, but eventually does so. Jeff would write a letter on 04/29/85 to his mother stating that, at 9 PM on April 18th,

Chris confided in him that he had spoken with the ghost, and that he tried to put the ghost to rest, and that the ghost seemed to have listened.

04/20/85 – Chris and Jeff run a 10K in town. Chris wins the race, Jeff finished in 7th.

04/21/85 – While listening to the radio in room C2D1, Jeff notes that Chris is watching a 'golden glimmer' of energy rise up to the ceiling. Chris tells Jeff that Tommy is saying 'good bye'.

04/26/85 – Chris, Jeff, Don Hunt, Linda, Beth, Ed and Judy all head out to Letchworth State Park. To date, it is the last time that they would all be together.

04/29/85 – Jeff writes to his mother and indicates that the ghost left on April 18th.

05/15/85 – Chris and Jeff move out of Erie Hall at the close of the Spring Semester.

www.ingramcontent.com/pod-product-compliance
Lightning Source LLC
Chambersburg PA
CBHW031425270326
41930CB00007B/575